DOWN ON
THE CORNER
ADVENTURES IN
BUSKING
& STREET MUSIC

CARY BAKER

DOWN ON THE CORNER ADVENTURES IN BUSKING & STREET MUSIC
CARY BAKER

A Jawbone book
First edition 2024
Published in the UK and the USA by
Jawbone Press
Office G1
141–157 Acre Lane
London SW2 5UA
England
www.jawbonepress.com

ISBN 978-1-916829-10-7

Printed by Short Run Press, Exeter

1 2 3 4 5 28 27 26 25 24

[above] Dom Flemons in Flagstaff, Arizona, 2004. *Courtesy of the Dom Flemons collection*

A resolute preservationist, storyteller, and instrumentalist, Dom Flemons has long set himself apart by finding forgotten folk songs and making them live again. His work has been recognized with a Grammy award (plus a subsequent nomination), two Emmy nominations, a USA Fellowship Award, and inclusion in an exhibit at the Country Music Hall Of Fame & Museum. Raised in Phoenix, Flemons comes from a family of civil rights leaders, Tuskegee Airmen, and preachers who were prominent figures in the Black community of Arizona. After graduating from Northern Arizona University (which presented him with an honorary doctorate in 2022), Flemons moved to North Carolina and co-founded The Carolina Chocolate Drops. After leaving the group in 2013, he established a solo career that has led him to collaborate with hundreds of artists in the Americana music scene. His latest project is *Traveling Wildfire* (Smithsonian Folkways), a follow-up to his 2018 Grammy-nominated album *Black Cowboys*.

FEEDING
THE STREET

FOREWORD
BY DOM
FLEMONS

WHEN I BEGAN BUSKING around the age of seventeen, I called it 'feeding the street,' and even though it was more challenging than playing in a venue, that was part of the fun.

In my hometown of Phoenix, Arizona, I was one of a few buskers to brave the hundred-degree heat with my guitar and banjo. During my high school and college years, I would stand on the corner at the neighborhood art walk on 1st and Roosevelt Streets, belting out songs ranging from Hank Williams to Cat Stevens, Lead Belly to Chuck Berry—or whatever suited my mood.

When I dropped my hat, it was showtime, and nothing stopped me from singing on the streets for a few hours at a time. Once I began to play in clubs and bigger venues, I never forgot the lessons in resilience and stagecraft I learned feeding the street. When you know that the audience doesn't have to give you their attention, your method of delivering a performance changes drastically to get it.

With my guitar under my arm and my harmonica in a rack, I mimicked the sounds of the 1960s folk revival that I had heard on records. When I began to read about the heyday of Greenwich Village and Boston, I knew that I wanted to have those experiences, so I took my music to the streets of Phoenix, and eventually, as I got into college, I'd busk all over Northern Arizona in places like Flagstaff, Prescott, and Sedona. As no one had seen or heard the type of music I was playing, my busking act began to evolve into a show where I played old styles of music for passersby, making the old songs come to life like a human jukebox.

The best part about busking, to me, was that there was no right or wrong way to do it. All I needed to do was set down my hat and sing.

While many buskers are known to be constant travelers, there is a strong busking culture that belongs to the local performers who become known through their immediate communities. Many of these buskers earned a name for themselves by being fixtures of a city, developing an audience that would consistently see them while slowly building, one fan at a time, from casual listeners to dedicated die-hards.

Every location has its own type of appeal for a performer, and many buskers can be found at big exhibitions, markets, and street fairs, all the way to natural amphitheaters. When I lived in New York City, I busked all over town from the Bronx down through Manhattan and in Brooklyn, playing in the parks and on the subway. I learned how to take break sections on the platforms so that my songs wouldn't get lost over the sound of trains going by. I saw every type of busker in New York City from insane preachers to horn-driven shout bands, the frantic sounds of the xylophone, the mysterious tone of the theremin, Peruvian pan flutists, and any number of guitar troubadours playing for change and feeding the street with their art and music.

When I was in North Carolina, I played on Franklin Street in Chapel Hill and got to learn the jive of the street people who lived out on the stoop before the area became fully gentrified. Many people who had roots in the rural parts of the state would come up and compliment my country blues picking. They would lend an ear to a nostalgic memory of their upbringing. Some of them even took a moment to spin a yard to give me context for their admiration.

Even as I began touring internationally with The Carolina Chocolate Drops, I would busk on my own throughout England, France, Belgium, and other places around the world when the mood hit me. While playing on the streets, you have full freedom, within reason, to play or say anything you please. Once you start, it becomes clear that your audience is both distant and close to you. If you play a song that is appealing, they may stay or go. Every audience member is now part of a much bigger theater that you, the busker, are providing for them. The desire of the audience becomes a new element of the performing experience. The synergy only multiplies when more people are involved. All of the sudden, a bigger crowd changes the busking experience from a one-on-one conversation to a majority vote. If you are a good busker, you can bring the crowd, give them a thrill, and finally disperse everyone in a timely manner, with a few extra dollars in your hat.

Music has always been about connecting with one another. Whether vocal or instrumental, there is nothing like a live musical performance and the impression it leaves on the audience. It can change the mind, melt the heart, or bring the hairs of the arm or head up on end in sheer excitement. There are many ways to experience music, but none are more organic and visceral than the sound of the busker standing out on the street and entertaining for everyone to hear.

I've seen buskers who are bare bones, holding a single battered instrument and having only the will to play for whoever passed their way. The master busker is not judged by musical quality alone but by their charisma and presence to enchant a crowd of strangers into their midst.

Busking requires no ego. In its most basic form, you or I could go to a street corner and start right now and begin working a crowd to a frenzy. There is a 50/50 chance it would work. Without something unique to grab people's attention, we are just causing a disturbance. When a real busker masters their craft, an audience of passersby will be spell bound by their talents and skills. First, the attention of the audience alone is the reward for the performer, but if they are really good, that attention will be rewarded with money. Sometimes it's coins and other times its dollar bills, but over time it accumulates. A busker will play anywhere between a few songs to several hours before they pack up. They sing out into the open air, their voices unrestrained by microphones or the sound limitations of an enclosed space, and it rings across the surrounding buildings.

In the following book, you will get a moment to meet a group of musicians who are all drawn together by the excitement, spontaneity, and potential financial gain of busking. Their methods are all honed from their unique environments and individual personalities and life stories. The chapters ahead give them the full respect they deserve because the nature of the profession leaves a lot of room for erasure. A busker can disappear as easily as they appear, without a single trace left behind. This book allows us to hear the full story of feeding the street, as it has been done for over a century in the United States. It gives us a glimpse into the lives of the buskers who have enriched our daily existence with music and performance art. It's a dollar in the hat, with the acknowledgment that the world is always a better place when busking is a part of the picture.

Special thanks to Cary Baker for giving a new voice to a music tradition that will continue to live on forever and will find new homes wherever the music takes it.

A BRIEF HISTORY OF
BUSKING

INTRODUCTION

BY CARY
BAKER

STREET SINGING, ALSO KNOWN AS BUSKING, has been a form of entertainment for centuries, as far back as ancient Rome. Historically, street performers would travel from town to town, performing for tips and relying on the generosity of passersby to make a living. The buskers could be comedic, theatric, political, or, of course, musical.

'Satirical songs were also a part of Roman life in a less political and exploitable way,' note authors David Cohen and Ben Greenwood in their book about the origins of street performance, *The Buskers: A History Of Street Entertainment.* 'It became the custom at funerals to sing songs about the deceased, drawing attention to his or her characteristics.'[1]

The term *busker* may have its root in the Italian word *buscare*, along with the Spanish word *buscar*, meaning to look for. The Spanish word traces its origins to the Indo-European word *bhud-skō*, meaning to win or conquer.[2] From there, it seems to have entered the English lexicon as what Merriam-Webster defines as 'a person who entertains in a public place for donations.'

One of earliest recorded instances of street singing is in ancient Greece, where musicians, jongleurs (defined by Merriam-Webster as an itinerant medieval entertainer proficient in juggling, acrobatics, music, and recitation), and actors commonly performed in public spaces. During the Middle Ages, troubadours and minstrels would travel from town to town, performing songs and spinning tales to crowds gathered in public squares. In *Big City Rhythm & Blues* magazine's 2022 busking issue, Dirk Wissbaum writes of how, in medieval Europe, 'poor peasants would play a pennywhistle or other instrument and dance a jig in hopes of making a little money.'[3]

The term *troubadour* was the word in Languedoc (a region and former province of southern France) for a finder or an inventor, but it came to mean a knight who wrote poetry and music performed in courts throughout the country.

In the USA, busking dates back to the nation's eighteenth-century origins. Benjamin Franklin, the venerable early American writer, scientist, statesman, philosopher, and, as it turns out, public orator, was himself a street performer, as he recounted in his autobiography:

I now took fancy to poetry, and made some little pieces. My brother, thinking it might turn to account encourag'd me, & put me on composing two occasional ballads. One was called the 'Light House Tragedy,' & containe'd an account of the drowning of Capt. Worthilake with his two daughters; the other was a sailor song on the taking of 'Teach or Blackbeard the Pirate.' They were wretched stuff, in the grub-street ballad style, and when they were printed he sent me about the town to sell them. The first sold wonderfully, the event being recent, having made a great noise. This flatter'd my vanity. But my father discourag'd me. Verse-makers were always beggars; so I escap'd being a poet, most probably a very bad one.[4]

Buskers became disseminators of news before the widespread use of a printing press, during which books were rare and costly. During the nineteenth century, the rise of industrialization and the growth of urban centers led to an increase in street performance. Singers, dancers, magicians, even acrobats took to the streets. This era also saw the emergence of new forms of street performance, such as the one-man band, in which a musician might play several different instruments at once.

In the twentieth century, street singing became particularly popular as immigrants brought their native musical heritage and instrumentation to the streets of the new nation. Among them was the Siberian-born songwriter Irving Berlin, who sang for pennies on New York's Lower East Side.[5] Comedian George Burns started in the same neighborhood, performing with the Peewee Quartet. The same thing was also happening in the Deep South, with pioneering blues and jazz singers like Blind Lemon Jefferson, Reverend Gary Davis, Blind Blake, Eubie Blake, and Louis Armstrong among the performers.

'Some of the oldest busking in the blues could be found in and around the towns that lie along the river,' Wissbaum writes. 'Especially in the Mississippi Delta, where during the 1890s until the depression, musicians could be found traveling to the many lumber, levee and turpentine camps found along the river's edge. It was here they would keep a low profile until Friday night, when the men came out to have a good time and spend a little of their weekly wages. The busker was there to entertain. [Delta-born Chicago blues singer] Honeyboy [Edwards] told several interviewers that very story. He was one of the many guitarists who went to those camps and entertained the working men there.'

Blind Lemon Jefferson, often referred to as the Father Of Texas Blues, played the streets of Dallas and East Texas. His brother, Alec Jefferson, recalled how rough it could be: 'Men were hustling women and selling bootleg, and Lemon was singing for them all night.' As Drew Kent further describes in his liner notes to *The Complete 94 Classic Sides*, 'Blind Lemon was singing for [street crowds] all night … he'd start singing about eight and go on until four in the morning…mostly it would be just him sitting there and playing and singing.'6

Another Texas blues legend, Sam 'Lightnin'' Hopkins, was discovered in 1946 while singing in Dowling Street in Houston's Third Ward by Lola Anne Cullum, a talent scout from Los Angeles's Aladdin Records. Imagine the odds. Cullum reportedly drove Hopkins 1,370 miles to LA for his first Aladdin session.

In the Southeast, '[Reverend Gary] Davis's curriculum at the Spartanburg School For The Deaf & Blind was based on a teaching scholarship he had,' explains Andrew Cohen, a historian and confidante of Davis's. 'In exchange for teaching guitar, he was able to learn Braille English, Braille music notation and most likely some other academic stuff, along with the school's obligatory "trade." Blind schools taught practical things: Macon taught piano tuning; Roanoke taught kitchen labor. In this case, the trade was mattress stuffing. Davis would return to local mattress factories when it was too wet or nasty to busk.'

It is more difficult to wield a piano onto the streets than a guitar, but that didn't stop Roy 'Professor Longhair' Byrd, who plied his craft on New Orleans's streets in the 1930s. According to writer and critic Robert Palmer, 'He taught himself to play piano on a battered upright some neighbors had abandoned in an alley. At the same time, he was tap-dancing in the streets for spare change and making occasional appearances as an orange crate drummer with a children's band.'7

During the Great Depression, many unemployed musicians and performers took to the streets to make a living. In the 1960s, the folk music revival led to a resurgence in street singing, as aspiring musicians took to the streets to perform the earliest American protest songs. Protest songs were paramount in the repertoire of folk musicians like David Bennett Cohen, who began playing in New York's Washington Square in the 1940s. 'One Sunday, I took my guitar,' Cohen told NPR's *Weekend*

Edition in 2011.'I didn't know anybody. Somebody came up to me and said, Oh, you play that? What do you got? I made a bunch of friends. It was an amazing place.'[8]

However, on April 9, 1961, the NYPD showed up with the mission of eradicating street performers. The protest was captured by filmmaker Dan Drasin in the seventeen-minute documentary *Sunday*. The film's buskers were victorious—and Cohen went on to sign on as keyboardist for Country Joe & The Fish.

Today, it is very legal to perform in Washington Square—and unusual not to see performers there. Located in the heart of Greenwich Village, Washington Square looks back upon a long history of outdoor performance, one of its colorful figures being David Peel, a street singer, marijuana activist, and close friend of John Lennon and Yoko Ono. Kris Needs set the scene in an article for *Classic Rock* magazine:

> Peel took The Fugs' taboo-shattering street chant ethos to Washington Square's gatherings which, by 1967's Summer Of Love, included love-ins but were increasingly being infiltrated by politically vociferous elements incensed by the escalating carnage in Vietnam and intent on causing as much havoc and social unrest as possible. ... Man, he captivated the crowds in the park, including the future Joey Ramone and his brother Mickey, who sometimes joined in on the songs. Danny Fields, who had been editing teen magazines and was part of Warhol's circle, had joined Jac Holzman's venerable Elektra Records as a publicist and resident 'freak on the street.' ... Elektra had never recorded an album live at Washington Square, so engineer Peter Siegel was dispatched to capture Peel and his gaggle of like-minded stoners who called themselves The Lower East Side, bellowing over guitars, harmonica, and basic percussion to create the *Have A Marijuana* album.[9]

Today, street singing is a common sight in cities throughout the world. And it hasn't remained low-tech: many of today's musicians and performers use the internet to promote their act, but the tradition of performing on the streets for tips and donations remains constant. Some cities have even established designated areas for street performers—New Orleans's French Quarter or Austin's East 6th Street, for instance— allowing them to entertain tourists and locals while preserving the character and culture of their city streets. Busker's Bunkhouse, a New Orleans organization devoted to aiding and even boarding (for up to three days) street performers, reports on its website that 'licenses and permits exist, but they are not required as of this writing. The city's noise ordinance prohibits public performance between the hours of 8pm and 9am; however, thanks to an email and letter writing campaign, it is not being stringently enforced at this time.'[10]

In the French Quarter, Royal Street's pedestrian mall, a haven to the city's rich talent pool, was due to be closed to automobile traffic, enabling musicians to perform unfettered. Unfortunately, at time of writing, that is not the case. According to New Orleans alt-weekly newspaper the *Gambit*, 'To this day, officials not only refuse to block off the mall from cars, the various police forces operating in the Quarter have harassed and threatened musicians who've tried to do it themselves.'[11]

Other cities have fought the tradition—even the entertainment capital, Los Angeles, where turban-wearing, roller-skating Harry Perry became the poster boy for preserving the right to play on Venice's festive Ocean Front Walk. The late activist Jerry Rubin (not to be confused his namesake, the Chicago Seven defendant) launched SHAPE—Save The Healers, Artists, Politicos And Entertainers—to help preserve the outdoor entertainment tradition.

In adjacent Santa Monica, where the 3rd Street Promenade pedestrian mall has become a busking hub, street performance is legal if the performer has a permit—and provided they maintain a ten-foot interval from bus stops and pedestrian crosswalks. Andrew Thomas, CEO of Downtown Santa Monica, Inc, has decreed, 'The Promenade is public space, and anyone is entitled to perform on the Promenade for donations if they secure a permit through the City Of Santa Monica. Because the street is public, the performance is protected by the First Amendment.'[12]

Farther back, street music was banned by New York Mayor Fiorello LaGuardia in 1935; the ban was finally lifted by Mayor John Lindsay on May 20, 1970. Among those affected in the interim was the aforementioned Reverend Gary Davis: 'Not so much that I liked it,' he was later quoted as saying, 'but that's the best I could do. I was glad to get away from it [street singing]. Cause there's too many different kinds of people you meet up with in the street … they call it beggin', panhandlin'.'[13]

Chicago, too, has a rich heritage in busking. In the 1950s, the South Side was alive with street-corner doo-wop vocal groups like The Magnificents, The Flamingos, The Moonglows, The Spaniels, and The El Dorados. Every Sunday from the 1940s until the 90s, Maxwell Street Market, due west of the Loop, became a stage to blues legends—initially Robert Nighthawk, Little Walter, Big Walter Horton, and Johnny Young, and later a second wave of blues performers including Maxwell Street Jimmy Davis, Blind Arvella Gray, and Little Pat Rushing. Sadly, a motion to list Maxwell Street among the National Register Of Historic Places was declined as a result of efforts by the encroaching University Of Illinois Chicago campus—efforts backed by Mayor Richard M. Daley. (An area located across the Dan Ryan Expressway on Des Plaines Street has been deemed New Maxwell Street Market and today features a new generation of blues, folk, and Mariachi performers.)

In 1982, musician and activist Cynthia Haring, aka Destiny Quibble, complained that she could not perform on the streets or subway platforms in Chicago as she had in Boston when she was a student at Berklee

College Of Music. This would change in 2017, when the city relaxed its anti-busking ordinances. On June 24, 2022, Haring announced on her Facebook page, 'It's been nearly forty years now, but we're still celebrating that victory of legalizing street and subway performance in Chicago, thanks to an amazing attorney named Rob Wynbrandt. Was in Chicago recently and made us happy to see the street and subway artists making a living as they should!'

In 2017, Chicago Aldermen Brendan Reilly (42nd District) and Brian Hopkins (2nd District) decreed that street musicians should be banished from the city's premier artery, Michigan Avenue, for most of the length of the city's Downtown and Magnificent Mile districts, including the stretch that runs along Grant Park. The proposed ordinance pertained specifically to performers who 'emit noise that is audible to a person with normal hearing more than twenty feet away.' Reilly later softened his ban, bowing to consensus: 'Facing an almost certain City Council defeat, Downtown Alderman Brendan Reilly (42nd) on Wednesday watered down his plan to silence street musicians on Michigan Ave. and State St. Instead of banning the music altogether on Downtown's two marquee streets, Reilly proposed limiting the music to the hours of the day when there is the greatest amount of pedestrian traffic. That is between the hours of 11am and 1pm and 5 and 6pm on weekdays and between 1 and 3pm on Saturdays and Sundays.'[14]

Austin, Texas—long touted the 'live music capital of the world,' and struggling to live up to the slogan 'Keep Austin Weird' amid becoming America's tenth largest metro area—has legalized street performance under a few reasonable conditions. Buskers must remain acoustic, emitting sounds no more voluminous than 85 decibels. Sidewalks cannot be blocked, nor can the sound be audible to residences or businesses after 10:30pm. And lastly: safety first! 'Make sure you're performing where people can safely gather without danger of stepping into a roadway.'[15]

Up in Missoula, Montana, the college city of nearly seventy-five thousand has co-opted Austin's slogan and is doing its best to 'keep Missoula weird.' A local street musician, Patrick Christianson, has been asked by municipal law enforcement to stop playing music on the sidewalks. An empathic city council member, Daniel Carlino, brought an ordinance to enable buskers and eliminate permits. 'Missoula is such a unique and special community to all of us. And I think as a local government, a couple things we can do to help keep Missoula weird is to help ensure everybody can still afford to live here in the future and to help ensure all Missoulians are able to express themselves as they wish.'[16]

Nashville, long the home of country music—and these days a hub of the music industry in general—has an equally relaxed policy on street singing. After all, some of its biggest stars emerged from busking origins. According to a report by Jason Lamb on Nashville's News Channel 5, 'There are no new ordinances involved; Metro is simply enforcing existing rules which have been on the books for a number of years. That enforcement includes asking businesses to remove ... obstructions to the public right-of-way, as well as some musicians who have been unlawfully setting up amplified or obstructive music equipment. Musicians, such as acoustic guitar or violin players, should not be impacted if they are not obstructing foot traffic or violating the noise ordinance due to excessive volume or amplification of sound. While we regret if any musicians are negatively impacted by the proper enforcement of existing laws and codes, public safety is our first and overriding concern in Metro Government. We hope that those musicians who are asked to move from the area are able to find work in some of the many live-music establishments in the Downtown neighborhood or beyond.'[17]

The streets have proven the birthplace of so much American music in the post-war era, from New York City's Washington Square and subway depots to Chicago's Maxwell Street, to New Orleans's French Quarter, to

LA's sunny Venice Boardwalk. The musical idioms are equally diverse: slide-guitar blues, sweet doo-wop harmonies, brass bands, bluegrass ensembles, solo folkies, indie-rock, and more. Some performers have found themselves in turf wars over location. Others have set up what might as well be their 'office'—buskers refer to them as 'squats'—for years on end. Some have needed to shift from location to location depending on local law enforcement, or in the event of a fellow busker poaching their location. And at least one busker with whom we spoke has never remained stationary, roller skates becoming a key element of his work uniform.

TRANSPORTATION HUBS including New York subways and the London Underground have long been ripe for buskers. In Seattle, SeaTac Airport has become a busking center, thanks to the efforts of the Gigs4U program, which books live music into the air hub. The city's Sub Pop label alone has put several of its artists on this stage, including Dinosaur Jr's J Mascis, Screaming Trees' Mick Pickerel, and Chad VanGaalen. According to the label's Bekah Zietz-Flynn, 'I was at both J and Chad's performance and heard a number of people pass by J and say, *Is that J Mascis?* I also threw down a hat when Chad was busking, and he made fifty dollars, which I thought was funny, because he was heading back to Canada and needed to convert the money.'

Busking has its own advocacy website, published and updated by Stephen Baird, called Buskers Advocates. Baird, a longtime promoter of musicians and others in the arts, is founder and director of Street Arts And Buskers Advocates And Community Arts Advocates. Based in Jamaica Plain, he is credited with restructuring Cambridge's Club Passim in 1995–97, co-founding the Massachusetts Bread & Roses Festival in 1986, founding and directing the Folk Arts Network from 1982 to 1996, and publishing the *New England Folk Almanac* and *New England Folk Directory* during the same period, among other achievements. His resolute advocacy has been cited in *Time, Newsweek, People,* and the *American Bar Association Journal.*

The Buskers Advocates site is an information resource center website that receives site visits from seventy different countries each day. Its mission statement declares:

> Street Arts and Buskers Advocates cultivates ongoing fundamental relationships between artists and communities by celebrating self-expression as a basic human right essential for the healthy growth of youth, individuals, and communities. ... A nonprofit organization dedicated to expanding public awareness, participation in and support of the arts through performances and festivals, exhibits and workshops, publications and publicity, educational forums, nonprofit arts management consultation services, and collaborative projects. ... A program of Community Arts Advocates, Inc., a nonprofit organization dedicated to expanding public awareness, participation in and support of the arts through performances and festivals, exhibits and workshops, publications and publicity, educational forums, nonprofit arts management consultation services, and collaborative projects.

While it isn't mortally possible to document every street singer who ever lived—even in the blues, folk and rock eras—a number of tales follow. The tradition began in ancient Greece and the streets remain alive with the sound of music. Nowadays, promoting a song to Spotify playlist compilers is a more efficient way to achieve success without leaving one's bedroom. But this is a book about those who have braved the elements, stood within spitting distance of their audience, put their own lives in danger, risked ridicule and theft, endured days of fewer and fewer dollar bills—and bet on their talent.

Some broke through; most did not. As Glen Hansard of The Frames, a Grammy-, Oscar-, and Tony Award-winning Irish busker who did break through, thanks to the 2007 busking movie *Once*, has said, 'As a busker, one thing that does not work is self-consciousness. A busker needs to be working. A busker needs to shed all ego and get down to work. Play your songs, play them well, earn your money, and don't get in people's way.'[18]

PART
ONE

ORIGINS

Says he where did you get your pretty little shoes, woman,
And your dress so fine?
Got the shoes off of Maxwell,
I got to dress up on Halsted, lord, lord.

'JOHN HENRY,' AS PERFORMED BY BLIND ARVELLA GRAY

MAXWELL
STREET PART 1

CHAPTER 1

A DAY
IN THE LIFE

AUTHOR'S NOTE: This chapter was originally written for the *Illinois Entertainer* in 1981. It has been updated, but I've opted to keep it in its original present tense in order to capture the experience of being there.

From the 1950s through the late 80s, Maxwell Street was a scrappy, sprawling flea market west of Chicago's Loop and south of the University Of Illinois's Chicago campus. On every warm-enough Sunday in the late 40s and early 50s, one could see blues legends like Robert Nighthawk, Muddy Waters, and Hound Dog Taylor; by the 70s, a newer generation of blues artists had populated the market.

By the early 2000s, the UIC campus had completed its southward expansion, and the original Maxwell Street was transformed. A 'new Maxwell Street' has since opened across the Dan Ryan Expressway on what is actually Desplaines Street. While it is a bargain shopper's paradise and outdoor stage to musicians of every musical idiom and ethnicity, it lacks the ambiance and grit of the old Market.

This story recounts a Sunday morning walk through the district in 1981. Please take a stroll with me, and I promise I'll get you back to the present by dinnertime...

JOHN HENRY DAVIS, leader of the Clarksdale, Mississippi Blues Band, is the self-proclaimed 'Mayor Of Jewtown.' His office hours are 8am 'til around 6pm every Sunday, in a vacant lot on the northeast corner of Maxwell and Sangamon Streets in Chicago.

When the Eastern European immigrants brought the institution of the flea market to the US in the early twentieth century, its prime motivators were Jews. It was largely a melting pot of Eastern Europeans who sold goods out of pushcarts. The bulk of the businesses were owned and patronized by Jews, and the area was commonly referred to—not altogether respectfully—as 'Jewtown.' The Great Migration from the South soon brought a significant Black population to the area starting in the 1920s—and with it came street musicians who brought with them the Southern traditions of blues and gospel music.

Although the flashpoint for the Great Chicago fire of 1871 was mere blocks away on DeKoven Street, Maxwell Street was miraculously spared. By the 1940s, Maxwell had become an outdoor stage to many of Chicago's blues greats: Muddy Waters, Howlin' Wolf, Bo Diddley, Chuck Berry, Robert Nighthawk, and both Little Walter (Jacobs) and Big Walter Horton. Bridging the gap between the immediate post–World War II era and the 1970s was Maxwell Street Jimmy Davis, owner of the Knotty Pine Grill, outside of which he would play when the winter winds weren't whipping.

Davis and his band, including guitarist L.V. Banks and bassist Steve Arvey, have been playing since dawn and word has it that guest star Muck Muck Man will be making an appearance around the noon hour. That leaves roughly ninety minutes to roam the periphery of the market before our return to 'Mayor' Davis and this purported street sensation, Muck Muck.

First stop: Little Pat Rushing's Blues Band.

Rushing's perch, going on three seasons, has been an isolated slab of cracked, banked concrete where once, presumably, stood a porch. The cement bandstand is located between Maxwell and 14th Place, Sangamon and Peoria Avenues—an unlikely but perennial mid-block oasis.

It's here that Maxwell patrons take a reflective moment and take in the surrounding environment with more than a rolling eye. It's here that you're going to get sufficiently rocked and funked by Rushing, his son (Danny), his daughter (Audrey), and sometimes his father.

You may have attended a Park West show on the previous evening with state-of-the-art sound. But here you're going to get untold decibels of raw blues power played through a minimal arsenal of amps and drums. And Pat, Maxwell's most technically proficient guitarist on a particularly good Sunday, grinds through a repertoire that combines the spirit of Maxwell forebears like Robert Nighthawk and latter-day Black heroes like James Brown. Constant is his guarded smile.

The audience is as diverse as any you'll ever see. A couple who'd be right at home in the city's Lincoln Park district—the man bearded and concealing an Olympus 35-SP camera under his windbreaker while his companion coyly counts quarters for the rather reserved hawker (who, upon a proper reprimand from Pat, becomes a tad more aggressive in his hat-passing).

On the south horizon is a disheveled Black man pushing a wheelbarrow, into which he eventually collapses and proceeds to bathe himself in an upturned flask of Wild Irish Rose. Another early bottle-hitter performs a one-man soft-shoe dance in front of the bandstand. His dance is one part vaudeville and another part dancing clear of empty Stroh's bottles, discarded Yummy orange soda cans, and trashed Eddie Kendricks singles. Pat's electric current, for which he pays between five and ten dollars every Sunday, emanates from an adjacent building.

One of the few that remain.

IT SEEMS LIKE only yesterday that today's vacant lots were someone's home or store. The Maxwell Radio Shop (831 W. Maxwell Street) went out of business in 1971 and was razed shortly afterward. At that store, in 1947, bluesmen Little Walter and Johnny Young made their first records for the house label, Ora-Nelle. The store owner, a middle-class Morton Grove resident, admitted 'til the day he locked his doors that blues was (in more or less his own words) unrefined low art, the antithesis of his hero, Frank Sinatra. Although he's gotten out of the store business, he still owns the tenement beside it at which Davis' Mississippi Blues Band performs. According to Davis, 'He won't let nobody else play right there.'

A weathered bungalow on 14th Street once set the backdrop for yet another Maxwell figure, Blind Jim Brewer. Films from the 50s reveal the green and white structure was once among dozens of the same. And in 1981, the bungalow (source of power for vocal mics, Lotus guitar, and Univox SR-120 rhythm box) joins the list of structural casualties. Undeterred, Brewer breaks into his Southern-inspired electric gospel music.

Just behind Brewer is a sign promoting East Chicago Heights' 'Primitive Baptist Church' and its Wednesday night services. Brewer and his accompanying guitarist perform a country blues-flavored rendition of 'Just A Closer Walk With Thee.'

For decades, a familiar Jewtown face was that of Blind Arvella Gray, the sightless singing drifter, who roamed the Maxwell and Halsted axes for nearly forty years prior to his death in 1980. Nine out of ten times, his tune was the traditional work song 'John Henry,' laced with his signature interjection of 'Have mercy, Mr. Percy' and reference to shoes and dresses bought on Maxwell.

Almost too coincidentally to be real, Maxwell had a second street corner minstrel, and she was Arvella's blood sister. 'Granny' (Clara Littricebey) used to be a fixture on the 1300 block of South Halsted with her repertoire of spiritual songs and simple acoustic guitar patterns Arvella taught her. Like her brother, Granny was the model of good will—never an unkind word, always a gesture of salvation for those less fortunate than she. A few years ago, Granny disappeared from the market. And Arvella, succumbing to gout, intestinal ailments, and a hard and largely thankless life, died on September 6, 1980. It was difficult, and a little sad, to imagine Maxwell without one or the other. Come 1981, however, Granny is back on the streets, accompanied by her husband—a gentle blind man—singing harmonies.

'Arvella would have wanted it this way,' she proclaims.

An era survives.

MAXWELL HAS PLAYED HOST to blues' most revered figures. Within the last ten years alone, it was possible to hear the likes of Big Walter Horton, Eddie Taylor, Maxwell Street Jimmy Davis, and Big John Wrencher—legends all. Horton, who made a very brief appearance on Maxwell Street with boogie forefather John Lee Hooker (who doesn't, as a rule, frequent the block) in the *Blues Brothers* movie, refuses to be photographed on Maxwell. At least his occasional streetside accompanist, a sour-tempered drummer called Porkchop with distinguished octagonal glasses, had a somewhat greater business savvy. A photo of him can be arranged. For a price.

Maxwell is also known for its Polish sausages, their presentation highly specific: a Maxwell Street Polish consists of a grilled or fried sausage (a combination of beef and pork) topped with grilled onions, yellow mustard, a pickle, whole green sport peppers, served on a bun. 'Maxwell Polish' sandwiches remain served throughout greater Chicago to this day. But they don't taste quite the same without the cacophony of live blues and flea market hawkers.

Nate's Kosher Sinai Deli is the place to go for serious deli food in Jewtown. A lox and bagel sandwich sets you back $2.25, and Nate—a robust Black man—carries both salty and Nova Scotia (unsalted) lox. It was there, theoretically, that Jake & Elwood Blues ordered their four fried chickens, white toast, and a Coke from waitress Aretha Franklin and cook Matt 'Guitar' Murphy. If you look very closely at the blue panel outside of Nate's, you can see where the words 'SOUL FOOD CAFE' were affixed for the filming.

In all probability, no one will burst into song while you're savoring your bagel and coffee—least of all into Aretha's 'Think.'

The *Blues Brothers* film was not the only immortalization of Maxwell on celluloid. There was a brief portrayal in last year's *My Bodyguard*, and an entire documentary filmed by University Of Illinois Chicago instructors Linda Williams and Raul Zaritsky called *Maxwell Street Blues*. The documentary premiered at Chicago's Facets theater for a ten-dollar cover, which entitled those who attended to partake in a fully catered party afterward. Entertaining attendees were John Henry Davis, Playboy Venson, Jim Brewer, and the whole gang. It seems only right that UIC give back to Maxwell only a part of what it's taken. The surface area of the market has slowly been eaten up for such necessities as UIC football fields.

John Henry Davis, projecting into the year 2000, doesn't feel Maxwell Street stands a ghost of a chance of survival. 'I hope it will, but I don't think it will last too much longer,' Davis said.

Showtime is approaching, and the crowds flock around John Henry Davis's corner. The band breaks into a funky shuffle, and a man bedecked in yellow hat, yellow shirt, and yellow pants emerges from a weathered car. Muck Muck has made his entrance.

'The money you put in the box belongs to the band,' he informs. 'The money you put in my hand goes to me. I'm into nickels and dimes. My shoes cost a nickel, my hat cost three cents, so you know I'm broke.'

Muck Muck proceeds to dance up a storm as L.V. Banks maintains a high-note guitar break, as if off a vintage Howlin' Wolf record.

'Now if *that* ain't worth a dollar . . . ,' Muck Muck says. A few audience members cough up the paper money.

Next, Muck Muck and the Davis band break into a song the guest star was said to have written in 1959, 'Hot Skinned Woman.' Another song, 'Skinned,' was pronounced as two syllables.

'What?' Muck Muck melodramatizes as he sings, 'She's back in town? She's stayin' on the third floor?'

He follows up with a song about his 'hot-skinned woman, whose eyes were like a pair of cherries and whose jowls hung down by her knees.'

Dollar bills ensue from all quarters.

Davis was quoted in the *Maxwell Street Blues* film documentary as fleeing Clarksdale, Mississippi, in 1955, in quest of the American dream. He may not have attained his goal, but he keeps the blues coming every Sunday morning on Maxwell Street.

'I play Maxwell because I know I'm going to make some money,' he says. 'If you have people in a club paying a tab, you never know.'

All the same, Maxwell is a world where next Sunday and next season are never assured. A square mile of urban blight, a flea market, a church, a concert stage. Maxwell Street Market offers experiences as varied as its constituents.

Will the next generation have the joy of sharing in the sights, sounds, and scents that are Maxwell's alone?

MAXWELL
STREET PART 2

CHAPTER 2

ARVELLA GRAY,
GRANNY LITTRICEBEY,
AND A MARKET SCENE'S DEMISE

ONE DAY AROUND 1970, during my adolescence in the Chicago suburbs, my father suggested that we visit the open-air flea market on Maxwell Street. He wanted to show me where his parents—Eastern European immigrants—used to take him shopping as a child. He described the area to me as being a generally run-down neighborhood to the west of Chicago's Loop, south of the University Of Illinois's Chicago campus, its southern border along largely Latino Pilsen neighborhood and its western border leaning up against Little Italy and several major hospitals. Thereupon, in generally unkempt storefronts—and, moreover, on card tables in the middle of the streets—are where his parents, a shoemaker and his wife, both of whom had arrived in the Windy City by way of Minsk, Belarus, used to buy clothing for their two sons during the 1930s and 40s.

All around, we could hear merchants hawking their new and used goods through distorted bullhorns. The aroma of Polish sausages, frying up year-around from numerous stands, was as pervasive as the cacophony of merchants haggling with customers over the price of a product like Bug Out! insect spray, sold out of the trunk of a car. I'll always remember my dad telling me, 'You'll only want to go there once, believe me.' Wrong he was: I returned to Maxwell Street every Sunday I could for the next fifteen years.

What had changed since my dad and his brother used to shop on Maxwell Street as kids was the presence of music—music on the streets, every Sunday morning. The musicians by now were nearly all Black, and they'd turned to Maxwell as a place to earn rent money after the blues taverns closed at 4am—some making a beeline to the area without stopping at home.

When my dad parked his car at the University Of Illinois lot, directly across Roosevelt Road from the Maxwell parcel, the first thing I heard, long before I could see where it was coming from, was the sound of a slide guitar—not just any guitar but a National steel resonator guitar. We followed the music and found ourselves standing on the west side of Halsted Street, midway between Roosevelt and Maxwell, where Blind Arvella Gray was playing the folk/blues song 'John Henry'—a song that seemed to have no beginning and no end.

Sensing that his audience was generally passing by rather than gathering around, Gray kept playing that one song for his entire shift. He'd even altered the lyrics to refer to the local streets, adding his own lines ('*I got the dress off of Maxwell / I got the shoes off of Halsted*') to the traditional refrain ('*John Henry was a steel-driving man, lo'd, lo'd!*'). When he stopped to catch his breath, I introduced myself and asked Mr. Gray for his phone number, which he cheerfully provided.

Before I could even get around to witnessing the other singers who played the Maxwell district that week—Maxwell Street Jimmy Davis, Little Pat Rushing, Jim Brewer and his wife Fannie, Big John Wrencher, John Henry Davis and the Clarksdale, Miss Blues Band at Maxwell & Sangamon; Porkchop Hines and Arvella Gray's own sister, Granny Littricebey, to name a few—I knew my life had turned a corner.

Before I forgot, I turned to my dad and said, 'We *are* coming back here, by the way! I want to come here *every* Sunday!'

Another time, while walking through Northwestern University's student union (I was still a high school student, but we lived near the campus), I saw a new newsprint publication called the *Reader*, which billed itself as Chicago's 'Free Weekly.' It was the first edition of the city's first alternative weekly newspaper. I picked up a copy. A few days later, I mailed an unsolicited manuscript—a feature about who else but Blind Arvella Gray. I titled the article 'Blues Over A Tin Cup,' even though his cup for spare change was actually a paper Dixie cup safety-pinned to the lapel of his jacket.

The *Reader* published my article as its cover story on January 7, 1972. I was sixteen, and my life as a writer had begun. But my quest to promote this blind busker did not stop there. One day I was looking in the Chicago north suburban Yellow Pages, under 'Phonograph Record Manufacturers,' only to find that one label of which I'd never heard, Birch Records, was located in the suburb where my family lived, Wilmette. I cold-called and asked what kind of records they released. I was told their specialty was old country artists who'd played on WLS-AM's vintage *Barndance* radio broadcast, including Patsy Montana and Lulu Belle & Scotty.

'Might you be interested in recording a street singer who plays down on Maxwell Street named Arvella Gray?' I asked.

It turned out that the owner, Dave Wylie, had not only heard of Mr. Gray but had seen him perform at a University Of Chicago Folk Festival. He readily agreed to record what would prove to be Gray's first and only album. A few weeks later, we drove from the northern suburb of Wilmette across the length of Chicago to the southern suburb of Harvey, Illinois, where, at Sound Unlimited Studios, we recorded an album all through the night. We drove back north as the sun was rising.

The resulting album received favorable notice, and Arvella spent his remaining eight years able to perform indoor ticketed shows at university coffeehouses and festivals. A 2005 reissue was reviewed on NPR and in the *New York Times* and *Rolling Stone*.

Unfortunately, most singers in Maxwell Street never received anything close to that degree of attention. Most played for spare change year-around, including during Chicago's legendarily cold winters. When one would cease to find them at their self-assigned spot on the Maxwell grid for weeks on end, it was safe to assume they'd become ill or passed away.

ARVELLA GRAY WAS BLINDED—per most reports—in a gun battle over a woman in Peoria, Illinois, though he told the story somewhat differently whenever asked. The scuffle also cost him two fingers on his left (fretting) hand, which is why he began to play slide guitar. Shortly thereafter, he moved to Chicago, learned guitar, and began to perform on Maxwell Street. In later years, he began to branch out to Englewood elevated train station on 63rd Street on the South Side, and in front of the Jazz Record Mart downtown, depending on the day of the week. A paper Dixie cup was affixed to his lapel, and Gray would invariably stop, mid-song, to interject an affable 'thank you' for contributions.

In the 1960s, he'd released two singles (civil rights anthems 'Freedom Rider' b/w 'Freedom Bus' and 'You Are My Dear' b/w 'Deborah') on his own Gray Records label, selling the 45rpm recordings on the street. They are both credited to 'Arvella Gray: Blind Street Singer.' In 1972, he recorded his first and only full album, *The Singing Drifter*, and that same year I interviewed him for *Living Blues* magazine. He recalled his introduction to music:

> After my mother died in 1917, started drifting. It didn't seem as if had any family ties, so I drifted into southern Texas. When I got there, began to work at a plantation owned by a fellow named

Eddie Wade. I visited him here in '63. He had the only guitar in the area at the time, and when he wasn't using it, I just monkeyed with it. I left there, started drifting, and joined the Ringling Brothers Circus. Then I lost my sight and I met quite a few blind people. I didn't associate with them or talk to them, but I saw what each of them were doing. In the meantime, ran into a problem. It wasn't really a problem. I was working, and had a wife then, and well I had a wife in Detroit, Michigan. I met a blind man who had a little mouth organ (harmonica). My wife gave him three dollars, you know, he was out in the corner. thought, *What the heck. If he can do that good, I might as well be blind.* Anyway, he was very neatly dressed, and he had his clothes on correctly, and everything. He had a watch and chain across on his vest, and he just looked like a fashion plate, I mean, I being that dressed up and everything. And I said that I wouldn't mind being a blind person as long as could do as good as he is, not realizing that I was going to get blind.

In the wintertime, I would get on the street cars, and I'd stand up with my back to the motorman. You know, there'd be someone in the back of the car, and I'd stand there sometimes, and as people'd go out, they'd contribute. I wasn't able to play more than just that one song, 'When The Saints Go Marching In.' In the summertime, I'd go on Maxwell Street. There were quite a few people there entertaining on the Street, and I thought I'd listen to them. I met one person, he say his name was Texas Slim, and he's the only one who kind of took me under his wing, and helped me.

All the rest of them didn't want to be bothered with me, so it was a number of them playing Daddy Stovepipe, a man named John Henry, and groups and things, and then you have your church groups. Way back when, Maxwell Street used to be like a dream, like a carnival, on Sundays. Now back in the 20s, when

I lost my sight, Maxwell Street stayed open all night. They had a different group of people there in them days. They hadn't learned how to steal and all that. If a hobo or a bum did come by, he'd take maybe a shirt or a suit, just what he could use himself. He didn't go out and peddle it. don't know whether they was stupid in them days or not, but that's the way they operated. They had three or four picture shows, and you get in there for ten cents, and you could stay in there all night. We slept in there. Early, early in the mornin', the cleanup people would come through and we'd all have to stand out in the aisle, and then we could go back. What made it so good back in them days is that they had silent pictures. Nothing to disturb you.[1]

CLARA LITTRICEBEY WAS BORN on August 30, 1913, in Temple, Texas. Of her unusual last name, she told me, 'My uncle had told me about the three Muslim words. One of them was Bey. My husband's name was Littries. On our marriage license, he wrote Littries at the top, Littrice below that. I adopted the Muslim name Bey, and it's my legal name now, Granny Littricebey. My real name is Clara Alma Allen Littricebey.'[2]

'I was an orphan at the age of three,' she explained. 'When my mother died, Arvella went to live with my aunt and then went out on his own. He came back to this aunt's house to see about me, as I was small. And then I didn't see him 'til 1933.'

Clara became a musician in a roundabout way. 'At the age of fourteen, I was out in a little town called Chickasha, Oklahoma. There was a man running for mayor named Lawson, and I did a poem about this man: *Lawson brought to this town a project we all know | To make the water softer which will help the town to grow*. Just a simple thing like that. Anyway, I had an eight-verse poem, and my uncle rewrote the whole thing, and then he took it to the mayor, and that helped the man to win the election.'

While in school studying social work, Clara found herself 'existing, not living' as a domestic worker. All the while, she would ask her brother to teach her guitar. 'I'd been following my brother many years, trying to learn things on the [guitar]. I used to love hearing him play, and I used to beg him after a day's work, but he didn't wanna. And I said, If I ever learn to play, I'll go [away]! So he purchased me a used two-dollar guitar and used to strum behind him. And I just kept strumming behind him until I got a beat I could do. And he pushed me out on my own, saying I [was] to either sink or swim. So just go out there and do my own thing.'

'I play out in the streets or in church—any church that asks me to play. I played Reverend Burgess's church at 96th and Burley, I've played at 64th Street and Harper, 65th and Cottage Grove. A girl named Debbie Jarle let me play for an hour over at the University Of Chicago. Then, the rest of the time, I play on Maxwell Street. And the reason I like to play on Maxwell Street is because I have a vast audience. I'm not housed in a little place with four walls. I get all kinds of people. Like, if I see Puerto Ricans or the Mexican people go by, I have two lines I sing to them. The reason I sing that is because if the Latin people are going to contribute to me, I might as well sing to them. If see white people come by, I try to sing the mountain songs.'

'I'm sixty years old now, born 1913,' she said, 'and still goin' strong.'

THE MAXWELL STREET blues scene remained active into the 80s and beyond. Chicago blues singer and harmonica player Billy Boy Arnold, a veteran of Bo Diddley's band, recalls that, at its prime, 'people would go over there and buy clothes and get bargains and stuff, and have sandwiches, and it was sort of a festive atmosphere. And musicians would go over there if [they were] in town and play on the corner. A lot of the people would pass by, and they would throw some money into their hats.'

Author David Whiteis described the scene in an article for the *Chicago*

Reader in 1988. 'Every Sunday morning, the energy of the Maxwell Street Market area rises phoenix-like from the rubble. The crowds, the hustlers, the musicians, and the entire cavalcade of sights, sounds, and smells still combine to transform the desolate wasteland into a once-a-week carnival.'[3]

As the years passed, however, the eventual demise of the original Maxwell Street location was inevitable. Real estate was pricey, abutting the university campus to the north, the Loop to the east, and a hospital district and Little Italy to the west. By the 1990s, the university had made its expansion plans clear, and they included the demolition of Maxwell Street.

Another city might have designated the area a historic district, along the lines of Memphis's Beale Street or New Orleans's Royal Street, or an entertainment district, along the lines of Austin's East 6th Street. And, in fact, a devoted collective of community members did petition for Maxwell Street Market area to be designated among the National Register Of Historic Places, both in 1994 and again in 2000. But the university fought the plan and proceeded with expansion.

Alongside *The Blues Brothers* and *My Bodyguard*, and Linda Williams and Raul Zaritsky's aforementioned *Maxwell Street Blues*, two further documentary films exist: 1964's *And This Is Free: The Life & Times Of Chicago's Legendary Maxwell Street*, directed by Mike Shea; and *Cheat You Fair*, directed by Phil Ranstrom and released theatrically in 2006. Each captures moments of music and mayhem typical of a Maxwell Sunday.

With an eye to preservation, the Maxwell Street Foundation, a 501(c)(3) charitable organization, was founded in 1993. Its mission statement? 'To preserve and interpret the history of Chicago's Maxwell Street neighborhood for future generations through public programs and special events.' Ultimately the organization's influence succeeded in preserving eight buildings and one façade for adaptive re-use and the dismantling and relocation of twelve facades in the University's redevelopment plan.'

There is a 'new Maxwell Street,' located not in the original location but rather east of the Dan Ryan Expressway on Desplaines Street, from Roosevelt Road to Harrison Street. The city's website touts it as 'an eclectic mix of handmade crafts, resale housewares and clothing, live music, family fun, and some of the best street food in Chicago.' Featured is a new generation of buskers representing every musical idiom and ethnicity. But the 'new Maxwell,' however earnest its intentions, could never match the authenticity of the original location, where musical history was served up every Sunday.

STREET CORNER SERENADE

CHAPTER 3

THE RISE OF
DOO-WOP
ON URBAN AMERICAN STREETS

THE STREET-CORNER ORIGINS of the doo-wop music genre can be traced back to the Black, Hispanic, and Italian neighborhoods of the major cities in the United States, particularly in the 1940s and 50s. New York, Philadelphia, Baltimore, Washington DC, Chicago, Detroit, and Los Angeles all featured street-corner harmonies in that timeframe, as did smaller municipalities like Newark, New Jersey, and Durham, North Carolina, as young singers gathered to harmonize and create music together.

Doo-wop emerged as a form of vocal harmony music that was often performed *a cappella* or with simple instrumentation, and it was typically characterized by tight harmonies, catchy melodies, and lyrics about love, relationships, and teenage life. Among the most successful songs of the genre are 'At The Hop' by Danny & The Juniors, 'Duke Of Earl' by Gene Chandler, 'Blue Moon' by The Marcels, 'The Lion Sleeps Tonight' by The Tokens, 'Stay' by Maurice Williams & The Zodiacs, '16 Candles' by The Crests, and of course 'I Only Have Eyes For You' by The Flamingos, which nods at street singing with the lines, *'I don't know if we're in a garden / Or on a crowded avenue.'*

Many of the most famous doo-wop groups—including The Drifters, The Platters, The Orioles, The El Dorados, The Ravens, The Teenagers, The Five Keys, and The Five Satins—began their careers as street-corner vocal groups. Their impromptu singing sessions allowed for experimentation and creativity, as singers would improvise and hone their vocal arrangements on the spot. Groups of singers, often teenagers or young adults, would assemble on street corners, in alleys, in school yards, or in other informal settings to sing and practice their harmonies. Some made their way to the hallways of New York's Brill Building, which was the nation's hub of songwriting, publishing, and label deals.

Mike Stoller, half of the legendary songwriting duo with Jerry Lieber—who co-wrote formative rock'n'roll classics like 'Stand By Me,' 'Spanish Harlem,' and 'On Broadway'—didn't recall seeing vocal groups on the streets. But when he went to work at the Brill Building, the men's restrooms were alive with harmonies. 'I would hear them in the men's room when we walked into the hallways,' he says. 'There were tiled walls, and they loved the echo. They would rehearse themselves in the men's room. It gave them a good feeling because they got that echo.'

In his book *Just My Soul Responding*, author Brian Ward provides examples of how some of these groups went from street corners to label owners' corner offices:

The street, with its bars, laundromats, pool halls, liquor stores, corner stores, shoeshine stands, barbershops, pawnshops, record stores, and storefront churches, formed a distinctive lower-class milieu in which this black entertainment culture operated. Black vocal groups inhabited and helped to define this vibrant, if far from untroubled, environment.

In West Baltimore, The Plants, heroes for about a block around Schroeder Street, signed with J&S Records in New York after they were heard singing backstage at the Royal Theater prior to a Five Keys and Moonglows show. ... Sometimes groups were discovered by chance, singing in and for their neighborhood. Legend has it that The Charms were spotted by [King Records owner] Syd Nathan at a park softball game in Cincinnati. The El Dorados were taken to Vee-Jay by their school custodian, who had heard them practicing in the hallways of Chicago's Englewood High School. Black Harlem impresario Bobby Robinson found The Mello-Moods 'singing on a stoop up in the Harlem River Projects,' and discovered the Channels in a Lenox Ave. rehearsal room.'[1]

As California-born, New York City–raised singer, songwriter, actor, author, and historian Billy Vera puts it succinctly, 'If you could sing, you wouldn't be beat up.' Things could get competitive, he adds. 'You know, some groups are better than others. And some were legendary. I mean, you know, some like a lot of the Italian groups would come over from Italian Harlem, which was on the east by the East River, or they would come from the Bronx, like Dion, and they came. A lot of it was gang-related. Dion was in the Golden Guineas gang. And there was the Fordham Baldies, another Italian gang. And in Harlem there was an Italian gang called the Harlem Redwings. The Harlem Redwings—they were the baddest. I knew those guys, man. They ranged from like fifteen to fifty in age. The Italian neighborhoods were separated.'

As doo-wop gained in popularity, it moved from street corners to recording studios. And many street-corner groups went on to record hit songs and achieve commercial success. However, the street-corner origins of doo-wop remained an important part of its history, and the genre's unique vocal harmonies and style were influenced by the creativity and spontaneity that emerged from these street-corner singing sessions.

The lead singer was usually a tenor, though sometimes a high tenor or a soprano (like Frankie Lymon). The bass would occasionally take the lead for part of a song, typically on up-tempo numbers, or contribute a talking bridge to the middle of a song. The lead in early doo-wop ballads frequently employed melisma—a gospel-derived vocal technique in which syllables are elongated to fit the meter of the song (such as the '*O-o-only You*' in The Platters' 'Only You' Falsetto parts were often used too, typically at the end of a song, in conjunction with a dramatic fade-out.

In New York—the mecca for doo-wop in the mid-1950s—The Harptones could be found on 115th Street, between Seventh and Eighth Avenues. One of the few female doo-wop groups, The Joytones, also sang at 115th and Seventh. The street is called 'a fertile nesting place for vocal groups' in Phil Groia's doo-wop history *They All Sang On The Street Corner*, though as Billy Vera explains, it was 'just where so many group members happened to live.'

The Four Diamonds made their base nearby at 134th and Seventh, while The Cadillacs could be found between 131st and 133rd Streets and Seventh and Eighth Avenues. 'I was friends with The Cadillacs,' says Vera, adding that she knew lead singer Earl 'Speedo' Carroll very well. 'I met him when he was on a break from The Cadillacs because they weren't making any money. So he joined The Coasters—and they *weren't* a street group, they were they were a studio concoction of Leiber & Stoller. But The Cadillacs, they *were* a street group.

'Then, up in the Bronx, you had The Chords. They made the original "Sha-Boom." And they sang on the streets. There's Morrisania. That's a section of the Bronx—Morris Avenue, around there. And The Chords were from there. The Mellows, with Lillian Leach, made "Smoke From Your Cigarette." The Crickets were from there—obviously not the Buddy Holly Crickets—and it's a fascinating section of the Bronx, so a little bit higher on the economic scale than Harlem, and then you cross into Queens. Jamaica was the Black section of Queens. And you'd have The Heartbeats,

[who] were yet another rung up the socioeconomic ladder, so they mostly practiced in their homes, you know. In their apartment. And they would *sing* on the streets. There was a park there, too—I can't remember the name of it, but The Cleftones would be there. The Heartbeats would be there; The Five Sharps, who evolved into The Videos, were there, and they were they're mainly a street group thing.'

Jay Siegel, a founding member of The Tokens, who topped the charts with the 1961 hit 'The Lion Sleeps Tonight,' recalls his group's origins on the streets and sands of Brighton Beach, Brooklyn. The group formed around 1955 and was originally known as The Linc-Tones and then The Tokens and The Coins, its membership initially including friend and neighbor Neil Sedaka. 'We started singing in school, in the gyms,' he adds. 'There was a different singing group on every street corner. I lived about two blocks from the beach, and we used to get together and sing, right on the beach. We didn't do it for money—we did it to get the girls! We just wanted to make music. We loved singing what we heard on the radio from the early days, listening to Alan Freed.

'Now they use the word *busking*,' Siegel continues. 'They have these great artists—they're terrific, and they have the guitar cases open or whatever, but no, we didn't do that. We didn't have a thought of making money. We were just enjoying singing the music. All of us really came also from really blue-collar families—none of us came from affluent families. We were all working-class people.'

Siegel recalls the group singing a song of South African origin called 'Mbube,' which by then had been adapted into a song titled 'Wimoweh' by the folk group The Weavers. While they were still singing on the beach and streets, The Tokens sang 'Wimoweh,' an early iteration of what would become their biggest hit, 'The Lion Sleeps Tonight,' for which English lyrics were added to the Zulu original 'Winnoweh' by lyricist George David Weiss at the suggestion of The Tokens' producers.

IN CHICAGO, groups like Johnny Keyes & The Magnificents (known for their 1956 hit 'Up On The Mountain') and The Five Echoes ('Lonely Mood') could be heard throughout the South Side, Keyes noting in his memoir, *Du-Wop*, that 'the lead singer was the one who knew the words.' Many vocal groups kept rhythm with a 'hambone' beat (made by slapping hands against the chest, a sound that proved influential on the beat of a famous Chicago South Side rock'n'roller Bo Diddley, who likewise started on the streets). While the original groups were predominantly Black, there were later ensembles of Italian and Puerto Rican extraction in many neighborhoods.

Robert Pruter, a noted Chicago rhythm & blues historian and author of the books *Doowop: The Chicago Scene* and *Chicago Soul*, cites Washington Park—located in the heart of the city's South Side, between 51st and 60th Streets and Cottage Grove Avenue and South Dr. Martin Luther King Jr. Drive—as a hub for live doo-wop. It was there that Samuel 'Smitty' Smith, who did A&R (artist and repertoire) for United Records and States Records, found The Dandoliers, who had a hit with 'Chop Chop Boom.' 'They were singing [in] Washington Park and Smitty drove by, took a listen to them, and signed them.'

Washington Park proved the perfect location for getting signed, as most of the Chicago record companies at the time were within a mile of 48th Street and Cottage Grove Avenue. Within a decade, most of them had moved to what later became the city's Record Row: South Michigan Avenue, between Roosevelt Road and Cermak Road.

Only ten blocks away on East 38th Street, between Vincennes and Langley Avenues, near the Ida B. Wells housing projects, were The Five Buddies. According to group member Ularsee Manor, interviewed for Pruter's *Doowop: The Chicago Scene*, 'That was our street, and any boy who came into our territory, they couldn't pass through unless they sang. From one territory to the next, there would be sing-outs. Instead of fighting, you had to sing to get through.'

'Different groups would have territories like gangs,' Pruter notes, 'and to be accepted into the other territory you had to sing real well.' Doo-wop's outdoor origins, he adds, were more utilitarian than theatrical: 'Many of them were singing on the streets and in the parks—but usually on the street—because they wanted to. Even though they were practicing, they wanted to do it in front of people.'

Bluesman Billy Boy Arnold, who played for a while in Bo Diddley's band, says the streets were just one of many rehearsal facilities for such groups: 'They would get together almost anywhere. Didn't have to be on the corner or the block or the schoolyard. Kids would get together, and that's how they would practice, you know?'

Billy Vera recalls talking to a member of The Dells, a doo-wop group from suburban Harvey, Illinois, who became R&B hitmakers in the 60s and are still playing today, despite the loss of four original members.

'I asked them, *Where do you get your shit from?*' he recalls.

'Well, we were singing on those corners,' the Dells member responded to Vera, 'and The Moonglows came by, [and they] were super professional. They were not a street-corner group. They certainly became a big group. And they were really well-schooled singers. And we were just fucking around. And so we went and auditioned for Chess Records. And Leonard Chess told us to not quit our day jobs ... because you sure can't sing. So The Moonglows sort of schooled us a little bit. How to harmonize and how to, you know, form this this this harmonies. And so we went in when we went to Vee-Jay, then by that time we could sing.'

'But,' Vera says in summation, 'The Dells began when they heard The Moonglows on the street.'

Chicago historian Paul Petraitis adds a bit of specificity. 'Thornton Township High School in Harvey, Illinois, was originally built at 154th Street and Columbia Avenue in 1899. Additional buildings [were added] in the 1930s. An underpass was likely built in 1942, when the school initiated its War Studies, remaining open eighty-seven hours a week.'

'We sang in the underpass because of the nice echo,' The Dells' Chuck Barksdale told Petraitis on June 8, 1990, during a ceremony for the 'landmarking' by the City Of Chicago of the old Chess Studio at 2120 South Michigan Avenue. 'I can't find a date for their years at the school,' he added. 'I'm guessing 1952–53 by adding sixteen to their birthdates.'

Fredrick Dennis Greene—professor of law at the University Of Dayton, vice president of production at Columbia Pictures, and perhaps most importantly a founding member of Sha Na Na—described the scene thus: '[Doo-wop groups] often rehearsed in hallways and high school bathrooms and under bridges; when they were ready for public performance, they sang on stoops and street corners, in community center talent shows, and in the hallways of the Brill Building. As a result many doo-wop records had such remarkably rich vocal harmonies that they virtually overwhelmed their minimalist instrumental accompaniment.'[2]

One survivor of the doo-wop scene was Dion DiMucci, lead singer with The Belmonts—three Italian lads who lived on or near The Bronx's Belmont Avenue. In an article for the *Guardian* newspaper, writer Michael Hann described the group as 'four Italian-American kids who grew up around Belmont Avenue in the Bronx's Little Italy [and] were like any of the groups of street-corner toughs who sang sweetly to the girls during Dwight D. Eisenhower's second term as President. Music was how they would all say the things they couldn't put into conversation, for fear of being kicked around the block.'[3] DiMucci, of course, went on to have a career long beyond doo-wop with the 60s hits 'Runaround Sue,' 'The Wanderer,' and 'Abraham, Martin & John,' plus a handful of critically acclaimed blues albums in the next century.

In South Los Angeles, there was a doo-wop scene that emanated largely from schoolyards. Vera, who was born in Southern California, raised outside of New York City, and returned to LA in 1979, says that doo-wop group members 'were identified in LA by what high school they went to. So there was Thomas Jefferson, aka Jeff High. The Jaguars were a racially mixed group with one Italian guy, one Hispanic guy, and two Black guys. They made "The Way You Look Tonight." Beautiful record. And they went to Los Angeles High School. But most of the music came from Jefferson High—they had a wonderful famous music teacher there Samuel Browne.'

In summing up the era of doo-wop on America's street corners, Chicago R&B historian Pruter feels that 'to a certain extent, [the groups] romanticized it a little in their memories about their street battles.'

Embellishment makes for a better story. But it usually comes from a kernel of truth.

BUSKING
BLUESMEN

CHAPTER 4
PRE- AND
POST-WAR

THE BLUES GENRE WAS BORN in the fields and eventually migrated to the streets. Southern cities like New Orleans, Houston, Dallas, Durham, and Memphis, and, up north, Chicago, St. Louis, and Detroit, became hotbeds for street-corner blues. Some artists eventually graduated to paying jobs at taverns and nightclubs. Some went on to have successful recording careers. Yet others played the streets all their days. Here we look at three blues artists who went on to make records and influence a new generation of blues artists.

BLIND LEMON JEFFERSON: DEEP BLUES FROM DEEP ELLUM

Blind Lemon Jefferson was born around 1893 (exact date uncertain) in Couchman, Texas. He is remembered as one of the first blues artists on record, his most widely covered songs including 'Please See That My Grave Is Kept Clean' (sometimes titled 'One Kind Favor'), 'Mean Jumper Blues,' and 'Jack O' Diamonds.'

Blind from birth, Jefferson began his musical career as a street singer, performing in Dallas's Deep Ellum neighborhood, a vibrant hub for Black musicians in the early twentieth century and still a nightlife district today.

He could frequently be found at the corner of Elm Street and what is now the Central Expressway underpass.

Jefferson's street performances took place primarily in the 1910s and 20s. He gained a following through his captivating performances, characterized by his distinctive vocal style and intricate guitar playing. His reputation as a talented musician and his unique approach to blues music led him to achieve considerable success during his short life.

In his article 'Deep Ellum Clues' for *Texas Highways*, writer Clayton Maxwell observed, 'Blind Lemon's music spoke to people. According to fellow Deep Ellum busker Huddie Ledbetter, aka Lead Belly—frequently Jefferson's guide—he and Blind Lemon were so popular when they'd play in Dallas, "the women would come running, Lord have mercy. They'd hug and kiss us so much we could hardly play." A musician's dream, regardless of the century.'[1]

According to Robert Palmer, in his book *Deep Blues*, 'He was a loose, improvisational, sometimes anarchic guitarist, and his jazzy single-string work bore fruit in the 1940s in the pioneering electric blues of T-Bone Walker, who grew up in Dallas and used to occasionally accompany Jefferson on those walks across town.'[2] In exchange for working as his guide, Jefferson taught Walker a thing or two about guitar.

While Jefferson's specific years as a street singer are not well-documented, his busking activities in the streets of Dallas contributed significantly to his development as an artist and helped shape his distinct musical style. He died at the age of thirty-six. He is interred in Wortham, Freestone County, Texas. The one kind favor he ever asked has been honored: his marked grave is kept clean.

REVEREND GARY DAVIS: FROM DURHAM TO HARLEM

'I was goin' up the street. Goin' up Lenox Avenue. Two o'clock at night. I'd jes' left from my friend preacher's house. Talkin'. Two fellows overtaken me. Thought maybe they was goin' my way. Ask me would I stop on a hundred an' thirtieth street wid 'em. I thought it was all right. Jes' good company, I thought. Then I stopped, got upon the stoop, you understan', an' one of 'em started foolin' 'round in my pocket. They have not git my money. I was turning too fast fur them to git that. Made me mad. Thas one night, if I'd a had me a pistol, I wouldn't a been settin' heah. I would-a killed both of them. I could eat a nail, I was so mad wid them. I didn't never give up, you understan'. I … I … they slapped me in the face. When I got that what I had in my pocket out I beat them to that, you understan'. When I got that out, wadn't nothing fur them to do. He close it down on my fingers an' hit me in the face. If he had ever got that near me, I'd-a kilt him. That was a pocket knife, you see.'³

Reverend Gary Davis, the singer and finger-picking guitarist also known as Blind Gary Davis, made his living as a street singer in the early part of his career. He was born in Laurens, South Carolina, on April 30, 1896, and was blinded as a child. He learned to play guitar and banjo as a young man and began performing on the streets of Southern cities like Spartanburg and the North Carolina cities of Asheville (in the city's Pack Square Park) and Durham (often in front of tobacco warehouses), as well as Atlanta, Georgia, since his mid-twenties. According to the Museum Of Durham History, 'Around this time, Davis broke his left wrist after slipping on the snow, but this accident would in fact aid his musical style since he displayed a remarkable ability to play unusual chord patterns not possible for a normal wrist.'⁴

According to William Lee Ellis, chair of fine arts and associate professor of music at Saint Michael's College in Colchester, Vermont, who wrote his dissertation on Davis, 'From Durham to Harlem, Davis busked most of his life. The cigar-chomping, blues-loving Rev, as the guitar world came to know him, only came to public prominence the last decade-and-a-half of his life. Some sixty years of hardscrabble living preceded that persona, decades filled with little but two choices to earn a living, busking on the streets for change and accepting what storefront congregations— themselves typically marginalized and indigent—could collect when he would preach.

'Yet it was on the streets where his social status as a person of color with a disability perhaps intersected most with his profound gifts. Street performing was an unforgiving environment for anyone needing to make a living as a musician, especially during the Jim Crow era. Vagaries of weather were the least of concerns. Like many of his busking peers, Davis also incurred the cruelties of humanity. Tips and guitars alike were stolen, he was run off by the police, harassed, fined, and arrested numerous times in New York City alone for the crime of public loitering.'

Davis's street performances often involved him singing and playing gospel and blues songs, sometimes in tandem with Piedmont contemporaries Bull City Red, Sonny Terry & Brownie McGhee, and Blind Boy Fuller. Davis was known for his virtuosic fingerpicking style and his ability to improvise on the guitar. He also taught guitar lessons to other musicians, including Woody Guthrie.

Durham flourished as a blues busking center through the 1930s, a period that noted North Carolina music journalist David Menconi described as the city's 'golden age' in an article for OurState.com. '[Blind Boy] Fuller was one of the musicians at its center. He would busk along with other players who congregated on street corners around tobacco marketplaces like Liberty Warehouse. The scene was especially bustling during the fall harvest, when Piedmont farmers would descend on Durham's warehouses to sell their crops. Once there, they had to wait around for hours or even days to do business—a captive audience, drawing musicians and bootleggers eager to sell their wares.'[5]

In the 1940s, following the decline of the Durham blues scene, Reverend Davis moved to New York City, where he continued to perform on the streets and in clubs. He gained a following among folk and blues enthusiasts and was eventually discovered by the music industry. He went on to record several albums and became a respected figure, but despite his success he never lost his connection to his street-performing roots and continued to perform on the streets of New York City throughout his career. He is cited as an influence by Taj Mahal, Eric Von Schmidt, and Larry Johnson, among others.

Late folk singer and activist Len Chandler recalled Davis's busking days in the documentary film *Harlem Street Singer*. 'Reverend Gary Davis used to play on street in this neighborhood and others all around Harlem, and it's not an easy thing,' he said. 'You have to be a certain type of aggressive, appealing, unique performer to be able to survive in this realm. Occasionally I would come to watch him play and he would have his guitar case open in front of him and he would just rock and play, and he would be snapping his fingers. But it was his intensity and his enthusiasm and the whole quality of his performance that was able to attract a crowd and keep it and make them give up a little money when they left.'[6]

Elsewhere, New York author and musician John Kruth described Davis's street performances in an article for the online publication *Please Kill Me*. 'Armed with his jumbo-bodied Gibson J-200, the Reverend would amble down to the corner of 138th Street and Lenox Avenue to broadcast the Lord's word. Although the street was rife with thieves and hustlers, Brother Davis soldiered on, day after day, through every kind of imaginable encounter, while singing about Jesus with a tin cup pinned to the lapel of his overcoat. There were days when he made nothing at all and other times, when his money-maker was shakin', he claimed to have brought in between $50 and $100.'[7]

Professor Ellis feels that, 'ultimately, busking gave Davis a public platform that validated his musical identity and purpose—all the while demanding that he be the best at it.'

REVEREND PEARLY BROWN: GOD LOVES A CHEERFUL GIVER

Pearly Brown was born on August 15, 1915, in Abbeville, Georgia. Like Jefferson, he was born blind. According to his late biographer, Jim Pettigrew, a schoolteacher recognized Brown's uncommon intelligence and ambition and set him up to attend the Georgia Academy For The Blind in nearby Macon.[8] He was greatly influenced by pre–World War II Texas bluesman Blind Willie Johnson.

John W. English's twenty-nine-minute documentary about Brown, *It's A Mean Old World To Try To Live In*, depicts him playing on the streets, usually with a resonator guitar, sometimes with bottleneck slide, and often bearing a sign that read, 'I am a blind preacher. Please help me, thank you. Rev. Pearly Brown, Americus, GA.' It was in Americus, a southeastern Georgia town of 16,230 by its 2020 census, that he made his home at 816 Ashby Street.

Throughout the documentary, Brown is impeccably dressed. Around his neck, he wore a brass necklace that read, 'God love a cheerful giver.'[9] In the documentary, he says, 'I've been singing in the street since 1939. Me and a whole lot of lot of blind guys, we used to work together. And many got to run us blind folks off the street, kick us off the street. There'd be some mean old folks around that time. Once they'd run you off the street…they was mean and low down. That stuff's still around right now.'

The film shows an amiable and humble man—a man of talent, and a man who found love. His wife, Christine, makes several appearances in the documentary. Brown went on to influence a new generation of Southern slide guitarists, notably Duane Allman and Dickey Betts of the Allman Brothers Band. Following Brown's death (and Duane's, for that matter), Betts referenced Brown in 'Everybody's Got A Mountain To Climb,' a track from the band's 1994 album *Where It All Begins*.

Reverend Pearly Brown was also an influence on singer/songwriter Lucinda Williams, who saw him play the streets of Macon on numerous occasions and listened fervently to his album *Georgia Street Singer*, which was given to her by her father, a poet and literature professor. 'I listened to him over and over and over again,' she says. 'I eventually learned some of the songs off of his records, but I really had to listen. He, his stuff was so primal, you know, that I had to listen to get the lyrics. When I look back on it, he was the real thing.'

'It was kind of an interesting circle,' she adds, 'because I went to see him singing on the streets, and then I ended up singing on the streets myself.' While Williams never busked in Macon, she would later perform on the streets of Austin, San Francisco, New Orleans, and New York.

Wet Willie was a Macon band at the leading edge of the early 1970s Southern rock scene that also included the Allman Brothers and Lynyrd Skynyrd. With origins in Mobile, Alabama, the band relocated to Macon around 1969. In 1974, they recorded their third album for Macon's Capricorn Records, *Keep On Smilin'*. The album's producer was the legendary Tom Dowd, known for his work with Derek & The Dominos, The Bee Gees, and Skynyrd. Wet Willie, in tandem with Capricorn's creative department, decided to take photos of the band interacting with municipal scenery around Macon, and were photographed against a store called Brown Liquor. During their explorations of Downtown Macon, photographer Al Clayton also captured an image of Reverend Pearly Brown with his famous handwritten sign that read, 'God loves a cheerful giver.'

According to Wet Willie's Jimmy Hall, 'That whole concept of him on the cover was kind of the label's creative department and the photographer's idea. So, okay, we're shooting some photos around the area downtown, and we see Pearly Brown, and the photographers said, This might be a cool idea. And we said, Yeah, we know, we've seen him before.

'So I go over and I say, Hey, this is Jimmy Hall and we're Wet Willie, and he said, Glad to see that you guys around! What's going on? So we talked to him, and we said, We're taking pictures for our album cover and we would love it if you would pose with us. So this photographer took a lot of pictures, including some close-ups of just him. [Capricorn] did a did a cover mock-up or put it together and said, This is what we came up with. So it ended up being Reverend Brown's picture in a kind of sepia tone, and a large version covering the whole cover with a small inset photo of the band.

'We decided, for his services, his time, and his likeness, we're gonna pay him some money, and I cannot remember the exact number, but it was a few hundred, from three to five hundred dollars. He was very happy with that. So the album came out, and soon after it hit the streets, our label got a call and then a letter from an attorney. And I just have a feeling he's the kind of guy who'd done this kind of work before; I could just hear him saying [to Brown], Hey, these white guys are putting your picture all over the cover and I think you deserve more money for this because it looks like your album, you know, with your picture on the front!'

An injunction was filed. Capricorn Records co-founder Phil Walden and his attorney were reportedly able to settle out of court. 'That was unfortunately not a great situation or interaction,' says Hall, 'because we all really appreciated what [Brown] did for us. I mean, I regularly listened to his radio show on WIBB-FM, where he would sing and talk and everything.'

In the end, both Wet Willie and Reverend Brown kept on smiling. Brown's musical career had its share of highlights, including appearances at both the Newport Jazz Festival and the Monterey Jazz Festival, as well as Carnegie Hall in 1966. He released two albums—*Georgia Street Singer* on Henry Oster's Folk-Lyric label in 1961, and *It's A Mean Old World To Try To Live In* on Rounder in 1975. English's documentary, which bore the name of Brown's second and final album, was released in 1977.

By 1979, he had ceased busking. Reverend Brown lived his final days at Plains Nursing Home in Plains, Georgia—famously the home of President Jimmy Carter. In 2010, he was posthumously inducted into the Georgia Music Hall Of Fame.

PART
TWO

The singer/songwriter thing was starting to happen.
Tom Paxton would be there, and I think Tom Rush
came too. All these groups of people playing music.
It was amazing. Everybody eventually showed up at
Washington Square Park ... including Bob Dylan. When
he showed up, everything changed. **DAVID BENNETT COHEN**

WASHINGTON SQUARE PARK

CHAPTER 5

SINGING THE RIOT ACT

AS PATRICIA J. CAMPBELL NOTES in her book *Passing The Hat*, 'The history of busking is the history of urban civilization. There have been street performers at least as long as there have been streets.'[1]

Nowhere in America was that truer than in New York. The city has hosted many types of musical buskers over the years: doo-wop vocal groups filled the streets of Harlem with harmonies in the late 1950s; Moondog on Sixth Avenue in the 60s; a long history of subway musicians; and a lively scene in Washington Square Park, a ten-acre parcel in Manhattan's Greenwich Village, located between MacDougal Street, University Place, Waverly Place, and West 4th Street. Its signature piece of architecture is the Washington Square Arch, designed by Stanford White in 1891.

Washington Square, with its carnival-like atmosphere, became a fully fledged busking haven in the early twentieth century. 'As a sign of appreciation, housewives would drop coins wrapped in paper down to the singers from their windows,' Joel Feinberg writes in his history of busking in the city.[2] By the early 60s, the park had become a leading outpost for musicians singing about social change.

'The singer/songwriter thing was starting to happen,' says New York folk musician David Bennett Cohen. 'Tom Paxton would be there, and I think Tom Rush came too, although he was a Boston guy. All these groups of people playing music. It was amazing. It was the Shanty Boys—Roger Sprung, Lionel Kilberg, and Mike Cohen. There was Eric Weisberg, Roy Berkeley, Dave Van Ronk, Joshua Rivkin ... my friend Dan Lauffer was there, and John Sebastian, Stefan Grossman, and Danny Kalb. They were all just singing songs. Everybody eventually showed up at Washington Square Park ... including Bob Dylan. When he showed up, everything changed.

'We were playing music outside, you know, and I guess you could call that busking,' Cohen continues. 'It was not really a busker place because people didn't collect money for what they what they did—what *we* did—but it was definitely a place where folk music was being played. I started going in 1956. That's where I learned so much about music. My whole musical vocabulary, pretty much, came from Washington Square Park and playing the guitar.'

Three decades earlier, on January 1, 1936, New York City mayor Fiorello La Guardia had effectively ended street performance, banning the licensing of street musicians. Debate ensued as to whether outdoor performers should be classified as 'artisans' or 'beggars.'

In his 2012 study of the ban, Robert Hawkins writes, 'Street musicians occupied an ambiguous space between begging and self-employment and, as relief programs provoked public concern over economic individualism, confusion between honest unemployment and willful dependency was a political liability for the mayor. Yet, while the mayor condemned busking as begging, citizens sprang to street music's defense, arguing the ban would force practitioners onto the relief rolls; while municipal policy proclaimed street music was no longer work, some New Yorkers suddenly believed the opposite.'[3]

This included musicians' willingness to fight for their right to perform publicly. In 1961, the New York Department Of Parks & Recreation decreed that the park be a quiet place. This did not sit well with outdoor performers, or their audiences. And it begat what is arguably the most storied busking protest of all time: the Beatnik Riot.

'This was the beginning of the 1960s,' said filmmaker Dan Drasin, who directed an evocative seventeen-minute documentary about the upheaval on April 9, 1961.[4] *Sunday* depicts a folk song concert and a demonstration about the right to sing folk songs in the park, after an application for permission to the park administration has been denied; eventually, the police enter to dissolve the protest.

David Bennett Cohen was present at the park that day. (He would move from his native New York to San Francisco later in that decade to become a member of Country Joe & The Fish, appearing on their FM hit 'I-Feel-Like-I'm-Fixin'-To-Die Rag' before resuming his life as a New Yorker). He recalls the riot as being 'very spontaneous. There was no planning. We just showed up. They said we couldn't. It was just, like everything else, an improvisation.

'The riots that happened because Mayor [Robert F.] Wagner Jr.—a Democrat—said we can't have folk musicians singing in public,' he reflects. 'We can't do that because [folksingers are] too radical. For some reason they didn't like folk music, or the lifestyle. So they didn't issue a permit [for public performance] that year. So we, you know, we went anyway. And, of course, we showed up, and so did the cops—cops are all around. We started singing and they started busting heads, you know … for singing. The *media* called it a riot. The ones who rioted were the cops …

'Everybody sings—even a baby sings. They didn't want us to sing "This Land Is Your Land." They didn't want us to sing any of the songs that you know. When the cops started rioting, they busted a few people, but, you know, Izzy [Folklore Center director Israel Young] really stood up for us and argued with them. Izzy was one of the most important people in the folk music scene at that time—the Folklore Center was a place where we gathered. It was just, you know, we were singing songs—what's the matter with singing songs? I think, at one point, we sang the National Anthem.

Right? Not quite a folk song. So, you know ... it was constantly back and forth with the cops.'

Cohen offers a humorous aside regarding Drasin's film. 'I took one of my girlfriends out to a movie in a theater in Greenwich Village. I looked up and I saw the movie that was playing was a short subject called *Sunday*. I had no idea what that was. So we were sitting in the theater, the theater goes dark, I hear this music, and I say, This sounds familiar. I look up and I see some friends of mine and at the end it [credited] music by David Cohen, and Jan Dorfman. It was us singing, so I did the soundtrack for it. So, of course, my girlfriend was very impressed.'

In 1970, the street performance ban was lifted under Mayor John V. Lindsey's administration, but subway performance remained banned. In the 80s, after some legal battles, the city implemented policies to decriminalize busking; musicians and performers were now legally able to perform in public spaces like Washington Square, which helped cement the park's reputation as a prominent location for busking.

Cohen, who has played a blues jam session every Monday night for the past thirteen years, still gets to Washington Square occasionally, and he acknowledges the change he helped effect. 'Now you go to Washington Square Park, and any time of the day or night you see people singing, right? I think [the fight for street performers' rights] changed a lot of things. It changed the way many of us looked at protesting. It changed the vibe of the city, because after that, the city backed down, and they issued permits. And then things started loosening up a lot more. As we became more politically aware, and more aware socially [of] what was going on in the world, we started banding together as beatniks and hippies. And, you know, it [had] a tremendous impact because, like I said, everything changed after that. And, in a sense, we won that battle.

'We used to have reunions at Washington Square Park every year,' he adds. 'And it was really wonderful.'

FAST-FORWARD TO six years after the riot of '61. Washington Square Park continued to teem with live music, and one of the artists attracting crowds was singer, songwriter, and guitarist David Peel. Peel, a Brooklyn native of Puerto Rican descent, was born David Michael Rosario; he took on the name 'Peel' based on a joke about how smoking banana peels was thought to get one high.[5]

During that time period, a young and passionate music fan named Danny Fields was working in publicity for Elektra Records. Fields, who years later would play a role in the discovery and development of the MC5, the Stooges, and the Ramones, among others, had the ear of label founder Jac Holzman, and one day he came to him with an idea. 'One of the things we loved were the drinking songs, like the Heidelberg beer song, so I said Jac in '68, Why are there no smoke-a-joint albums or songs? And Jac said, What a great idea! I said, What would we put on it? Let's think of possible content for this concept.'

One Sunday, while strolling through Washington Square, Fields serendipitously found his vision for that album. 'I was in Washington Square—I lived in the Village—and there was a street singer with a group of twenty people hanging around, and I heard him sing, *I like marijuana*. I said, This guy is great!

'In fact, in my paranoia, I believed everyone there was from a record company and they're all the way and they're all gonna jump on him and sign him up because he was so good and original and funny and *streety* and brash and *pushy*. So I'm just gonna try and get like closer to him, and then when all these other record company executives pounce, they're gonna have to get in line behind me. Well, of course, when he finished, everyone had left *but* me.'

Fields asked the singer to lunch at Max's Kansas City and then took him back to his apartment, where he recalls that the TV was on, showing President Lyndon B. Johnson announcing that he would not seek reelection. That Monday, Fields informed Holzman, 'I think I found the content for this marijuana album.'

'Jac lived on 12th Street and Fifth Avenue,' Fields recalls. 'And I lived on 20th & Fifth. So I said, Let's meet here in Washington Square next Sunday, which is his day. So we watched David for a few minutes, and [Jac] said, This is really cool, and I think we should record it right here in Washington Square!'

Holzman in turn assigned producer Peter K. Siegel—a folk and blues musician with his own history of playing Sundays on the Square—to oversee the recording. Fields remembers the day the album was recorded. 'They brought a Nagra [tape recorder] down and they got the electricity by screwing with one of the lampposts for the street in Washington Square and ran a power wire to that and spliced it up. So we stole money from the city of New York to make this record, which is kind of wonderful and it's kind of *not* wonderful—but, you know, perfect, as it should be!'

'I was using the power that came out of the base of the lamppost,' Siegel remembers. 'I believe, at least at that time, that most if not all of New York City lampposts had a faceplate at the base. There was a plug in there that you could plug into. I had a permit that allowed me to do that. And suddenly all my equipment stopped. I looked around, and there was a cop holding the plug from my extension cord up in the air. And he said, You can't record here, you know? And I said, Yes, I do have a permit. I took out the permit and showed it to him, and he looked at it and said okay, so I plugged it back in, and we proceeded.'

Peel was recorded in his natural habitat—two sets' worth. And, by 1968, times were clearly changing. 'I think that was an active spring and summer for anti-war protest,' Fields recalls. 'One of them was covered in *Time* magazine, and the reporter [described] a protest that started in Times Square [and] ended at Grand Central Station ...

'The story said the hippies marched into Grand Central Station, led by a street singer who was singing, *Have a marijuana*. They were talking about Peel, of course. Now, David had a speech impediment. He was [singing] out of the side of his mouth. The guy thought he was saying, *Have a marijuana. . . .* The *Time* magazine reporter misheard it, which is understandable . . . and I thought, *Wow, this just sounds like an album title!* So we're gonna take this error and put it on, that's it.

'*Have A Marijuana* would be the title of the album. My fervent wish was that teenagers, kids, college kids all over the country would have it in their rooms, and—because I wanted it in really big type—their parents see it and drop dead of a heart attack.'

Siegel corroborates how taboo an album whose subject matter was marijuana seemed at the time. 'We were paranoid about putting our names on the album,' he recalls. 'So I arranged to have David Peel shout out the credits at the end of the album.'

For bringing Peel to Elektra, Fields was rewarded 'a tiny-teeny fraction of a penny discovery fee, but . . . I bought a color television set with the check, you know. It supposedly sold between five hundred [thousand] and a million.' The album crested at #186 on the *Billboard* 200. 'But it existed,' Fields says. 'All I cared about was, it existed. And hey, on the front of the album, it says *recorded live on the streets of New York*. And hey, it cost $1,500 to record, so it more than made back its money.'

An Elektra follow-up titled *American Revolution*, also produced by Siegel, appeared in 1970. 'The second album was recorded in a studio, but I also went around with another tape recorder and got street sounds and people talking on the street,' he says. 'Marshall Efron was an actor and comedian who was a permanent fixture at WBAI in New York. And I got him to come play the role of a cop on the second album. We had a lot of fun with it. At that time, David Peel had a drummer and a bass player, so it was more like a rock'n'roll album, but with additional sounds that I recorded on the street.'

John Sinclair, the Detroit-based activist and poet (and, in the late 60s, manager of the MC5), was famously incarcerated for possession of two marijuana joints in 1969. He called Peel 'a giant at what he did.' Peel partook in the John Sinclair Freedom Rally held December 10, 1971, at the University Of Michigan, Ann Arbor.

Peel may be the only artist to have been discovered not once but twice on Washington Square. The next time was by none other than recent New York transplants John Lennon and Yoko Ono. Fields was no longer involved at that point, but he recalls, 'John and Yoko had just moved from England to New York, and they were looking around for avant-garde talent to attach their names to. They walked over to David Peel, who I was no longer working for. I just thought, *Well, this is funny.*' The resultant album, released on Apple Records in 1972, was entitled *The Pope Smokes Dope.*

'New York was Mecca for folk,' says Fields, 'whether it was at Folk City or in Washington Square. This is where Phil Ochs and Eric Anderson and all of them were nurtured. I like to think David is part of that too ... there should be a plaque in front of that tree, right? The record about marijuana in 1968 [was] the first ever on a legitimate label to talk about this substance which now is widely available in every smoke shop in the city.'

But, Fields says, while music is now legally accepted in Washington Square Park, it is no longer what he considers 'legitimate' music. 'It's over, replaced by squawking saxophones and no more songs. I mean, jazz is the opposite of songs. [A song] like David was singing... that's over. I don't know why. Maybe it has something to do with social media, but people don't seem to be singing their hearts out in public and attracting a following.'

RAMBLIN'
JACK ELLIOTT

CHAPTER 6

NOT BUSKING,
JUST SINGING
FOR THE FUN OF IT

RAMBLIN' JACK ELLIOTT, now in his nineties, continues to ramble, true to his appellation, playing venues, theaters, and festivals. The 'Ramblin" in his name—reportedly given to him by folk music contemporary Odetta— also suggests, correctly, that he's been around. Indeed, the Brooklyn native, born Elliott Charles Adnopoz on August 1, 1931, has lived all over the United States and Europe.

Inspired by rodeos he saw in New York City growing up, the son of a Jewish surgeon ran off to join Colonel Jim Eskew's Wild West Show rodeo. It was during this stint that he encountered his first singing cowboy, rodeo clown Brahmer Rogers. Elliott made a point of teaching himself guitar, banjo, and singing. His first performances were on the street.

Years later, Elliott met and derived deep inspiration from Woody Guthrie. Elliott himself would much later inspire another great legend of the American folk evolution, Bob Dylan, in whose rambling ensemble, the Rolling Thunder Revue, Elliott would appear from 1975 to '76. He would accrue a recorded output of more than twenty albums—most of them solo releases on labels like Topic, Folkways, Prestige, Vanguard, Reprise, Red House, HighTone, and ANTI-. He won a Grammy in 1995 for his album *South Coast.*

One aspect of his career that is whispered rather than emphasized is that the Jewish Brooklyn surgeon's son who changed his persona to a country boy of sorts, played the streets. 'But not in Brooklyn,' he's quick to point out. Nor did he busk for long, he adds. But he did play New York's Ground Zero of street singing, Washington Square, in the 60s, back when it was inhabited by some of the pioneers of the Greenwich Village folk scene.

'I played for a New York City for an audience of Sunday afternoon-goers in Washington Square Park,' he says. 'but that wasn't busking—that was just singing for the fun of it. There was barely any passing the hat around for money. So I did it occasionally.'

Further recalling his time in Washington Square, he adds, 'I wasn't there when they had the riot. But they had some close calls with the police because it became necessary to purchase a permit to perform music in the park on every Sunday afternoon. And after three or four years of that stuff, some people objected to it. Mainly, the police didn't like the idea of such a large crowd gathering up, but there was never any unkind gestures or violence or anything.

'I know one time I was getting ready to go to California with Woody, we did pass the hat around the crowd and got about eleven dollars in Washington Square Park. That money contributed to the gasoline expenses for the trip, and the food stops, the coffee, and the sandwich between New York and California.'

Of course, eleven dollars would barely cover two coffees today.

Busking in Washington Square around 1953 also connected him with two future associates, Guy Carawan and Frank Hamilton. With his new friends, Elliott rambled to North Carolina—initially to a whistlestop called

Mesic, which had a population of around two hundred at the time—to visit some of Guys' relatives.

'One night, the first person we met down in Mesic was a farmer and a fisherman and he took It out shrimping in his boat and gave us supper and we had a night of music out there on the porch,' he recalls. 'That guy, Frank, sang some wonderful songs. And the next morning we headed west for the Smoky Mountains, where we met a lot of hillbilly musicians. And, yes, we did a little busking there, and on the street in North Carolina—in some little farming towns, in western North Carolina, Asheville and Maggie Valley.'

Maggie Valley was named after the founder Jack Seltzer's daughter, Maggie Mae. 'Maggie's old man, Ted Sutton, played five-string banjo. His favorite song that he kept repeating [was] *I catch them, feed them, milk them in the morning blues.* That was just a refrain from some song. I never heard the rest of it; he just used to like to repeat that one phrase. And then I have another favorite song called "Knot Hole." And he would shout out every half hour or so. He'd say, *Knot whole, knot hole. Y'all have seen one that's all through the old Knot Hole.* He was quite a character. And we gave him a ride home to where he lived up in Maggie Valley, where we got to meet Maggie, and they put us up overnight to sleep in their little tree house. We had to climb up a ladder to get into the tree house. And Maggie was waiting for us with a rolling pin because we were real late getting home. We got to witness a family feud going on right there in the bedroom. But nobody got injured real bad.'

During the early 60s, prior to his first meeting with Bob Dylan, Elliott spent time in Europe, busking his way through England, France, and Italy. 'I was in Europe for six years, driving around singing,' he says. 'It was difficult to do any busking in London, especially, because one had to purchase a permit to busk. They issued you a permit to perform on a certain portion of a certain street—a certain one address and another address, and that was the limit of your location.

'In busking there, we could ask for money and put the hat out on the ground for a little money. And there was one place in London where it was legal for *anybody* to busk without a permit—the *only* place where it was legal—and it was about a block away from the Tower Of London, near the Tower Bridge. It was an established routine. And it was only on Sundays, I believe, that they went to that particular location. There were three or four or five other people doing the busking. Some people drew art on the pavement with different colored chalk and they would do chalk paintings on the sidewalk and put the money in their hat.

'We had many adventures all over Europe,' he adds. 'They had the worst wine in France, but it was free. We saved up enough money [that] in only two years, we were able to buy an Italian motor scooter. Brand new at the factory. It was only $240.'

Back in the USA—specifically California—Elliott met Derroll Adams, who was chosen to be the best man at one of Elliott's weddings. 'He was a pretty fine banjo player from Oregon,' he recalls, 'and he didn't know anybody else in Oregon that could teach him how to play a banjo. Uh, you learned it from listening to records of Bascom Lamar Lunsford.' He and Adams busked on the West Coast for a while.

Elliott does not look upon his street singing experience with particular fondness. 'I don't particularly enjoy trying to sing out on some street corner hoping that somebody's gonna give me twenty cents in a hat,' he says, adding, 'There are romantics and there are incurable romantics. I'm a romantic but I'm curable!'

It was during a busking episode in England, however, that Elliott caught the eye and ear of a future singer named Mick Jagger.

'I had played plenty of concerts indoors for money at a school where Mick Jagger was living as a child,' he says. 'And he was I guess around maybe ten or eleven years old. And my wife June and I were on the railroad platform, waiting for the train to take us back to London. There were these children on the opposite platform, waiting for a train going the other way—they're going to school, and they were all wearing school uniforms. We had to wait for over half an hour for our train to come in, so I got the guitar out of the case, started playing, and, of course, I was wearing a cowboy hat—I *always* wore a cowboy hat.

'I sang a cowboy song. And one of the kids turned out to be Mick Jagger. I met him about twenty years later, when they were playing in Toronto. Mick told me that . . . he saw me—he was one of those school children waiting for a train on the opposite platform. He saw and heard me singing and playing the guitar and got excited about it. Said he ran round out the very next day and bought himself a guitar.'

While Jack carved a legacy from his ramblin', the lad who heard him across the tracks hasn't done too badly with his own career, rolling.

OLIVER SMITH

CHAPTER 7

AN ORDINARY MAN'S
LUCKY DAY

IN 1966, PETER K. SIEGEL was walking around near Elektra's offices on West 51st Street in Manhattan. He may have been headed to the Sam Goody's record store, where he'd frequently buy LPs. Or he may have been walking home. Whatever his destination, he heard a singer on the sidewalk who turned his head.

He forgets exactly where the singer was perched. 'I think it was probably on Seventh Avenue or Broadway, in the forties. That's what I'm guessing.' In any event, he stopped to listen. There, a white man who appeared to be in his mid-fifties was standing with his service dog, playing vintage country, folk, and blues songs in Midtown Manhattan.

Siegel, who was twenty-one or twenty-two at the time, doesn't want to say he 'discovered' Smith. 'I'm generally not sympathetic for the term *discover*, but I did meet him and record him, all in one day.'

But let's not get too far ahead of the narrative. 'I heard this voice,' Siegel continues, 'and it was busy out on the street. But I found my way through and heard him singing. And I knew immediately that he was really good.

I had listened to a lot of old-time country records, and I had listened to lots of Gid Tanner in The Skillet Lickers. I already had a whole batch of recordings by Tanner in The Skillet Lickers, which featured Riley Puckett.'

That's who this stranger reminded him of.

Siegel introduced himself. The singer said his name was Oliver Smith and that he was a native of the Atlanta, Georgia, metro area. He told the story of their meeting in what would become the liner notes of Smith's first and only album, as penned by *Little Sandy Review* editor and pioneering rock critic Paul Nelson (who, in his later years as an A&R man, would go on to sign The New York Dolls to Mercury Records):

> I was walking down around 43rd Street and Broadway when I heard this street singer. I always listen to street singers, and I could bear him block away! He was playing a modern country song, 'Crazy Arms,' I think, but the guitar runs and the voice suggested an older style. I asked him if he knew any old songs. He said yes and played [the country classic] 'I Only Want A Buddy, Not A Sweetheart.'
>
> 'It sounds like you've been listening to Riley Puckett,' I said. '*Riley Puckett!*' he said. 'I used to play with Riley Puckett all the time!' He seemed impressed by someone who had *heard* of Riley Puckett and played me about half a dozen more old-time songs. I asked if he'd ever been recorded. 'No,' he said. Would he record tonight, I wondered? 'Well, I'm doing pretty well here tonight,' he said. 'I might make ten or fifteen dollars.' I told him that recording fees were far more than that. He said that, in that case, he'd be interested.

Smith is quoted in Nelson's notes as well, further attesting to his humble, work-a-day nature:

[Smith's] speech is relaxed, both considered and considerate, his language gentle and Southern, yet, like James Agee's, almost Elizabethan at times in its unexpected turns and phrasings. He constantly underplays, to really incredible degree, the drama and uniqueness of his own life: 'I am just an average person with a wife and daughter. I sing and play the best I can. I specialize in this old-type music. There's not much more to be said.' Here is Smith, with his typical, straightforward modesty, summing up the first fifty-five years of his life, covering, at one point in the monologue, in a single sentence, his entire thirty-seven years of street singing.[1]

Siegel decided to get the singer from Georgia into the studio that same day. 'I wanted to do it right away,' he explains, 'because I thought if I didn't do it right then and there, I might never find him again. I told him I would pay him for the session. Union scale at that time was sixty dollars for a three-hour session. And that overcame his objection about [whether] he would have preferred to stay and make money on the street.'

Siegel put in a call to Mastertone recording studios on West 42nd Street. 'It was where Elektra made all its records. I called them up and said, I want to make this record. They had a couple of hours of time, and they let me come over and be the engineer and producer, if you will.

'He was a very powerful performer,' he says of Smith. 'I mean, I don't know how much it comes across on the record, but my impression at the time was he was just he had a loud, projecting voice, and he had this Gibson—I think it was a J-45. And he was just real powerful.'

Siegel wasn't fully authorized to sign artists to Elektra at that point. He'd also produced for Folkways Records and for County Records, a small Virginia-based label specializing in old-timey and traditional bluegrass music. 'I wasn't thinking it was something that Elektra would want,' he says. 'I had in my mind that I could place it with County Records.'

Nonetheless, he was nearby to the Elektra office, so he decided to give his employer first refusal on the project.

Elektra founder Jac Holzman had made a career of being musically open-minded. At some point, his New York–based label, initially known for the folk music of Theodore Bikel, Ed McCurdy, Oscar Brand, and Judy Collins, morphed into a Los Angeles rock label that signed The Doors and Love. His personal motto—also the title of his eventual memoir—was 'follow the music.'

'I didn't persuade Jac to do anything,' Siegel clarifies. 'I may have told him that I recorded this guy, and I'll probably give it to County Records. But when [Jac] heard it, he said he wanted it.'

Smith was accompanied in New York that day by his wife as well as his dog. They lodged at an inexpensive hotel in Midtown. He described himself to Siegel as an itinerant musician, and told him he had recorded two sides in the pre-war 78rpm era that were never released.

'After I recorded him, and when Jac said he wanted it, I was able to call them at the hotel,' Siegel recalls. 'I think I call them or get in touch with him somehow. Maybe I went over there, I don't remember. But anyway, he and his wife came into the Elektra office and signed a recording contract, and then he was off again. That's what his life was.'

The eventual album contains fourteen of the seventeen songs recorded that day, among them a few originals, including 'Manhattan Blues,' and a few country classics, such as 'I Only Want A Buddy' and 'Just A Closer Walk With Thee.' Siegel describes Smith as 'sort of a white songster sometimes the blues sometimes you get ragtime and sometimes you get old country songs.'

Elektra released *Oliver Smith* in 1966. Siegel never heard from his 'itinerant musician' again. And that would be the perfect place to end the story … except that shortly thereafter, the nominees were announced for the 1966 Grammy Awards. And there, in the folk category, were Ravi Shankar,

The Chad Mitchell Trio, Peter Paul & Mary, Pete Seeger, Richard Farina, Nashville blues busker Cortelia Clark, and—can it be?—Oliver Smith!

Siegel looks back on that night. 'As I recall, I think Felton Jarvis of RCA gave a spoken introduction at the beginning of the album, about how Cortelia Clark was a street singer. And then he said, Now let's go out on the street and listen to him! And you hear these car horns and street sounds. But they sure sounded like it was a studio recording with street overdubs. Cortelia Clark had some of the same types of progressions that Oliver Smith used. And I thought it was interesting: two street singers, competing for the same Grammy Award!'

Close to six decades after the day Smith caught his ear, Siegel remains proud of their work together. ' [Smith] was a journeyman musician,' he says. 'He was a professional musician. I don't think he was thinking of it as his big break. I think he was just there to do his best singing. And I do remember they were pretty much all first takes, you know, I mean, he just went right through it. I mean, he must have sung this so many thousands of times—he just sang them beautifully from beginning to end. And I didn't really do anything but, you know, I put some mics up and I press the record button.'

Smith went on to make one more recording, five years later: *Street Singer*, released by Triagle Far Records. According to discogs.com, the LP was recorded in Jacksonville, Florida, by Ken Davidson of Kanawha Records, cut in April and May 1971 on a Nagra recorder loaned by the Smithsonian Institute. Two Jacksonville area musicians assisted: Roy Jones on lead guitar, and Bob Patterson on twelve-string guitar.

MOONDOG

CHAPTER 8

THE ROAD TO
CARNEGIE HALL,
AND THE SIDEWALKS
ALONG THE WAY

LOUIS THOMAS HARDIN, better known as Moondog, was an American composer, musician, and poet who gained recognition for his unique style and performances as a busker on the streets of Manhattan in the 1950s and 60s. Born in Marysville, Kansas, on May 26, 1916, he was blinded in 1932, aged sixteen, after an accident with a dynamite cap. He found his way to New York City in 1943 after first spending time in Batesville, Arkansas, and Memphis, Tennessee.

Although he was a Midwesterner, Hardin's work wardrobe included Viking-inspired clothing, often featuring a horned helmet. (He would later learn that helmets worn by actual Vikings did not have horns.) He would play his homemade percussion instruments, including drums and self-designed instruments like the *trimba*, a triangular percussion instrument. His captivating performances and distinct appearance drew attention from passersby, making him a beloved if curious figure in the city.

'He stood there like a statue, and through a lot of bad weather,' recalls longtime New York resident Fred Gruner, who saw and interacted with Moondog on numerous occasions.

Hardin's choice of perch was no accident. 'He chose to anchor his act on Sixth Avenue in midtown Manhattan because so many jazz clubs and record labels were located in the area at the time,' wrote Jim Farber in the *Guardian*. 'He became so well-known for occupying that spot that an advertisement in the 60s for the nearby Burlington Mills clothing company read, *Come see us—right next to the Hilton Hotel and Moondog!*'[1]

In a recent *New Yorker* feature, Amanda Petrusich described his imposing regional presence. 'For some people, Old New York is subway tokens and street crime; for others, it's merely Greenwich Village without a salad franchise on every corner. In the 1950s and 60s, the musician and composer Moondog stood on the corner of Sixth Avenue and 54th Street, wearing an elaborate Viking costume, selling his political broadsides and musical compositions, eating chocolate bars and chugging grapefruit juice out of a jug fashioned from an animal horn. Moondog is a potent symbol of Old New York, both as a collective fantasy and as a real and absent place. He translated the clamor of street life into song.'[2]

He would often sell his homemade recordings directly to passersby on the streets. These recordings showcased his original compositions and his unique blend of classical, jazz, and Native American music influences. By selling his music directly to the public, he established a connection with his audience.

'New York streets fascinated him,' notes Ljubinko Zivkovicso in an article for *Living Life Fearless*. 'He decided that is where he had to be, but located close to the source of music, and that source was Carnegie Hall. So he located himself, his instruments, Braille composing tool, and his music at the corner of 51st Street and Sixth Avenue, close to Carnegie. Artur Rodzinski, then the conductor of New York Philharmonic, noticed Moondog (hard to miss at over six feet tall) hanging constantly at the Hall's musician's entrance and invited him to rehearsals. When Moondog presented some of his music to him, Rodzinski offered to conduct an orchestral work of Moondog's.'[3]

That evening at Carnegie Hall in 1974 would prove to be the most significant moment in Moondog's career. The performance marked a breakthrough for him as he transitioned from street performances to a formal concert setting, showcasing his innovative compositions and garnering him critical acclaim and recognition from the music community.

Interviewed by Jason Gross for *Perfect Sound Forever* in May 1998, however, Moondog explained why playing in the streets may have been his fastest path to renown:

> I made my living that way, and I got exposure. It really worked because I hadn't been on the streets for more than a few weeks of the fall of '49 when I was written up. By January of '50, I was sitting in the doorway of Spanish Music Center on Sixth Avenue (which isn't there anymore), owned by Gabriel Oller. He said, 'I like the music you're making. I made records. Would you like to make some singles?' We did three singles together, and then I got other offers, including a Columbia album. The first one was with a forty-piece orchestra that [producer] Al Brown got together. He really did a lot for me.'[4]

Los Angeles Times classical music critic Mark Swed, who wrote an article comparing and contrasting Moondog with twentieth-century Hungarian composer Ervin Nyiregyhazi, paints a picture of an often-antagonistic figure. 'During his first years in New York in the early '40s, he sort of fit into the bohemian world. He was a proud bum who wrote his own quirky music, invented his own quirky instruments, made his own quirky clothes, and panhandled,' Swed writes. 'It took a while for Moondog to develop his style, but by the late 50s he had become a New York icon, with his clothes sewn of square patches of fabric and leather and his Viking helmet. He had his spot in Midtown on Sixth Avenue, where he played his music, recited his poetry, and begged for money. Duke Ellington, Benny Goodman, Dean Martin, Charlie Parker, Cassius Clay, Leonard Bernstein, and Marlon Brando dropped by . . . Philip Glass took Moondog in for a year. But sooner or later, Moondog bit every hand that fed him. He was intolerant. He worshiped Nordic culture. He was antisemitic and racist. He married a couple of times but had a reputation for being gross and inappropriate around women.'⁵

Glass himself wrote a preface to Robert Scotto's definitive biography, *Moondog: The Viking Of 6th Avenue*, noting:

The *Village Voice* had a piece about Moondog needing somewhere to live, so I trekked out to his usual spot, in front of the Warwick Hotel, at 54th and Sixth, and invited him to stay at the house I was living in with my wife, JoAnne Akalaitis. A few weeks later I get a call from Moondog from a pay phone; he sounded cautious but says he'd like to come check out the room.

I look out the window and the sight of Moondog crossing the street startled me. He was such an imposing figure, about six foot eight if you count his Viking headpiece, and he was *so* confident in his walk you wouldn't think he was I blind. I wondered how, as a blind man, he managed to cross the street without an instant of hesitation until he showed me how he listened to the traffic lights; I had never heard them before in this way.⁶

At one stage, there was talk of Moondog recording an album with Charlie Parker, but before these plans could ever come to fruition, Parker passed away. It was due to this early death that Moondog wrote the piece 'Bird's Lament,' dedicated to Parker. The composer recorded it for his self-titled album from 1969, and it would become one of his most famous pieces.

In his biography, Scotto describes a day in the life of Moondog on his turf. 'The crowds begin to pass by, old friends and voices, new acquaintances; he sells a little poetry, an old record or two, his perpetual calendar; he passes out broadsides and announcements. He is at this spot because it is at the center of an industry (ABC, CBS, NBC, MGM, studios, record stores, agencies, all situated within a few short city blocks) and because he loves the people here, loves to talk with them, not at them, to listen, to cherish the novelty of sounds, to seek out new wrinkles in the fabric of the human garment. ... Taxi drivers, truck drivers, secretaries from the surrounding offices, all send greetings.'[7]

John Kruth, a musician and author who grew up in New York, recalls seeing Moondog on his way to concerts at Carnegie Hall. 'Carnegie Hall is where I saw Ravi Shankar and Ornette Coleman. The oddest show I ever saw there was *An Evening With Groucho Marx* in May 1972. Loving the genius/Dadaist/comedian as I did, the sight of Moondog standing on the corner in full Viking regalia after the show was second only to the first time I witnessed Sun Ra's Mothership. It was as if he'd suddenly appeared from another dimension and double-parked his galleon somewhere down the block on 57th Street.

'I stood listening, enthralled as the old man with a long white beard sang some nonsensical operatic ditty. I had no idea he wrote symphonies. I just assumed, like most people who briefly stopped to gawk and drop a few coins in his cup, that he was another street freak trying his best to scrounge up some lunch money in the most creative manner.

'Whenever I'd take a date up Central Park, I'd always walk past Carnegie Hall to see if Moondog was on the street,' Kruth adds. 'I found him down the block sporadically, holding court. As a teenager, I was too shy to talk with him, but I always dropped some coins into the blind visionary's cup. I soon found his records, which were refreshingly original and brilliant.'

In 2023, a tribute album was released: *Songs And Symphoniques: The Music Of Moondog*, by jazz-chamber ensemble Ghost Train Orchestra in collaboration with The Kronos Quartet. Also featured are vocal performances from stars such as Rufus Wainwright, Jarvis Cocker, Petra Haden, Marissa Nadler, and Joan As Policewoman.

Ghost Train Orchestra's Brian Carpenter, who also hosts a radio program on WZBC-FM Boston, says of Moondog, 'He was a sort of legendary cult figure in New York City. Everyone knew who Moondog was. He was a sort of tourist attraction—people would fly in and tell the cab driver to take them to Moondog. But few knew he was in fact a highly unique and adventurous composer who would go on to inspire countless others, including Philip Glass and Steve Reich. An American original.'

Moondog's busking career left a lasting impact on the music industry. His unorthodox compositions, use of unconventional instruments, and rhythmic experimentation inspired many musicians, not only Glass and Steve Reich but the minimalist music movement as a whole. His influence is felt today in various genres, and his street performances and compositions continue to inspire and captivate artists and listeners alike.

SATAN & ADAM

CHAPTER 9

ANGELS OF HARLEM

THE MUSICAL DUO SATAN & ADAM was composed of Sterling 'Mr. Satan' Magee, a Black singer, and Adam Gussow, a white harmonica player, scholar, and author twenty-two years Magee's junior. Their unlikely union began in 1986, as part of a five-year busking partnership on the streets of New York City, and ultimately endured for more than three decades, until Magee's death in 2020.

Magee was already an accomplished blues guitarist when Gussow encountered him, having played with many legendary blues and R&B musicians such as James Brown, King Curtis, Big Maybelle, and Joey Dee & The Starliters, before he started performing on the streets. Gussow, on the other hand, was a young harmonica player who was just starting to make a name for himself in the New York City music scene.

One day in 1986, Gussow was driving across 125th Street in Harlem when, just past Seventh Avenue, he chanced upon Magee playing guitar and hi-hat cymbal in front of the New York Telephone Company office. Impressed by Magee's skills, Gussow approached him and asked if they could play together. Magee agreed, and the two began busking together on the streets of Harlem.

Their performances were raw and electrifying, blending Magee's fiery guitar playing with Gussow's soulful harmonica riffs. They quickly gained a following, and their reputation as one of the best blues acts on the streets of the city spread quickly. In the summer of 1987, members of the band U2 happened to pass Satan & Adam; they were so taken with the duo that they included thirty-nine seconds of Magee's composition 'Freedom For My People' in the film *Rattle & Hum*.

In 1991, Satan & Adam released their debut album, *Harlem Blues*, on Flying Fish Records. It was well-received by critics and catalytic in establishing them as a legitimate touring blues act. Despite this success, they continued to perform on the streets of Harlem for several more years, their busking career now legendary in the city's music scene.

A good place to begin with Satan & Adam is filmmaker V. Scott Balcerek's documentary, *Satan & Adam*. But it's important to Adam that we clear up one conceivable misconception: his encounter with Magee in October 1986 was not his first foray into busking. By then, he'd already had extensive experience playing on the streets. 'In fact,' he explains, 'I met Mr. Satan at the very tail end of a long process that the documentary leaves out for the sake of narrative compression.' His novel *Busker's Holiday* presents a fictionalized account of this period.

'My time as a busker began in the summer of 1984, at the tail end of a five-year relationship that was about to explode,' he recalls. 'I went to Europe with a friend that summer as a backpacker, basically. I considered myself a guitar player/harmonica player. And I brought along a couple of harps, stuffed into my backpack. On my second day in [Paris], rather than hanging out with my buddy, I went to the place known by buskers as the Beaubourg—the Pompidou Center. I ended up jamming with a Danish guitar player whom I fictionalized [in the novel]. A lot of the stuff in that book is made up; I brought in things from different parts of my busking career. But that day in June of 1984 felt like a transformative moment in which I went from being a guy who was relatively inward-turned. I exploded outward. Busking—the existential risk and creativity of busking—just brought that to the surface and connected me with an audience. And it connected me with that guitar player and the scene he was part of.

'So, I had a long, rambling adventure that summer. When I got home, I sat down, and in the space of fourteen weeks wrote a four-hundred-page novel that was the very first iteration of what later became *Buskers Holiday*, although none of the stuff that was in it ended up making it to *Busker's Holiday*. But the energy was there. The point is, I felt incredibly energized by the busking breakthrough, as though my life really were beginning again. If you've had that sort of spiritual rebirth, and if busking is what did it, then the question then is, well, what happens next? And so, over the next several years, through the late summer of 1986, I tried to figure out who I was as a writer *and* as a busker.

'A very important moment for me was in the spring of 1985, when I ran into the man who ended up becoming my blues harmonica teacher, my mentor. His name was Nat Riddles. I write at length about him and about this experience in my 1998 memoir, *Mister Satan's Apprentice*.'

Riddles, a Black New Yorker six years older than Gussow, proved a key influence on him, taking the young harpist on as a protégé. 'He was a model for me, Nat was,' Gussow says. 'I'd watch him do his thing out on the streets, down in at the Cube on Astor Place. Without him kind of coming along and saying, *You're good, but here's what you need to know in order to get better*, I would not have ever played with Mr. Satan.'

Subsequent busking encounters involved a pair of guitarists named Bill. First there was Bill Taft, described by Gussow as 'an Atlanta area guy, kind of like a Bob Dylan crossed with the Talking Heads. He was kind of a wild man. He's still around and we're friends. He was a surrealist kind of Bob Dylan/Robert Johnson figure. We played all fall [of 1985]—that was when I really became a busker.'

Then came Bill Collins. 'Bill was a kid, a redheaded Irish kid from Pelham, The Bronx. And I was seven or eight years older, and he and I played all over New York. We played Washington Square Park; we turned our amps up and the cops came and stopped us. We had big crowds. We played down in the subways. So, with Bill Collins, I felt like I was really busking. And then I bought him a plane ticket. I said, You've got to come to Paris—we've got to do this for real.

'In June '86, he and I went to Paris. We had two months over there. We lasted about three weeks together, and then we kind of got pissed off at each other, as buskers sometimes do. He went his way, I went mine. We're friends now. He's never come home! He stayed in Paris. He has a group these days called Swingin' Paris.'

Collins remains a Parisian to this day, but Gussow returned to the States. 'I'd decided when I got home at the end of that summer [of 1986] that I'd done it. I was done with busking. I'd lived that life. I'd gotten it out of my system. I was done. And at that point I said, I need to get a straight job. So I got a job as a tutor for seven dollars an hour at Hostos Community College in the South Bronx.

'There's two ways to get there from where I was in Uptown Manhattan. One was to go around down the East Side Drive and then across the 145th Street Bridge to the Grand Concourse. [The surrounding area was] bombed-out South Bronx. I mean, Hostos was fun, but the environment was burned-out South Bronx. The other way to get to my job was straight through Harlem. Now, I had played in the clubs in Harlem, starting kind of like late '85 through summer of '86. Before I went to Europe, I played in those clubs. I got a kind of reputation, almost [as] a minor sensation: I was the white boy who comes in and, you know, plays with Jimmy "The

Preacher" Robins and Jackie Soul and Tippy Larkin, a trumpet player who was bandleader Milton Larkin's son. So I had a bit of a name down there, mostly because nobody else was playing harmonica in Harlem in those days, white or Black.

'And all this is a prelude to that day when I was driving through Harlem and I saw Mr. Satan for the first time. This was in mid-to-late October of 1986. I had seen him once before, when he was busking with a trio—guys named Mr. Marvin and Pancho Morales. Marvin was on guitar and Pancho was on drums when I saw him in 1983. So it'd be three years earlier, when I was walking with my girlfriend, he was playing that night on the south corner of 114th Street & Broadway, with his trio. And it was extraordinary music.

'He was drinking on that night; he was strumming with an incredible groove. So there they were. This is a moment long before I'd thought about being a street musician. I just knew my relationship was going south. And I was called to it. I do think there's an element of calling. And I suspect that almost everybody who busks says the same thing: it was just something [they] had to do.

'So I see him three years later, as I'm driving to work, and I say, *That's the guy!* I don't know his name, but I remembered him from having had a trio. Now he was alone, and he was playing not just guitar but a hi-hat cymbal, which was just kind of sitting on the concrete. And he was doing it on the upbeat one-two-three-four like that kind of thing, and playing this amazing guitar. I got out of my car, and I turned to the guy who was standing next to me, an older Black man, and I said, He's amazing. Who is that? And the guy looked at me and said, That's Satan. *Everybody* in Harlem knows Satan.'

Jumping well ahead of the narrative, Adam immediately thought of a duo name: Satan & Adam. But the two had yet to meet. 'So I asked the guy, Would he let me sit in? and he said, Yeah, he will. What do you play?

I said harmonica, and we had a conversation. And he said, Yeah, Satan will let you sit in ... but can you play? And I thought, well, I'd had just enough experience in the clubs in Harlem. So the idea of playing blues before a Black audience was not a new thing. And I'd done a lot of busking, both in Downtown New York and over in Europe. But playing on the street in what a military person might call a highly exposed position? That was new. That was *exciting*. It was like, *I better go home and practice!* So I went home that night and practiced.'

Adam showed up at Satan's spot again the next day. 'I waited until he took a break, and then I went up to him and said something like, I really enjoyed your music, and he said, Thanks. And I said, I'm a harmonica player, any chance that I could sit in on a song or two? I won't embarrass you. Magee thought about the offer for a moment, and then he roared, Come on up!'

Gussow plugged in, whereupon Satan announced that he was going to do a song called 'Mojo.' *If that's 'Got My Mojo Workin',' Adam thought, I think I can do that.*

'And then he did his own version, so we had that first encounter, it felt like it went on forever. It probably went on for five minutes, and then it was over, and the place exploded. What I remember distinctly, though, is that even before I played a note, there was the sense something's going to happen here. Now you need to remember, this is 1986. Just before the Howard Beach thing. So there was a lot of racial tension in the air. But I [told myself], nobody's worried about me, right? And they weren't, people were happy.

'When that first jam was over, it was like this *explosion*. And he was like, Come on up with your tips, everybody in here. And he didn't know what my name was. And he said, How about a hand for Mr. ... and I said, Adam, and then he said, And you know who I am—I am SATAN. That was the first day we played together.'

Satan & Adam were born that day.

In a short time, Adam figured out Satan's history. He had recorded several near hits on Ray Charles's Tangerine Records label. He'd played guitar with a who's who of R&B legends. By the 1970s, he'd shed his birth name and demanded to be called 'Satan.' By 1983, his street act was an acknowledged attraction on 125th Street alongside the New York Telephone Co.

The details of the duo's prolific twelve-year history are well-documented in both Balcerek's documentary and in Gussow's memoir, *Mr. Satan's Apprentice*, so I asked him to talk about busking in a more general sense—a few memorable moments, his thoughts on where busking as a practice is headed, and some advice to future buskers.

'If you want to busk, there are three key things you have to pay attention to,' he says. 'You have to pay attention to the weather, because if it's raining, you get in trouble. I have a story or two about that. Especially if you've got electric amps, right?

'You have to pay attention to foot traffic. In other words, what you need is a place that has enough people coming by you that you can make some tips. So the weather, foot traffic, and the police. And all three things were working in our favor on 125th Street. We have to be careful because we played in all seasons. We'd play after it snowed sometimes; I mean, we were crazy that way. But obviously there's certain months that are better for it and rainy days are not good for that; we obviously would never play. The foot traffic 125th Street in the middle of Harlem—you couldn't do better. It was incredible there . . . everybody went by there, including some famous people. The Apollo Theater was a block away. And the police didn't give a damn about us because they had so many other things on their minds. The cops never said, *Turn it down*.'

This was not the case a few miles south in Central Park. 'If you were to try to play a Central Park, for example—and I've tried to busk there—be careful, because the cops are there: the environmental cops, the ones in green uniforms who were in charge of monitoring sound levels . . . they pointed up to the apartments up there and they said, If we let you play, those people will call my supervisor.

'I've never actually been in a position where somebody threatened to confiscate my equipment. I've been really lucky that way. I know for a lot of buskers that's a real thing. That's a problem. I tend to just not put up any resistance, and once they realize you're not going to put up resistance, they're always pretty nice. But anyway, those three things are important. And so we got lucky in Harlem.'

Then there was the ever-present issue of Satan & Adam being a racially mixed duo based in predominantly Black Harlem. Adam tells of a rare altercation. 'There was one moment that was seriously negative, and it set me back a lot, which was in the summer of 1989, two weeks after Spike Lee's *Do The Right Thing* was released. I was playing with Sterling on 125th Street and a couple of Black men came up. One of them was younger, maybe closer to my age, and he had what I think of as the Malcolm X–type glasses, and one of them had a knitted cap like the men who were Muslim tended to wear. So the young guy came up to Sterling and asked, Why are you letting this white boy play with you? Sterling began to defend his right to have with him anybody he wanted to. The guy said, basically, You know what you are, old man . . . you are a Negro, which was like he was cursing him out as an old Uncle Tom. I had never heard anybody diss Mr. Satan like that.

'I suddenly got fearful. I mean, *What's going on here?* This is not like any response I've ever had here in Harlem. People were overwhelmingly friendly toward me. Harlem was a self-contained kind of world, as cosmopolitan as it was.

'Next thing you know, the guys come up to me. [One of them] goes, What do you what are you doing here? And I said, I'm playing with him.

He says, Yeah, I know what you are—just one more white boy come to rip off the Black man's music. And then I began to talk to him, and we had a kind of back and forth where I made it clear that I valued [Black music]. I didn't respond as he'd expected, partly because I've been reading a lot of African American lit, so I was pretty conscious, in a sense.

'It was an incredible challenge. The guy ended up sort of backpedaling, the Malcolm X guy—not apologizing, but sort of backpedaling in terms of his heavy come-on thing. He and Sterling were kind of yelling. Sterling said, Let the young man alone, he's here with me. And then the older guy came up to me. I said, Look, you've seen me here for a while. You know people are okay with what I'm doing. He said, in this very inverted syntax, I can't say there might not be some young brother who just might, you know, not want to see you out here.

'It was like a threat—a veiled threat, but not so veiled that I couldn't hear it—and I looked out at all of those cars cruising by with the rap booming out of the windows in the dark, you know. It's like I had to suddenly think, *Is it possible somebody could just lower a window and shoot the white boy? A drive-by, you know. Could that happen?*

'Yeah, I had never thought about that. So, in terms of buskers and violence and the cops, where the buskers play, what kind of dangers do they confront—that was a pretty heavy thing. And I had not felt frightened in Harlem up to that point. Once I got over it, then it was like I was normed in a weird way.'

Gussow nowadays leads a mainly academic, off-street life as a professor at University Of Mississippi in Oxford. He ponders the changes brought by advances in technology that may affect his street-corner successors.

'When I was doing it in the mid-to-late 80s, people had change, and they had bills. So a dollar bill, whatever it was equal to then, it's probably worth three dollars now—that's what you'd make: the change and the bills. And occasionally a note from somebody with a gig, or maybe a girl might sort of want to give you a phone number—I had that happen once or twice. [Now] we're in an increasingly de-cash economy, right? So I would say buskers have adapted. Do they have QR codes?

'Here's the other thing. If you have a cash app, it's all legit. Every cent you make, it's all on the table, right? Somebody out there is collecting data on how much money you're getting through that cash app. Five dollars now would be more like the dollar people used to give. A dollar now doesn't seem like very much, although it did add up back in the day. I would be very interested to know—from the standpoint of longtime buskers who's been doing this for a while—how the cashless economy has gotten them adapting.

'One thing that's really changed busking is social media. I've been able to go online and find some exceptional musicians, male and female, more young than not, but just exceptional performances that now go viral because of the visual technologies. Today's world is very different from the world of 1986. In 1986, portable video cameras were big and unwieldy. A few people were starting to get them, but it was a rare thing. They might take a still photo, but nobody was spreading them around the world. Streaming is all relatively new. And the visual technologies just weren't there, back in the day. So the expectation was that if somebody came up with a video camera, maybe they were part of a movie crew, they would ask you first: *Do you mind if I take some photos?*

As for Satan & Adam's two disparate audience sectors, Gussow maintains that the duo never altered their approach between sidewalk and festival stage. 'The single biggest difference between being buskers in Harlem and being a touring act was the radical shift from, in effect, an older Black audience to whatever was in the on the contemporary blues festival circuit, an [audience that was] much more white than not, although not entirely. But we played the same music. We didn't change the music.'

SATAN & ADAM remained a duo for twelve years, recording a series of albums together—two on Flying Fish, one on Rave On Productions, and three on Adam's own Modern Blues Harmonica label. They toured Europe and Australia and played key jazz, blues, and folk festivals, including the Newport Folk Festival. They also appeared on the cover of *Living Blues*, subtitled 'The Journal Of The African American Blues Tradition,' making Gussow one of the few white musicians to grace the magazine's front page.

Sadly, things changed in 1998. Magee disappeared and suffered a nervous breakdown. He had left Harlem for Brookneal, Virginia, and was located at a care facility in Gulfport, Florida. A Tampa-area blues harmonica player named T.C. Carr eventually learned that Magee was living in the facility and patiently helped him find his way back to music.

In the meantime, Gussow found a new life of his own, having similarly left New York. He became a professor of English and Southern Studies at University Of Mississippi in Oxford. Since 1998, he has authored six books, including his busking novel and his history of Satan & Adam—the latter receiving the Blues Foundation's 'Keeping The Blues Alive' award.

Magee was rehabilitated enough that the duo could resume work in 2007, joined by drummer David Laycock. In 2013, they performed at New Orleans JazzFest, before proceeding to record their final two albums.

Seven years later, in September 2020, Magee died while in hospice care of complications from COVID. These days, Gussow performs in a new trio, Sir Rod & The Blues Doctors, featuring Magee's nephew, Rod Patterson, on lead vocals. The Satan & Adam sound, born on the streets, continues to live on.

MARY LOU LORD

CHAPTER 10

TUBES AND TROLLEYS,
SQUATS AND PITCHES

SINCE ITS INCEPTION IN 1987, the annual South By Southwest (SXSW) festival has drawn thousands of media tastemakers to Austin, Texas, each year. By 2018, just prior to the pandemic, it drew close to 161,000 registrants, with upwards of 2,000 performers playing official showcases. Among the breakout performers over the festival's thirty-plus years: John Mayer, Amy Winehouse, She & Him, Haim, Lizzo, Leon Bridges, Polyphonic Spree, Hanson, Arctic Monkeys, Janell Monae, Spoon, Fastball, and, in a legendary parking lot recital, The Flaming Lips.

For those who have attended SXSW, it's not uncommon to be walking down Austin's East 6th Street and be asked by a friend or even a stranger, 'Hey, are you going to see Franz Ferdinand?' (one of the buzz bands of 2004). You may not have heard of the band at that moment, but you comply, because heeding such tips is often key to optimal navigation of the festival.

At SXSW 1995, however, a lot of the week's street buzz focused on an artist who didn't always have an official showcase.

'Hey, have you seen that singer named Mary Lou Lord playing out by the Driskill Hotel?'

Those who know Austin geography know that the Driskill, one of the city's most prestigious hotels since it opened in 1886, sits at one of Austin's most trafficked corners, at East 6th & Brazos—the eastern edge of the city's nightclub district. Lord set up directly in front of the Littlefield Building, located across from the Driskill. She would typically play until 3am, attracting hotel-bound passersby after the bars closed at 2am.

Lord had just signed with the resolutely indie Kill Rock Stars label, having released her first seven-inch single ('Some Jingle Jangle Morning When I'm Straight') in 1993, followed by a self-titled EP in 1995. That year, she recalls, she went out on tour with Elliott Smith, formerly of the band Heatmiser but now embarking on a solo career. 'He was my opener. And we applied to SXSW. We both got rejected. We were going through the Texas area anyway. I said, We're gonna crash that bitch! So we went. He and I had never been to Austin before. So we set up in front of the hotel and just played, and people found us!

'It was really fun—it was St. Patrick's Day—and Elliott and I played all these Irish songs I didn't even know he knew, and we had the best time. So, every year after that, I kept going. And so, you know, I got written up. Everybody loved it because I kept coming back.

That year's SXSW program book noted, 'For over a decade, Mary Lou Lord has been charming the punters on 6th Street with her battered Martin Guitar and amplifier. From indie to major to indie, Mary Lou has always stayed true to her busking roots and is much happier playing guitar on a street corner than in any club.'

One night, Lord was joined by a rather famous busker from the UK. 'I remember one night when I was busking, Billy Bragg walked by. I said, Hey Billy, how about a busk? He kept walking and replied, Yes, maybe later. Three or four hours later he returned. I let him use my gear, and he played for about an hour, including the brand new songs from *Mermaid Avenue*,' his album of unrecorded Woody Guthrie lyrics, set to music by Bragg and Wilco. 'That was super fun!'

Longtime *Austin American-Statesman* music critic Peter Blackstock, writing in the *SXSW Scrapbook*, a hardcover volume of moments and memories published in 2011, applauded her eclectic repertoire. 'Just to be clear, Lord was hardly one of 6th Street's infamous human-jukebox cover bands. She had immaculate taste in the songs she chose to interpret, from Richard Thompson's "1952 Vincent Black Lightning" . . . to the Elliott Smith throwaway "I Figured You Out" (literally: he'd thrown it in a trash can and Lord retrieved it), to Pete Droge's instantly memorable "Sunspot Stopwatch."'[1]

'I did have several [official] inside gigs,' Lord says, 'but I just loved playing outside. I was selling a lot of CDs and making a lot of money actually. I played SXSW about eleven years in a row . . . I just loved it. And then it started to get really, really kind of, um, what do you call it? Corporate? Yeah, corporate.'

Her origins as a busker, however, have far longer roots, traceable to her time living in her native Salem, Massachusetts, and nearby Boston in the 1980s. She would often perform on the streets of Harvard Square, playing acoustic guitar and singing covers of songs by artists like Neil Young, Joni Mitchell, and The Velvet Underground.

Even prior to that, as a student at Berklee College Of Music and a fan of the band Rush, Lord interned at a couple of local businesses peripherally catering to the music industry. The first was called Ted Charles Associates, which booked bands into conferences. Mainly she 'picked up toilet paper for the office' and ran other errands for the firm. One day she passed the Salem Theater in town and the marquee touted a coming attraction: R.E.M.

'What's that movie *R.E.M.*?' she inquired as she entered the theater, only to be informed that it wasn't a movie but rather a band. She left the agency to work for the theater, and her first assignment was to keep the members of R.E.M. entertained, as the theater's electricity had gone out. She was given a budget to take them to dinner.

Lord estimates that maybe twenty people attended that 1983 concert, but for her, seeing the band that would soon become America's premier indie-rockers was nothing short of a revelation: 'I just fell in love with this music, and I was, like, *Jesus, this is cool shit. You don't have to be an incredible jazz guitarist to be great.*'

Soon, Mary Lou and her roommates, Deb and Shirlé, were busking in a subway station in Boston to pick up some extra money. They'd play at Government Center station along the Blue Line, which largely transported riders to the airport. 'And then,' she remembers, 'I met a guy at Berklee, and he was an incredible trombone player and was from England. So, I found a little school in London called the School Of Audio when it was new—now, it's a big, big enterprise. I went to this little school to study engineering and production and stuff and be with my boyfriend at the time, the trombonist, and because his visa had expired, so I was like, *I'll just move to England.* I lived there and we lived in a squat [an empty house occupied by squatters] where there was a meter in the basement where if you put fifty pence in, you could get electricity for like a week.'

Ah, but how to earn those fifty pence pieces?

'I'd sleep [at the squat] at night, and then in the day I'd go to school, and then after school I didn't wanna go home, because it was freezing, so I would hang out in the subway. And I would watch the buskers. I did this every day. I think it was at the Charing Cross Road tube that I would watch this one guy in particular named Mark. We became friends, and I just sat there doing a little homework or drawing. He asked me one day, Can you watch my equipment while I go to the bathroom? And I said okay. While he was gone, I played the guitar. Shirlé had taught me a few chords. I wasn't very good, but I played the guitar, and someone threw a pound coin in—and I was like, *Holy shit! Ding, ding, ding,* right?'

A busker was born. But she needed a tool of the trade: her own guitar.

'I took all my savings and bought a shitty Hondo—a cheap guitar.

I didn't even have a case, but I had a little wicker basket, and I was like, *Okay, I'm gonna go and I'm gonna try busking by myself,* and I knew like four songs the whole way through, and they were really long songs.

'It was always Fairport Convention and old English ballads that had two chords and a million words. I'd discovered Sandy Denny at that point—I was really into all that stuff. I found a little spot and I started playing, and I was making a little bit of money here and there—money for the electric meter in the basement, which was fine with me. About two hours into it, [I realized] you can play the same song over and over and over because people are moving.'

One day, not too long after she started, Lord discovered the busking life was not without its snafus.

'This dude came down, and he had one arm, right? And he was huffing, like he had this big black ring around his mouth. And I swear to God, he had a dog with three legs—this little tripod dog—and he's got one arm. So he sits down next to me, and I'm like, *Oh, jeez,* and we looked like a pathetic little gypsy family. Eventually they fell asleep—the dog and the man—and I'm still playing. And probably about an hour or two later, he wakes up and he stands up and the dog stands up and shakes, and he stretches his one arm out and turns toward me and I'm like, *What the fuck is he doing?* He's standing right in front of me. I'm like, *What are you doing?* He whipped out his dick and he pissed all over the fucking money. And I'm like, *What the fuck?*

'I had my guitar still on me, and I started off down the platform looking back, going, *Oh my God, I just got robbed by this guy pissing on my money,* and I look back and he's picking through it, and I'm like, *Oh no.* People wanted to hang out, you know?

'I learned a big lesson on that first day. I was just so naive, you know,' she sighs. 'No street sense at all.' But she would gain increased street sense with every passing day. She started learning more and more songs, adopting Central London's Holborn Underground station, right under Fleet Street, as her main 'pitch,' which meant 'a lot of lawyers and people like that' would pass by. 'I remember this one guy came down—I'd see this guy every day with his briefcase and his suit—and he said, you know, You're always playing the same song. Do you know any other songs or the same three songs? And I'm like, No, I really don't. I remember he took his jacket off, put his briefcase down, and he showed me a song. It might have been [John Lennon's] "Working Class Hero."'

Lord stayed in London for a year or two, then returned home to Massachusetts. By then, emerging technology had sent a lifeline to buskers everywhere. 'I got a Maxi Mouse amp, and that was a game changer. Before that, I was just singing acoustic over the train. These amps are battery-operated and a little bit bigger than a lunch box. And they had a plug for the vocal and the guitar. I got one of those, and now I could sing over the trains. I didn't think that I would do it, but I just kept going, and it became my job.'

She also found her musical direction—less earnest folk, more lo-fi indie-rock. 'I discovered people like Daniel Johnston and all that sort of lo-fi indie stuff that was easy and acoustic and awesome and kind of all spun out from R.E.M. and all that stuff. And I'm like, *God, this music, you don't have to be a technical wizard to do this, and you don't have to be as dorky as the, the, the snobby folk people, right?*'

On her return from the UK, Lord was busking in Boston when an audience member named Robert Haigh introduced himself. He was the music director at WERS-FM at Boston's Emerson College. Picking up on her love for Sandy Denny and British folk, he offered to introduce her to a friend whose music he thought Lord might like—Shawn Colvin. 'Shawn became a friend of mine and a real inspiration to me,' she says. 'She didn't have a record deal yet. I thought it would be so good if I play all of her songs in the subway. So I learned and performed her entire song catalogue—at least until she got a record deal.'

For Lord, inspiration often came from unlikely sources. During a trip to San Francisco sometime around 1988, while playing at the Powell Street trolley turnaround, an audience member looked a little sketchy. Not that she hadn't grown accustomed to this by then. 'This dude was watching me. He wore a trench coat. He had really greasy, gross hair—the quintessential creepy-looking guy, right? But he was there to see me every day. One day he said, Hey, I, I live right over there and you *gotta* hear this song. It's a special song! He was so committed to me hearing the song. He was a bit creepy-looking, but he was sincere. So I said, All right, I'll go.

'It was, like, my last day there anyway, so we went to his apartment—a bit creepy, but very neat and tidy. Just a little single bed, a desk, and then a boom box and a bunch of cassettes. He said, Here's the song, here's the lyrics, read the lyrics. The song absolutely blew my mind! In fact, it was the best song I've ever heard! I learned it. It was "Vincent Black Lighting" by Richard Thompson. And I was like, *Holy shit*. I was so happy that I'd trusted him enough through the music, and I got a lot of mileage out of that song. And I just *love, love, love* playing it. I didn't play it very well, but the song is so good that the lyrical merits of it override the fact that I'm *not* Richard Thompson. And everybody has loved that song.'

During another trip to Northern California, this time at the corner of Telegraph Avenue and Bancroft Way in Berkeley, Lord had another interesting encounter involving an audience member. 'I had a nice group of people watching me, and a guy came along who didn't have any shoes or a shirt on. He was kind of a homeless guy. A little nutty. And he was dancing around and reached in his [empty] pocket, and he pulled it out and made a gesture [as if to say], I would give me money, but I don't have any. And I'm like, It's okay. I played a few more songs and then the man was getting more and more frustrated, like, Look, I don't have any money. And this went on for a while. Finally, he reached down and pulled his pocket off of his pants and he threw the empty pocket in my case. He then walked away, and as he was leaving, he gave me a thumbs-up. I have this man's pocket but still, because it was just, like, such a cool thing for him to do, and it just said a lot.'

Lord has given much thought to the ethics of busking. And part of that is the intentional omission of drums. 'I'm not really into whole-band busking because I have a thing about [respecting] people's space, and drums can get really, really loud. I'm not the biggest fan of people busking on drums. I just think that they're not really designed to be played outside on sidewalks, know what I mean? If you're gonna be a busker, you gotta realize that it's *people's* space too.'

She's also watched as her daughter, Annabelle Lord-Patey, now in her twenties, has become a busker in her own right. 'She's in college, getting her master's in music therapy. She's doing great. I showed her the ropes and I told her, Work smarter, not harder. So what she does is play before or after concerts … Neil Young played, and she busked outside a venue and people were like, *Oh my God, this is great*, because she's playing, like, these Neil Young songs. She did that after Pearl Jam too, and Jimmy Buffett, and Billy Joel … so she works smarter, not harder.

'So the tradition continues, and I'm glad she knows this skill because (a) she'll always have a friend and (b) she'll always have a job. Be your own boss and play when you want and put in the time as much time as you want. It's a great, great thing to have that skill. She even told me, Mom, you gotta get a Venmo and a QR Code.'

Lord ended up taking her daughter's advice.

'I played last Halloween, and I had my first Venmo—and sure enough, all this money came in, along with little notes like *Awesome* or *Love that song* or *You're so cute*. And it was like, *bing bang boom*—suddenly there's big money—like, twenty dollars and stuff like that—now that people don't carry cash anymore. I had no idea that the kids use this stuff!'

PART
THREE

THE SOUTH AND THE MIDWEST

My dad tells me that when I was a kid in New Orleans, he went into a liquor store and left me outside on the curb. I had seen kids tap dance in the Quarter for change, so I just started dancing... I realized that I was the kind of person who could be expressive and be rewarded with it in a public space. **KETCH SECOR, OLD CROW MEDICINE SHOW**

CORTELIA CLARK

CHAPTER 11

FIVE 'N' DIME
STREET SINGER

IF YOU HAPPENED TO WANDER through Downtown Nashville between the late 1940s and the 60s, you might have encountered the blind street singer Cortelia Clark. Michael Weesner—later a record producer for RCA, Columbia, and Bell Records, among others, as well as a music publisher, TV and movie special-effects expert, boat repairman, and builder of an airplane—was a child when he first laid eyes on the singer. 'I remember going down to hear him play with my mother when she would go shopping,' he says. 'Everyone went to Downtown Nashville at the time. I'm guessing I was five or six, seven—pretty young—and asking my mother if I could go hear the guitarist. He mainly sold shopping bags—brown paper bags for ten cents. That's how he made his money.'

Clark was born in Chicago around 1906. Little is known of his early years, although some reports have him arriving in Nashville at age eleven to attend a school for the blind. It's also been reported that he began performing around 1955; Weesner disputes this, noting that the musician 'told me directly that he was singing for troops waiting in line for the movie theaters at the end of the war—that would be World War II. So basically in 1945 or '46, he was playing for tips from the troops waiting in line to get into the movie theaters that were on Church Street in Downtown Nashville.'

Some say Clark lost his eyesight following surgery in the mid-1950s, but Weesner believes he'd been blind from birth. Either way, he became a fan to the degree of going out on the ultimate limb on the blind street singer's behalf.

Nashville is best known for its country hits, of course, and Weesner had done some independent production for RCA Records on Music Row. And while Cortelia Clark was a bit different from some of RCA's other projects that year—Chet Atkins, Roy Clark, Charley Pride, Jim Reeves— Weesner nonetheless brought a tape to his friend, Bob Ferguson, an RCA producer and songwriter commonly regarded as a founding pillar of Music Row.

Ferguson had worked with Connie Smith and Dolly Parton, among others. He loved what he heard and assigned staff producer Felton Jarvis, who in turn had worked with Elvis Presley, Willie Nelson, and Jerry Reed.

'I recorded the demo at Globe Studios—took him into a little independent studio,' Weesner recalls, 'and then I took that tape to RCA, and after he was signed to RCA, that's when we recorded him on the street.'

By now, Clark was playing out in front of the Woolworth's on North 5th Avenue (since renamed Rep. John Lewis Way). The five-and-dime location now a registered historical landmark, carried a lot of racial history with it. The website for Woolworth's, which is now an independent restaurant and theater, tells its story:

> At a time when this part of the country was still operating under the Jim Crow laws and customs of the 1890s, African Americans were prohibited from eating at public lunch counters…
>
> On April 19, 1960 … four thousand Nashvillians, including young John Lewis, marched in silence to the courthouse and confronted Mayor Ben West. Among those marching was Fisk

University student Diane Nash, who is credited with asking Mayor West if he felt that segregation at the lunch counters was morally right. Mayor West answered no, and the official process of desegregation at downtown lunch counters began.[1]

Weesner and Jarvis wanted to capture the unvarnished ambiance of Clark's outdoor performances but decided to record the album a few blocks west at the original Pancake Pantry, located on 8th Avenue in Downtown Nashville. Felton, Weesner, and the engineer sat inside while Clark sat outside and performed. The resulting RCA album is full of car horns, the screeching of tires, and chattering passersby. Released in July of 1966, it was titled *Blues In The Street* and credited to 'Nashville's Authentic Original Street Singer Cortelia Clark.'

Clark is pictured on the cover with cane, tin cup, and sunglasses, though Weesner says he did not wear sunglasses as a rule. 'His eyes were very white and opaque,' he notes. 'Those glasses were put on him so he'd be more photogenic for the album cover.' Also somewhat misleading is that the LP's twelve tracks are all credited to Clark, though he did not write the country blues and jug-band standard 'Walk Right In' (generally credited to Gus Cannon and Hosea Woods, both of Cannon's Jug Stompers).

The first track in the sequence, meanwhile, is actually a short spoken interview between Jarvis and Clark. In it, Clark boasts that he 'makes a pretty good living,' to which Jarvis inquires, 'How much money do you make?' Clark hesitates none in responding, 'I have made as much as twenty-five or thirty dollars a week.'

Weesner visited Clark at home on a few occasions and remembers him being 'very poverty-stricken, living behind the capitol in Nashville on Jefferson Street in basically a hovel … outside plumbing, including getting water from a faucet in the … it was in a slum neighborhood that later got cleared by urban redevelopment.'

Despite living in relative squalor, Clark reportedly did not see the RCA recording as his meal ticket to a better life. 'It was just another adventure—something to do,' Weesner says. 'He made scale for playing, and also SAG-AFTRA scale for singing. And that was a large boost. But it was only a few hundred dollars—six or seven hundred dollars. That was the real money that came from the album. He got a lot of publicity but, uh, but not much money.'

The ultimate act of publicity would occur early the following year. Weesner, a Recording Academy member, knew a little something about Grammy eligibility and voting blocs. So he submitted Clark's album in the 'Best Folk Album' category. At the time, folk was an under-the-radar category—certainly beneath Music Row's country-music radar.

'The way that voting goes is, you nominate your artist, right? RCA nominated Cortelia [because] he was the only one that they had in that category here, or at most two. Okay. I knew a lot of people in Nashville in the business. And I knew a few in LA and New York. I got all the national votes. So when it came down to the next round of voting, I got all of Nashville a little bit out of New York, a little bit out of LA, and that's how we won the Grammy with very low sales. I mean, it's truly political.'

How low was low, in terms of sales? About fourteen hundred units.

Cut to the tenth annual Grammy Awards ceremony, which, as fate would have it, was to take place that year in Nashville, at the Hillwood Country Club, on March 2, 1967. Clark's heady competition in the folk category? Pete Seeger, The Mitchell Trio, Mimi & Richard Farina, Lead Belly, and even one other blind street singer: Georgia country artist Oliver Smith (profiled elsewhere in this volume).

Did Clark attend Music's Biggest Night, happening 7.3 miles from his North Side Nashville home? Unfortunately, no.

'He had been at a fraternity party about a week before,' Weesner recalls candidly, 'and had been incontinent. So, basically because of that, I decided that he shouldn't go, and that was purely my decision. I'd wanted him to go, but I decided that that that could be embarrassing, you know—not exactly [what] I wanted people to know about. So Felton Jarvis accepted the Grammy and received a plaque as a producer.'

At the very least, Clark might have had the chance to record a follow-up. 'There was a question about a second album,' says Weesner, 'and RCA turned it down. I taped a second album with some musicians. That was sort of interesting. It was never released. I still have the tapes here somewhere—I have four shipping containers of tapes here at the farm.' (He resides forty-five minutes outside of greater Nashville.)

Did Weesner remain in touch with Clark after the Grammy win? 'Well, the rest of his life was very short after that,' he sighs. 'He died in 1969 at age sixty-three. He never got to improve his living situation as a result of any of this. He lived and died in poverty. I suspect his common-law wife, uh, drank the money pretty quickly. Cortelia would take a drink now and then, and that's how he died. He and a friend had been drinking at the house in the wintertime—early December. A kerosene stove blew up on him, burned them both badly, and despite good care at the hospital, he did not survive. He died at Hubbard Hospital the day before Christmas.'

Singer/songwriter Mickey Newbury later penned a tribute song titled 'Cortelia Clark.' The tune recounts his life and sad end, and then asks, 'Can you save a street in glory for Cortelia Clark?'

OLD CROW
MEDICINE SHOW

CHAPTER 12

CURBING THEIR
ENTHUSIASM

'YOU NEVER KNOW who you're going to meet on the curb,' says Ketch
Secor, co-founder, singer, fiddler, and banjo and harmonica player in Old
Crow Medicine Show. 'And I think that's part of what makes busking such
a good branch to reach for, when you're looking to climb. For me, it was
the first available branch.'

The alt-country string band's early music was influenced by traditional
folk and bluegrass music, and the members often played on instruments
like the banjo, fiddle, and mandolin. Their high-energy performances and
catchy songs quickly gained them a following, and they eventually began
playing in bars and music venues.

Formed in 1998 in Harrisonburg, Virginia, Old Crow's roots can be
traced back to busking and street singing in the late 1990s, when founding
members Secor and Chris 'Critter' Fuqua, who began playing music on
the streets of Canada, Boston, New York, and elsewhere. In 2004, the
band released their debut studio album, *O.C.M.S.*, which includes several
of the songs they had been performing on the streets for years. It was a
critical and commercial success that helped to establish the band as one
of the most exciting and innovative acts in American roots music. In the

ensuing years, they have released seven more albums, including two that have cracked the Top 5 on *Billboard*'s mainstream country chart, 2012's *Carry Me Back* and 2014's *Remedy*.

Long before the band formed, Secor's first busk outside his Virginia hometown was at Taste Of Chicago, the Windy City's annual culinary and music festival in Grant Park. 'I was fifteen,' he reflects, 'and I was going on a train ride to Washington state—Seattle—coming from Virginia. So when I got to Union Station in Chicago, I had about a ten, twelve-hour layover, as one has to catch those Western trains, and it just occurred to me, *Well, hell, I'll just go down there, and I'll find me a place to play*.

'Something I felt that was really important about being a busker is that I played acoustic music—[you were] out there with the birds and the traffic, the sirens and streetscape. Another reason to go out there acoustically was, you could put it on your back—everything that you needed to go do a job was all at your disposal. All you really needed was your wits, and whatever instrument you packed, [and] that open case.'

While some artists repaired to the warmer climates of New Orleans, Austin, or Los Angeles to busk, Secor spotted opportunity where others had not—to the north, notably in Canada.

'I remember going up to busk in French-speaking Canada, which was really lucrative for me, learning the French word how to tip—*pourboire*. We played in the T stops (MBTA subway stops) in Boston. And knowing to quit when the train rattled through—getting your lay of the land as a busker meant reading the signs of the streetscape.

'Busking was the richest, almost meditative or sacred kind of act for me as a hungry musician in the 1990s. I thought that the curb was a more authentic place to go have the experiences of a young musician. I liked it. Its grittiness and its rawness ... kind of made me feel more alive in my conviction to play music. So it was kind of self-fulfilling, you know—as much as I would go out on the curb, it would make me want to play more. It made me want to be successful. I wanted to fill the case [with tips] doubly. By the time I could clean up in one town, I wanted to move to the next town.'

His relationship with street performance dates back to a specific incident in his childhood. 'My dad tells me that when I was a kid in New Orleans, he went into a liquor store and left me outside. I was about four years old. And if you know my dad, you know that he is the kind of guy that would, like, unabashedly leave you outside and assume you would be fine. So, anyway, in about 1982, Dad went into the liquor store and left me alone for five minutes out on the curb. I had seen kids tap dance in the Quarter for change, so I just started dancing. And Dad said that when he came back out of the shop, somebody had thrown coins at my feet ... I realized that I was the kind of person who could be expressive *and* be rewarded with it in a public space.

Busking continued into Secor's teens, still focused on points north of native Virginia. 'When I was eighteen, we went out on our first big busking trip, to New England. It was the winter of 1997. Our first shows were all outdoors in January in New Hampshire, Quebec, Maine, Connecticut, Massachusetts, and Vermont. It's really, really cold—*really* cold. We cut the fingers out of our gloves we played in our long johns, but we were a string band. And we knew that busking was the way to get a place to sleep indoors. The band was called The Route 11 Boys—we'd grown up on Route 11, which goes all the way to Quebec—so we sort of like the runs from New Orleans to Montreal.

'We called ourselves The Route 11 Boys, and [we were] kind of a quasi-busking band of merry misfits. I read a lot of Henry David Thoreau when I was a kid. I thought that a lot of Walt Whitman and Woody Guthrie and all those things were like a kind of song of myself that I was singing in my teenage years. And busking was the thing that I found that was the most genuine expression of everything I was reading. So anything that made me feel like Allen Ginsberg, Kerouac on the road…

'I perceived that I grew up in a time that wasn't cool, and that cool was over. So I went to the streets because I knew that the streets were still rockin'. The curb was still totally punk rock. You know, everything on the curb was free and loose, and it was just like it used to be … there was nobody trying to make it. *Making it* meant a half a pack of cigarettes and a bottomless cup of coffee.

'We would go up north—we figured that we had a commodity, being a Southern string band in the north, right. It never occurred to me to go busk in Richmond, so I figured we'd go to urban 'scapes of the north, like Windsor, Ontario, [which] I first hit the winter of '97. I thought that that town was gold—and speaking of gold, one of the things that I first learned as a busker was that in Canada, you were better off because of the *toonie* [Canada's two-dollar coin]. Everybody wants to throw a *coin*; nobody wants to throw a bill. Throwing a bill, that's what you struggle with, because you crumble it [so you] can hurl it … it's not a hand-to-hand transaction. A tip in an alms box is for a blind man, right? You don't even have to say thank you.

'The crumpled bill is one way to go, but people like to throw coins. I learned this as a child in New Orleans—they want to hear the *plank*. The plank is the indicator that the transaction has been sealed. It's done once you hear it coming. There's no payoff to throwing a greasy dollar bill all balled up. And in Canada, you have your choice of throwing a coin worth double that, right? The *toonie* is a busker's godsend. I learned in the 90s that Canada was the place to double your money, [because] their change is worth, what, eight times as much as American change. The highest valuation of American change is a quarter. In Canada, it's eight times that!'

One of the band's big breaks came when folk legend Doc Watson—

himself a street singer as a teenager—heard them busking in North Carolina. Secor tells the story.

'[Old Crow] had been a band for about a year and a half, and we were in Boone, North Carolina—we lived on the outskirts of it. On the 5th of July in 1999, we set up to busk in front of this drugstore, which is a place that we sometimes worked at, usually in smaller numbers. One thing about the economics of busking is that you have to decide, because everybody has to get paid equally. You have to decide what the most amount of people you can [play] with. If it's three, well then you can make a lot more money than if it's four. So generally we'd [show up] as a duo that would go down to busk at Boone Drug. But on the 5th of July, we were really hungover, and everybody felt sick. So it was more like busking as a kind of [full] group exercise—kind of a detox buster. We probably made about sixty, seventy, eighty dollars.

'We were thinking about packing it in when this woman came up to us and said, 'Are you going to be here for a while? My daddy loves this kind of music.' And I said, 'Ma'am, I really don't know. We'll be here as long as the tips keep flowing.' And she kept [tipping] us, and I took it as a good sign to keep playing. We played for about forty-five minutes longer. She came back, and I saw her park across the street in that same red Jeep Cherokee. And this time she had her dad with her, Doc Watson—she brought him to see us. And Doc listened to us play and gave us a gig on the spot. You know, he said, I want you boys to play the festival I have in honor of my son.'

Playing onstage at MerleFest, which is held every April in Wilkesboro, North Carolina, is not all they did. They actually busked—on the festival grounds. 'We were busking there because the slot we had was onstage, and it was easy to see that busking was *better* than the stage. So we did this show at MerleFest, and we set up our own stage, which was basically us busking. We wrote it on a cardboard sign. We talked a lot about it. And that's when the *Opry* discovered us—a woman named Sally Williams. She brought us to Nashville in the summer of 2002.'

Williams managed the sidewalk in front of the Opry, Secor notes, and booked the band for an outdoor show at the Opryland Plaza. 'They had decided they were going to put a stage up there for the first time and try and get tourists to come to the mall and to the Opry ahead of the show and hang out and maybe see a show. And then our busking set sort of [gave visitors] another reason to stick around. So we would set up there on Friday and Saturdays. And we would play about a four-hour show. And then, once it was dark, we'd all go down to Nashville's Lower Broad district and busk down there. And then [we'd] stay in a twenty-six dollar motel room, and it was a big party. It was quite a life!'

Country and bluegrass star Marty Stuart happened to see the band and offered his mentorship. And, soon after that, they were playing the Opry stage at the Ryman Auditorium. They received a rare first-time-out standing ovation and a call for an encore.[1]

Of course, playing in front of the Opry is not like serenading Music City's more urban curbs. 'Nashville is one of the worst busking towns out there,' Secor says. Yet somehow they succeeded where others had failed. 'We've set up on Second Avenue, right at Commerce across the street. There's a place that had dollar beers; they advertised dollar beer, but then when you actually went in there, they just pour like half a beer into a Dixie cup. Still, when you're trying to spend all that change, that'll buy a lot of dollar beer.'

Now and again, a record company employee, straight out of a marketing meeting, will suggest that Old Crow busk promotionally.

'Somebody is always having a brilliant idea that they'll take us out to the curb again,' Secor shrugs, 'but I think the last time I really played on the curb was with Molly Tuttle down in Key West, just for the hell of it. It's in my blood, so I do it. For me, it's a kind of birthright—and I want to make sure I *still* have that right. So I'll open up my case, I don't know, maybe a couple of times a year, or once a year or something, just to remember ... that and that music still belongs in public spaces. Everything I do is from that perspective. I just felt like it all began with trying to prove yourself on the curb, be the best performer that you could be, without any whistles or bells—just with a cardboard sign or open case and whatever you can bring. I just figured, if you can do it there, you can do it anywhere.'

TIM EASTON

CHAPTER 13

THE WORLD
AS AN ACOUSTIC
STAGE

TIM EASTON'S LIFE as a busker can be traced back to the years he spent in Europe in the 1990s, playing on the streets and in the local pubs of London, Dublin, Paris, Madrid, Amsterdam, and Prague. It took a while to garner attention, but eventually he got to the point where he was invited to perform at music festivals—with actual stages—throughout Europe. He looks back happily on the Europe of the 1990s. 'Beer was twenty-five cents a glass. McDonald's was just getting there. It was an amazing time to be there.'

Born in Lewiston, New York, and raised in Akron, Ohio, Easton spent some formative years in Tokyo and studied for a BA in liberal arts at Ohio State University before making his way to Europe. It was while living there that he found that he had shared an improbable parallel life experience with a legendary busker-turned-movie-star.

'It was a funny thing when I saw the previews for [the movie] *Once*, where Glen Hansard—a former busking buddy of mine back in the day—falls in love with a Czech girl. And I was like, *That's my life story!* My Irish friends laughed and asked, Do you think you were the only street musician to fall in love with a Czech girl? And I had to agree—there were many, many of us. It's just that, for me, it happened in Prague ... and man did she break my heart ... and she therefore made a songwriter out of me!

'The reason I took to street performing was because I wanted to be a songwriter but all I could do was sing the songs of my heroes. I needed to live the life that led to the songs. I needed to have life experiences. James Joyce said *inspiration is memory*, so what was I going to write about as a teenager? All my heroes, like Jack Kerouac or Woody Guthrie or Sonny Terry and Brownie McGhee, were from the streets. They weren't afraid to get right down in it and learn a thing or two about life and how to perform.

'You get used to singing right through the distractions out there when the world is in your face. Look deep into the town square scenes of many old paintings from the Renaissance and you will often find a street performer with a woman dancing nearby. Busking has always been a part of society. Everywhere I go today, I often look at the world as an acoustic stage and wonder what it would be like to set down the guitar case and just start singing right there and now on that spot.'

Degrees of revenue, he says, have much to do with song repertoire. 'The guys who were singing The Beatles and Eagles down the road? They were making plenty of money. They had a bigger audience than I did. I was kind of stubborn, singing ancient folk music.'

Easton considers playing music outdoors as a continuing education. 'Busking was a mandatory thing for me because I needed to learn how to capture a crowd. I also wanted to learn how to write songs, and since I did not have enough life experience I went to Europe and played on the streets. Over there, the towns are more conducive to foot traffic since they were built before cars. I did that on and off for seven years before I wrote the songs that would comprise my first solo album, *Special 20.*'

Though he had the bulk of his busking under his belt by the time he returned to the United States, Easton's dizzying itinerary continued. He played the streets in Columbus, Ohio, where he attended college, and in New York's Washington Square. He then crossed the country to live in California, where he would often play the streets of Santa Cruz and San Francisco, earning tips and selling his self-released albums, before settling in Los Angeles, which is where he became serious about making records.

'I made that first album, and it has a kind of busking vibe to it. And I sent it to Cameron [Strang, the founder of New West Records]. I met with him around the first week I moved to LA, and he signed me—I literally got to Los Angeles and got signed like a week later. It was crazy. I didn't have any time to establish myself. I began playing at [LA music venue] Largo right away, without having to play the streets first.'

The New West pact resulted in four albums: *The Truth About Us* (2001), *Break Your Mother's Heart* (2003), *Ammunition* (2006), and finally *Porcupine* (2009). During that period, he toured behind Wilco, Lucinda Williams, and John Hiatt.

Easton, ever a rolling stone, left LA in 2003, first to briefly couch-sit in Athens, Georgia, and then back west to join the burgeoning bohemian desert enclave of Joshua Tree, California. By 2013, he'd concluded that East Nashville possessed both the creativity and access to commerce that he yearned for. Trading yuccas for poplars, he has remained there since.

New West Records itself left LA for Nashville during the same timeframe, likewise finding new energy in the creative spirit that's suffused Music City since the 1990s.

Twelve solo albums later—including several on his own Campfire Propaganda label—Easton digitally released a new album, *North American Songwriter Volume 1 & 2*, in 2023. Despite his hard-earned gravitas as a recording artist, he continues to embody the spirit of a busker, citing the freedom and spontaneity of street performance as a source of inspiration for his music.

'My busking days were long behind me before I got to Nashville,' he says. 'But I've contemplated it from time to time, especially on the [John Seigenthaler] Pedestrian Bridge. Every now and then, I still see a good spot to set up and play.

'To this day, I always give a tip to the first street performer I see in every new town I visit. It is a tradition of mine, because I have been there, trying to turn the tourist money into my food—and *beer*—money. It is a way of life for so many, and I do not take it for granted. I had some very rough nights where I had to sleep in the park, and other nights where I was living the romantic dream of the true troubadour. All of my favorite bands today did a bit of busking at one point in their life of songs.

'Because of that life of standing on the shoulders of the giants who did it before me,' he concludes, 'I will be able to play music for as long as I wish. Folk music never goes out of style.'

Easton is now at work on his memoir. Its title? *Busker.*

NEW ORLEANS
PART 1

CHAPTER 14

BLUES
WITH A SIDE OF
BOURBON

FOR MORE THAN A CENTURY, musicians—along with their fans—have flocked to New Orleans, where some of the most exciting, intimate, and spontaneous musical moments happen on the street, as well as in the city's abundance of clubs. 'Dating back to the 1800s, you had wagons that would circle the Quarter and would have these battle-of-the-bands between two jazz bands,' Renard Bridgewater, community engagement coordinator for the Music And Culture Coalition Of New Orleans (MaCCNO), told the *Gambit* in 2002. 'It was all very happenstance.'[1]

A singer named Old Corn Meal, or Signor Cormeali, was active on the streets of New Orleans in the 1830s, often standing beside his horse and cart, sometimes in front of Bishop's hotel, selling cornmeal between songs, the best known of which was 'Old Rosin The Bow.' In 1837, he received his spotlight moment as one of the performers in a St. Charles melodramatic production entitled *Life In New Orleans*. His biographer,

Henry A. Kmen (also the author of one of the first histories of the city's music, *Music In New Orleans: The Formative Years, 1791–1841*), called this 'the first appearance of a Negro on the white stage in New Orleans, indeed perhaps in the United States.'[2] The *New Orleans Picayune* punningly referred to the singer's 'meal-odious voice,' while the *True American* newspaper considered him a 'genius.' According to Kmen, 'It was realized that under other circumstances, Corn Meal would be worth more than the tips he got from street audiences.'

New Orleans music history expert Bruce Boyd Raeburn, curator emeritus at the Hogan Archive Of New Orleans Music And New Orleans Jazz, says that Old Corn Meal 'ultimately went from the streets where he was hawking wares to the Opera House on St. Charles by the end of the decade. There are some great films from the 1920s [capturing] black kids playing in the street on homemade drum sets and dancing to it. The serenading tradition was pretty important in both the Sicilians and the "Creoles of color" communities. It was where someone was having a birthday party or some event or just someone you knew, got out there with guitars or fiddles or whatever and serenaded them and then wait for whatever kind of reaction you got—which could be a chamber pot, or it could be to get invited up for a drink. So those nineteenth-century and early twentieth-century traditions are kind of the threshold, I think, for the modern era. And there were, of course, lots of guitar players in the streets in the 1920s, some of them recorded. [They were] forerunners of Babe Stovall and Snooks Eaglin.'

According to Robin Rapuzzi, washboard player in present-day New Orleans band Tuba Skinny, 'The oldest New Orleans busking band probably would have been the Razzy Dazzy Spasm Band.' The band with the assonant name—helmed by Emile 'Stalebread Charlie' Lacoume—did indeed perform in the streets of the Storyville district in the 1890s and early 1900s. 'If you walk into the casino on Canal Street,' Rapuzzi adds, 'you'll see a photo of them on the wall. It was pretty cool; they made homemade instruments. They were kind of like a jug band or string band.'

In fact, a 'spasm band' was an actual thing, loosely defined as a musical group playing a variety of Dixieland, trad jazz, jug band, or skiffle music. Per Wikipedia, the term applies to 'any band (often made up of children) who made musical instruments out of found objects not usually employed for such.' Historian Raeburn adds, 'You'd find like equivalents in England, in the streets and whatnot. They're usually thought to be street urchins who are just busking for money—borderline begging—with people either paying them to play or pay them to stop. Lacoune's is probably the most famous one; The Boozan Kings were another. It was a thing.'

Raeburn notes that these ensembles typically utilized 'homemade drum sets with pie plates and an orange crate for a bass drum with a foot with all sorts of little contraptions on there. That's something that goes all the way, at least from the 1920s, because, you know, the trap set hadn't been around for all that long. And this is a homemade version of a trap drum set.'

Author Laurence Bergreen describes the scene in his definitive biography of Louis Armstrong:

> Street musicians, usually adolescent boys, were another important feature of the Storyville musical scene … The best known of these groups was the seven-man Spasm Band, and soon other spasm bands sprang up throughout Storyville. This was the era before recordings, so there is no way to know exactly how the spasm bands sounded, but on the basis of descriptions left by those who heard them, they were early, primitive jazz bands, short on sophistication but long on novelty. … They frequently punctuated their music with howls and growls and wild calls to one another, or to their audiences gathering on the sidewalk outside the brothels and gambling joints, their rude cacophony drowning out the sweet sounds emanating from within. The spasm bands would play for a quarter, a nickel, even a penny.[3]

As a teenager, Armstrong—one of the most pivotal figures in the development of jazz—performed with a quartet of boys on the street. According to the Busking Project, 'The most common tale that biographers tell is the story of Armstrong as a young boy dancing for pennies in the streets of New Orleans, who would scoop up the coins off the streets and stick them into his mouth to avoid having the bigger children steal them from him.'[4] When somebody called him 'satchel mouth,' it begat his lifelong nickname, Satchmo.

'Obviously, one of the things about New Orleans busking history that's a little different is brass band activity,' Raeburn says, 'because they were playing in the streets, and a lot of them had corner locations. I met [one] when I was doing a gig in 1983, and he went by the name of Barcelona Red [real name: Chris Mason]. He was an alto sax player. And the thing he told me was that he would do his spot, because everyone respected his spot. How they worked out territory is another interesting facet of New Orleans busking history.'

'There were always stories of some of the most original jazz bands in New Orleans playing off the back of a tailgate of a wagon in the French Quarter—promoting their gigs in the hall later that evening,' Rapuzzi says.

Poet and activist John Sinclair, a Detroit native who spent several years in the 1990s and 2000s in New Orleans before relocating to Michigan (and then spending time in Amsterdam), recalls seeing Jackson Square buskers nearly every day. 'That's an industry, right?' he asks rhetorically.

KID ORY

Legendary trombonist Edward 'Kid' Ory was one of the architects of New Orleans's reputation as a jazz hub. Born on Christmas day in 1886 on Woodland Plantation in LaPlace, Louisiana, to a French-speaking family of Black Creole descent, Ory migrated twenty-nine miles downriver to New Orleans at age twenty-one. He became one of the best-known jazz bandleaders in the city, providing employment to many key players in the Crescent City's jazz scene, including Louis Armstrong (who was thirteen years old at the time), Joe 'King' Oliver, Johnny Dodds, and Jimmie Noone. He is credited with introducing the 'tailgate' style, in which the trombone plays a rhythmic line beneath the trumpets and cornets. The tailgate style was used on R&B records besides traditional jazz.

Babette Ory, the trombonist's daughter and today a respected chef in the Los Angeles area, wasn't alive when her father played the streets of New Orleans, but she has become an expert not only on her father's history but that of the city's street singing origins. At the age of two, she traveled with her dad, by which time he'd become a jazz ambassador for the US Information Service. She describes the scene from 1900 to 1917, during which Kid Ory made his name on the New Orleans streets:

'Everyone who lived up and down the river and at the various plantations, and who would come into New Orleans, would hear the carpetbaggers, and they would hear the church singers and all the different musical genres of people, ragtime and everything. What they would do is, they would go and start skiffle singing and make their own instruments out of cotton seed, oil cans, and whatever else they could find. They would put on their strings. Once they felt good enough on the plantation, they would go to New Orleans and try out their new techniques and learn new techniques.

'After the 1900s, at the turn of the century, most of the young kids were starting to become teenagers, and they were actually able to purchase instruments like my dad, who got his first real non–Civil War trombone. They went to the music store in New Orleans and bought real instruments once they had enough money. So they would start busking with their first instruments. My dad was discovered by [cornetist] Buddy Bolden playing this instrument on Jackson Avenue. Right after that, my dad took his homemade band, or his brown-skin band, and they'd busk on the street.

Then they figured out, hey, they could get a wagon. They could elevate their busking and be a level up, and they could have a horse draw it.

'So they're moving around, not just going from corner to corner [but] from district to district. They can advertise on the side of the wagon because telephones were just coming in, and my aunt had a telephone—she bought a house on Jackson Avenue, and my dad would stay there. They elevated busking from going from street corner to street corner, and from plantation to plantation, taking it to the next level with a horse-drawn wagon. Then they got motorized wagons and flatbed trucks. And then they would tie themselves to the competitor's wagon, because they would get competition.

'It was just like Mardi Gras—you're having a parade, and it slowly starts growing. First it's just people walking, and then all of a sudden you see something being drawn by a horse, and there's a celebration going on around the wagon. And then this burst of music comes out from it—you're just walking along the streets of New Orleans, and all of a sudden this wagon passes you by.

'At the same time, they would advertise for a dance the next day, and they would get people they would promote dances or have picnics in City Park, or they would advertise for funerals or whatever other social events might be happening—a wedding or whatever—and they would get dressed up in their full, finest regalia, you know, with clean button-down shirts . . . the whole thing. They look very *dut*, which is the Creole term for a dude—that was *dude* before the dude of Quincy Jones—the original dude. They wanted to always look clean and presentable, and organized, you know, to do other gigs.'

In 1919, Kid Ory relocated to Los Angeles. The busking did not stop there, despite the city's legendary reputation for automobile commuting over New Orleans's pedestrian orientation.

'Basically, my dad did not record in New Orleans,' Babette notes. 'He didn't record until he moved to Los Angeles in 1919. And then, in 1921, he made the first jazz recording by people of color for the Spikes Brothers (Jeb Curry Spikes and Reb Spikes), who had a record store at 12th & Central. They recorded at a studio on Main Street in Santa Monica, and then they [made] wax cylinders and sent the wax cylinders to New York to be made into records—and half of which melted going through the Mojave desert. But the busking continued, because they still had to promote dances, even though it was not just on street corners anymore... they had raised the bar to be in the wagon. In LA in the 1920s, I think they did it once or twice to promote [a show they were playing at a club on] Washington Boulevard in the Culver City area.'

SNOOKS EAGLIN

Sometimes, the stuff of legends lacks a basis in facts. Take Snooks Eaglin, for instance. Born in New Orleans on January 21, 1937, Eaglin was one of the city's most respected blues and R&B artists, active from the 1950s until his death in 2009. But his first LP, *Snooks Eaglin: New Orleans Street Singer* (Folkways, 1958), seems to have branded him a busker for life, despite the fact that his ten subsequent studio albums feature his full ensemble. And while he certainly did perform solo on the streets in his early years, most living Crescent City experts remember seeing him indoors and onstage in the company of other musicians.

Several of Eaglin's later associates, including Hammond Scott—co-founder of Black Top Records, which released many albums by the artist—never got to see him playing on the streets.

'I never saw Snooks do that,' says Scott, a lifelong Louisianan. 'I don't know where he would have played on the street, because wasn't the type of person to set up a cardboard box or something and sit out on the curb in the Quarter. He and his wife were too paranoid about everything—as soon as he started being more prosperous, the first thing they did was move out of town and get their own house and live out past the airport in St. Rose. They were very paranoid about crime. They had a lot of very odd idiosyncrasies about how money was handled. He was one of the only artists I ever worked with that was paid fully in advance for most of his jobs, and he had several reasons for that. One of them was not trusting being paid, no matter how reputable the person was. And secondly—and I tried to reason with him about it—they thought that if they had money on them and they left a gig, that they might be robbed.

'He liked having a band behind him much better, because he could still play multiple parts on the guitar, you know, so bass lines and rhythm and leads and fills and all that all under his… he had such an idiosyncratic technique with his hands. So, I mean, certainly he probably had occasion to play on the street, but that was not his normal habit.'

Fellow New Orleans bluesman Little Freddie King says of Eaglin, 'Me and him never did play together, but we were friends, and I used to go where he used to play up on Philip and Clara Streets, years and years ago. I always did like that man. Then we used to play JazzFest, and we'd be booked on the same on the same gig. I always like to listen to Snooks. We used to talk, we used to be at the Louisiana Record Factory. We played there.'

In his liner notes to the 2005 reissue of *Snooks Eaglin: New Orleans Street Singer*, musicologist and author Elijah Wald attempts to set the record straight:

On his own, Eaglin [could be seen] not only singing country numbers, but playing jazz and Latin instrumentals, as well as old folk and blues tunes that would have been of no interest to hip young dance crowds. When he didn't have a dance gig, he would sometimes play on the streets of the French Quarter, and one day, on the sidewalk in front of Krauss's department store, he caught the ear of Harry Oster, an amateur folklorist from New England.

Considering Eaglin's tastes, his preference for working with bands, and the fact that he has never made an acoustic recording except when it was demanded by a folk record label (and those [more than] fifty years ago), it is not surprising that many of his present-day fans have underrated or even dismissed his solo work, complaining that Oster inappropriately tried 'to reduce Snooks to a solo "street-performer" type of attraction,' in the words of the poet and historian John Sinclair.'[5]

BABE STOVALL

Babe Stovall was a first-generation Mississippi bluesman whose style derived from the better-known Tommy Johnson, originator of such classic blues as 'Big Road Blues,' 'Canned Heat Blues,' and 'Cool Drink Of Water Blues.' A Mississippi Delta stalwart, Stovall relocated to New Orleans's French Quarter in 1964 and entertained both in cafes and on sidewalks.

Stovall's discography contains a handful of albums: the eponymous *Babe Stovall*, released on Verve in 1964; the similarly self-titled *Babe Stovall*, issued by the UK's Flyright label released in 1976; plus three posthumous releases, *The Old Ace: Mississippi Blues And Religious Songs* (Arcola Records, 2004), *South Mississippi Blues* (Rounder Records), and *Babe Stovall: The Larry Bornstein Collection* (2009). He is said by some to be the inspiration behind singer/songwriter Jerry Jeff Walker's 'Mr. Bojangles.' He passed away in 1974.

New Orleans blues singer and guitarist Little Freddie King remembers seeing Stovall—eleven years Johnson's junior and thirty-three years King's senior—performing in clubs and on the streets in two very different Deep South cities.

'I did play with Babe Stovall actually,' he says. 'He was my daddy's friend in McComb, Mississippi. I'd get in my car, you know, and I used to go and get that corn liquor and stuff out the Tylertown, Mississippi, and

I used to ride with them in the car and they would drink and play, you know, and that's when I first met Uncle Babe. And after that, time passed on. By the time I got down here [to New Orleans], I didn't know what had happened to Uncle Babe.'

Cut to the very early 70s. 'I was going to a club there on Ursulines & Marais. I used to go in there every evening [after] I got off from work and, get a little drink. So there [Stovall] was, standing on the outside, still playing the guitar. I didn't know who he was at first. I went on inside and I ordered my drink, and my friend said, Fred, did you see Uncle Babe out there? I said no. He said, Did you see a man out there with a guitar? I said, yeah, I know Uncle Babe, but I didn't know he was down here. So I went back outside to talk to him a little while and got to see him play to guitar a little while. He was a good gospel player, and he was a good, good blues player. I used to enjoy with him on Orleans Street there, by the Tremé supermarket. And we set our buckets out there, for tips and stuff, and we [would] have a good crowd, and we made real good money some days.'

LITTLE FREDDIE KING

Little Freddie King was born in McComb—also the hometown of Bo Diddley, with whom King toured in 1976, and blues singer King Solomon Hill—on July 19, 1940, and was a cousin of Lightnin' Hopkins. At age fourteen, he moved to New Orleans, where he was inspired by 'Boogie Bill' Webb and Polka Dot Sim. He recorded his first album for Louisiana's Ahura Mazda label, also known for its Robert Pete Williams and Scott Dunbar LPs, but it was never released. He has issued a total of sixteen albums since then. One of them was recorded live at JazzFest, an event of which King is a forty-two-year performing veteran.

Before he became a consistent touring and festival attraction, King played on the streets of New Orleans. But did he ever have run-ins with the law for playing on the street?

'I had that problem playing down there by Claiborne & Magnolia. I went in and played—and this was the first time I went to jail—and a lady was upset. Her husband had just passed away, and [she claimed] we were disturbing the peace. I saw the lady call the police. The Black Mariah van is coming down—a great big van—and [the cop] said, Come on, Fred, let's go. I said, What you lockin' me up for? He said, You're disturbing the peace. He grabbed me and my whole band and slugged us into that Black Mariah van.'

King says that, by 1974, he had made the transition from street singer to club and concert attraction. 'I'd play all the little places in New Orleans, like the Dew Drop In,' he recalls, 'and I'd cross the lake to places like Arabi.' His recording career picked up as well—still performing into his eighties, he now boasts a discography of seventeen albums, several of them recorded live.

NEW ORLEANS
PART 2

CHAPTER 15

DAVID & ROSELYN, GRANDPA ELLIOTT,
AND MORE

DAVID & ROSELYN

David Leonard met Roselyn Lionhart while in the Air Force in 1959. They both played in a touring Air Force music ensemble. 'They were the two most interesting people on the bus to talk to,' their daughter, Arlee Leonard, surmises. 'They fell in love and were married six months and six days later—the last day of 1959.' According to Arlee, now in her sixties, 'They are still like schoolkids in love.' We witness this as the interview unfolds. In fact, David and Roselyn—and Arlee, who serves as her parents' unofficial spokesperson—routinely finish each other's sentences.

David, who sings and plays guitar, harmonica, and trumpet, earned a BA in Anthropology from the University Of California and did graduate work at Wayne State in Detroit. Roselyn, who sings and plays guitar and banjo, among other instruments, and studied drama and folklore at Wayne State followed by anthropology and sociology at Oakland Community

College. Their education is a point of pride: 'My dad's a UC Berkeley grad,' says Arlee, 'and almost got a master's at state in Detroit but didn't quite finish. They have three college-educated kids. Two with master's.'

They have played music on the streets for more than half a century—forty years of those in New Orleans, although they've also called Detroit, the Bay Area, and Los Angeles home. *Variety* wrote of them, 'David & Roselyn report on ghetto life . . . as sincerely as Woody Guthrie and Leadbelly wrote for their times.' In his national bestseller *Charles Kerault's America*, author and broadcast Charles Kerault describes them as 'old pros': 'She plays guitar, mandolin, and several African instruments—kalimba, marimbula, and ekwe—and he plays guitar, cornet, and harmonica. They both sing. They are very good, and their open guitar case fills quickly with cash whenever a crowd gathers.'[1] They have released eight CDs, most of them on their own Da Ro Productions label, commencing in 1981, with copies sold primarily as busking merch.

According to Arlee, 'My mother opened her guitar case in 1974 in Jackson Square. She was depressed that our bus was taking a lot of long time to get repaired. And she just sat down in Jackson Square to feel better by playing her guitar. They were already singing the blues. They were already performers and Michigan having learned the guitar in the early mid-60s; they were playing a coffeehouses in Michigan when I was a little girl. But then people started putting money in her guitar case, and that was a nice little lightbulb moment that happened in Jackson Square in 1974.'

They weren't living in New Orleans yet, however. 'They started coming through regularly,' Arlee continues. 'We were still living in Michigan then, and then we moved to California again. I was born in the Bay area, and we moved to [LA's] Topanga Canyon. They started after working at the Great American Food & Beverage Company [a 70s restaurant chain] as singing waiters for a minute. They actually started busking on Venice Beach.

[above] Blind Arvella Gray on Maxwell Street, Chicago, 1972. *Cary Baker*

[below] Clara Littricebey at the corner of Maxwell and Halsted, 1972. *Cary Baker*

[above] Reverend Gary Davis's 1960 LP *Harlem Street Singer*, and a poster for the 2014 documentary film of the same name.

[below] Maxwell Street Jimmy Davis performing on the Chicago street that gave him his name, 1972. *Cary Baker*

[above] Little Pat Rushing on Maxwell Street, Chicago, 1972. *Cary Baker*

[left] *Living Blues* magazine issue number 11, winter, 1972–73, featuring the author's report on the Chicago scene of the time. *Author's collection*

[above] David Peel recording live in Washington Square, New York City, 1968, as producer Paul Siegel looks on. *Tina Tinan*

[left] Oliver Smith's Grammy-nominated Elektra LP.

[opposite] Moondog on the streets of Downtown Chicago, 1975. *Saul Smaizys*

[above] Mary Lou Lord, busking in Austin during the South By Southwest festival, 2014. *Steffen Paulus*

[below] Satan & Adam (Sterling Magee and Adam Gussow), Downtown New York, 1989. *Corey Pearson*

[above] George 'Bongo Joe' Coleman with music writer Lawrence Skoog and his son in Alamo Plaza, San Antonio, 1968. Photo by Chris Strachwitz, courtesy of the Arhoolie Foundation [below] Cortelia Clark performing outside the Pancake Pantry in Downtown Nashville, c. 1967. Courtesy of Sony Music Archives

[above] Poi Dog Pondering, Guadalupe Street, Austin, Texas, 1987. *Jean François Berneron [below left]* Lucinda Williams, Guadalupe Street, c. 1974. *Photo by Gary Bishop, courtesy of the Austin City Limits Archive [below right]* Violent Femmes, Milwaukee, Wisconsin, 1982. *Karen Keene [opposite]* Tim Easton, Bolgna, Italy, 2019.

[above] Tuba Skinny, New Orleans. *Sarah Danziger* [below left] Wild Man Fischer's 1969 Bizarre LP, *An Evening With…*

[below right] Cover artwork for Ted Hawkins's 1986 album *Happy Hour.* Courtesy of Concord Music

[left] Fantastic Negrito in Oakland, California, 2018. *Gabriel Turek*

[below] Peter Case and Bert Deivert, San Francisco, 1973. *Bert Deivert*

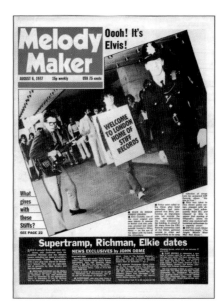

Melody Maker

AUGUST 6, 1977   15p weekly   USA 75 cents

Oooh! It's Elvis!

WELCOME TO LONDON HOME OF STIFF RECORDS

What gives with these Stiffs?
SEE PAGE 22

Supertramp, Richman, Elkie dates

NEWS EXCLUSIVES by JOHN ORME

[left] Elvis Costello outside the CBS Convention, London, July 26, 1977, as featured on the cover of *Melody Maker.*

[below] Billy Bragg busking in support of the homeless charity Shelter, London, 2013. *Katy Stoddard*

[opposite] Harry Perry, the Kosmic Krusader of Venice Boardwalk, 2014. *Nikki Kreuzer*

[above] Madeleine Peyroux performing on Rue de Buci, Paris, c. 1994. *Courtesy of Madeleine Peyroux*

[right] Glen Hansard (The Frames, The Swell Season, The Commitments) busking on Grafton Street, Dublin, 2006. *David Cleary*

[above] Grandpa Elliott recording beside the Mississippi, 2018. *Courtesy of Playing For Change* [below] New Orleans street musician David Roe and his group the Royal Rounders busking on Royal Street. *Courtesy of Playing For Change*

[above] Playing For Change
founder Mark Johnson recording
in Bamako, Mali. *Courtesy of
Playing For Change*

[right] David & Roselyn busking
on Royal Street, New Orleans.

DAVID & ROSELYN

'We were some of the first ones out there. There was Harry Perry, the guy in the white turban on his roller skates. My parents were starting out around 1976–77, playing Venice Beach, playing up in Westwood near UCLA, and playing on Hollywood Boulevard. By the time they stopped playing [the streets] in New Orleans, they were averaging eight hundred dollars a day or a weekend.

'Then I went off to college. My sister went off too. We were born in 1960 and '62. [My parents] had two more kids, in 1977 and '80. They were living in a van, commuting between SoCal and New Orleans, and the kids more or less went to school in New Orleans. Since the 80s, New Orleans and California back and forth, and then they bought a house here.'

From the start, they were activists as well as musicians. 'They were activists from way back. They came down to Louisiana in '63, to register as voters, leaving me and my sister with relatives in Michigan, like with my grandmother. So they've been activists forever. And when I asked them what it was like to fight City Hall here [in New Orleans], my dad said *refreshing* and my mother said *necessary*.

'They were making a good living in New Orleans—Royal Street, Jackson Square—working in the evening. That's when people had had a few drinks and were looser with their cash. And then the city is like no busking after 8pm. And they're like, *That's ridiculous. You're gonna cut our income in half.* So they would work on fighting noise ordinances *and* time ordinances.'

'We won everything that we fought,' Roselyn chimes in. 'It's civil rights, after all, right? I was fighting for color, I was fighting for free speech—which is what music is, by the way, in case you didn't know. Music is free speech.'

They credit New Orleans civil rights attorney and busking advocate Mary Howell for their court victories. 'She's sweet and she's sharp,' says Roselyn. 'I like that combination.'

Roselyn's knowledge of current affairs, politics, and community policy is second-generation. In March of 2012, she found herself opposing New Orleans City Council member Jackie Clarkson. Arlee asks her parents 'what it was like to kick Jackie Clarkson's butt.' Not missing a beat, David responds, 'Well, it was scrawny!' Roselyn adds that when Clarkson 'found out that my mother had been a city councilwoman back in Michigan, [it] just freaked the shit out of her.'

Roselyn's mother, Arlee explains, was the first Black woman on the city council in Flint, Michigan. 'A Cadillac dealer's wife was a white woman that the Republicans put up to run so that my grandmother wouldn't have the distinction of being the first woman. So the first Black woman went up on the city council at the same time—they were both one-term people. But my grandmother, my mother's mother, was always an activist and a lady of many firsts—first lady funeral director in Flint and much more. But Jackie Clarkson, who is also [actress] Patricia Clarkson's mother, was a real pain in the ass on the city council! She thought street music was, as she put it, *déclassé*... she thought it was trash. But in fact, music originated that way,' on the streets.

David & Roselyn set out to educate the Council. 'Sure, I don't know if they *learned* anything, but we *taught* them!' says Roselyn. They took their instruments with them and took them out of their cases.

David picks up the story. 'We realized why we don't like this [the council meeting]—because it's so boring, you know. So we entertained them! We second-lined them. And they got up and danced! It was marvelous.' The end result? 'In the end, music is freedom of speech,' Roselyn says. 'And they said they had to agree.'

There was also the question of amplification. 'They didn't like us using our amplifiers,' David says, 'even though we turn it down low enough. It was just enough so that our instruments and our voices could be heard.' (At one point, he demonstrated to the council how an *un*amplified trumpet was sometimes louder than an amplified trumpet.)

David & Roselyn continued to power through bad days and good.

What was a bad day for a busker? 'Bad times is when it rained, or it was cold and windy. That's hard,' says David, to which Roselyn adds, 'And it was a drag sometimes when you had some idiot that came up and wanted to chase you away because they because they decided that busking was *déclassé*.' They laugh at the thought.

Arlee puts things in perspective. 'People would move to the French Quarter and then complain about the *music* in the French Quarter. Don't move here if you don't like it! It was here before you came—and it'll be here when you go bye.'

What was a good day for a busker, then, I ask—a hundred-dollar bill? 'Oh, we got a few of those,' Roselyn replies. But even better: 'We ended up on *The Gong Show* in 1977, and that was a result of being seen in the streets…and we won!' *The Gong Show* was a Sony Pictures Television that ran from 1976 to 1980 and 1988 to 1989; the winners were generally the most outlandish performers spotlighted in each episode. David & Roselyn later performed on an all-star version of *The Gong Show* too, but they didn't win that one.

Generally speaking, though, they simply felt most at home on the streets.

New Orleans musician and WWOZ DJ Marc Stone remembers a day he spent busking with the pair. 'It's a nice day and we're on Royal and we've got a good crowd, and there's this skinny old belligerent drunk, and David and Roselyn are telling him off—*fuck you* or whatever—and he gets up and he seems to walk away, and then we've got a nice crowd of people. All of a sudden, I see David get out of his chair, mid-song, which is something he never did. And I get up, and the guy is pissing on the back of a Jeep in front of everybody, and David gets up behind him and kicks him in the ass so hard. He's a skinny little dude. [David] rips him to the ground.

Meanwhile, the guys from [doo-wop group] Jay-Ray & Gee are coming down the street, and this time they're wearing, like, matching sweats with the Jay-Ray & Gee logo, looking athletic. They all throw their hands up and yell, *Field goal!'*

'One of the things that they liked about street performing was that they could make their own hours,' Arlee elaborates, 'and they didn't have to deal with unscrupulous club owners or cigarette smoke.'

Roselyn picks up the conversation. 'Yeah, we do play a lot of clubs.'

Arlee: 'They would spend time in Europe. They got taken to Asia for film projects. They worked in Colombia, they worked in Australia, different parts of Europe. And they could play on the streets sometimes when we were traveling. They would have club dates [that evening], but then they could also go and play on the street whenever they wanted to, as well.'

Roselyn: 'And we were world performers, world travelers. We had a great time, and the nice thing is that we didn't have to pay for it. We convinced the promoters and club owners it was all an advertisement: *Oh, we saw them on the street, we just have to come and see them again!'*

Above all, Roselyn and David won respect from fellow musicians. 'We were respected by other musicians because we were good musicians,' Roselyn says. 'We had good voices. We sang in tune, we sang in time, and people came and listened to us and paid us for it. We were interesting. Of course, there were all those who didn't like us because we were an interracial couple, but they were either amusing or annoying. When they were amusing, we enjoyed them, and when they were annoying, we ignored them.'

Arlee tells their story as though she were a third wheel in the duo, and at times she was, especially while growing up in Los Angeles. 'I would sit in with them when I was in town, or I'd have them sit in with me when I had gigs in town,' she says. 'I was already a teenager when they started really playing the street regularly. And so I was going to high school, and we just come out for fun and sing a few songs or something. My younger brother and sister were free-range kids at Venice Beach, and they never got kidnapped because they were very free-range. People tried, yeah—they would scream and yell, Where are your parents? or something. [I'd say,] They're right over there!'

Arlee also points out that she's on some of their CDs. 'My now-husband recognized me on one of their CDs and I was like, *Oh yeah, I forgot*...hey, did I get paid?'

'Yes,' Roselyn responds, 'room and board!' The three share a laugh.

Are they still busking?

'Not so much, since COVID,' says Roselyn. 'We don't wanna get sick. There are still calluses...I can still see them on my hand, but they're not as big as they were.'

GRANDPA ELLIOTT

Grandpa Elliott, born Elliott Small, was a soul and blues singer known for his soulful performances on the streets of New Orleans. Born in the city on November 1, 1944, he gained international recognition for his captivating street performances, most notably through his involvement in Playing For Change, a global music initiative that connects musicians from all over the world (discussed in more detail in this book's epilogue).

Elliott's street singing career began in the 1980s, following years spent in New York, where he recorded several singles. He became a beloved fixture in the French Quarter and was often seen performing on Royal Street, near the famous Brennan's restaurant. His music was deeply rooted in the blues and soul traditions, and he possessed a rich, gravelly voice that could move audiences to tears.

'The whole Grandpa thing was very much an act when I knew him in the 90s,' musician and DJ Marc Stone recalls. 'He was a master at drawing and holding a crowd. One day he ran down the litany of his facial expressions and voice characterizations for me—I was in stitches. Then there was the time I figured that since he was not on his regular spot, I could just set up and play for as long as I wanted, telling him to wait when he arrived. That also could have ended in stitches, had he not given me fair warning by running across Royal Street toward me with the massive bike chain he normally wore around his neck, swinging furiously above his head. It was easy to hear through the babbling Grandpa act and realize that he was a very experienced and savvy musician with excellent ears and musical range. He could sing a wide variety of music well, had excellent pitch, and had the sweetest and most controlled harmonica sound I may have ever heard.'

New Orleans musician, producer, and Ernie K-Doe biographer Ben Sandmel remembers Elliott's street performances. 'For years, when walking through the French Quarter, I loved hearing him busking on the corner of Royal and Toulouse. He sounded great, so soulful, such a crowd-pleaser. The song I remember most vividly was their rendition of "Stand By Me." As a programming consultant for the New Orleans Jazz & Heritage Festival, I recommended Grandpa Elliott to [festival director] Quint Davis, who booked him to perform in 2010. When Elliot died in 2022, there was a lively second line on the streets of the Quarter in his honor.'

Elliott's heartfelt rendition of the Ben E. King classic 'Stand By Me,' recorded on the streets of New Orleans, became a key representation of the Playing For Change project and its mission to unite people through music. The organization's co-founder, Mark Johnson, remembers the first time he heard Elliott sing 'Amazing Grace' on the street. 'It gave me chills and tears,' he says. 'He'd been performing on the streets in New Orleans for over sixty years. He started as a tap dancer. He would just stay there all day, all night—twelve hours of sitting in his spot just to then start his day.

Sixty-six years old and sixty years on the street. One of the most profound musicians I've ever met.'

Johnson asked Elliott if he knew the song 'Stand By Me,' to which Elliott laughed, 'Who doesn't?'

'So then I put headphones on him,' Johnson continues, 'and he sang on that song—and that was the beginning of our journey together. We spent the next ten years traveling the world together. We made the album called *Sugar Is Sweet*. But we did so much more than that. We toured five continents together. He played concerts for over a hundred thousand people [in] Brazil; they treated him like Elvis. He would have billboards and was like a legend in in Brazil and in many other countries. He toured the world in airplanes and tour buses and all of that, but he always seemed most comfortable just playing on the street.'

In a 2019 interview, Elliott told the *New Orleans Times-Picayune* that Johnson 'changed my life. He made me lift my head up.'[2]

'I think he was finally getting back what he'd been giving to people for so long,' Johnson adds. 'The interesting thing about being a street musician in New Orleans is [that] it's a very divided city, with race and money. And he was the one—he was everyone's grandpa. It didn't matter who you were—he was gonna sing a song for you to make your day better.

'My favorite moment in my life would be walking him out onstage with the Playing For Change band, which was made up of all musicians that had never met. It was a band of eleven musicians from ten countries, and Grandpa was the leader. And when I'd walk him out onstage, he'd get these huge standing ovations, and he would just squeeze my hand because he [was blind and] couldn't see the crowd. But he could feel it … I knew in that moment he was feeling back that love he'd given to so many people.

'Grandpa Elliott went on to inspire more people than I could ever count.'

MESCHIYA LAKE

In 2018, New Orleans music magazine *Offbeat* called longtime former busker Meschiya Lake 'the figurehead, the homing beacon for the zeitgeist of the Frenchmen Street trad scene.'[3] For DJ Gwen Thompkins, meanwhile, 'She brings an early jazz sensibility to songcraft and presentation that marks her as a top-drawer cabaret singer, blues belter, and honest-to-goodness, modern-day chanteuse.'[4]

Lake, a Southern Oregon native, came to the Crescent City by way of South Dakota, where she won a singing contest at age nine, and later played in the state's South Dakota Opry. She quickly found kindred spirits—and an audience.

'My first thing on the street was just me and my friend Kyle,' she recalls. 'As a duo, it wasn't really too hard [to find good places to play]. You just go where it was busy where there's a lot of foot traffic.'

Lake gained particular renown during her long stint with the street ensemble Loose Marbles, who played Royal Street and eventually splintered into new ensembles such as chanteuse Meschiya Lake's Little Big Horns Jazz Band and Tuba Skinny. 'With the bigger bands, you really kind of needed to do it in the pedestrian mall on Royal Street because ... really big crowds would form and block traffic, if there was supposed to be any traffic, which would make it difficult for people to tip and for us to do our show.'

The band would often flee hit and humid New Orleans summers to play another busking vortex, New York's Washington Square. 'We went from New Orleans up to New York City, stayed there for about six months, then we went to Europe for a month or two months, and then we went back down to New Orleans. Busking is not super great in New Orleans in the summer. It can be unbearably hot during the day, and tourism really dies down. You kind of just go with the crowd. Summers are great in Washington Square. So we would just kind of travel and go where the crowds were.

'There were so many good days,' she reflects. 'I mean, if I made a hundred dollars solo busking in a day, that was an okay day. But we used to rake it in with the Marbles.'

Other days didn't pan out as well. 'The competition got so fierce on the street and there were so many bands out busking that we used to do split shift,' she says. 'And so one band would play two hours [in the morning], and then another band would come in and then play two to four. So the morning band would have somebody get the spot the night before.

'I remember it was my turn to get the spot. I was on a date with a gentleman, and he dropped me off at the courthouse steps at 3am, and I slept on the courthouse steps with a little pink razor in my hand [until] it was time to busk at 11am, and I was like, *This just isn't worth it for the two hundred dollars that we might make today.* And I've got regular gigs.

'Some people would chain chairs to fire hydrants and things, to get the spot. We all kind of thought that that was cheating a little bit because he would, like, be out there in person at 3am and take shifts to hold the spot down.

'I don't know what it's like out there now. There are so many new experiences—you're always meeting new people from all over the world. And it really, it can kind of act like a bridge between people, where, because you're putting emotion into your music, it connects people. I think it makes you more approachable, gives you something to talk about. So it really opens a lot of doors and brings people closer together.'

Lake also busked around Europe, in England, France, and Ireland—specifically Cork, where she moved for a time in 2018, and where the busking ordinance curiously emphasizes that street performers 'must have a sufficient repertoire to avoid constant repetition.' She has since returned to New Orleans but spends much of the year in Asheville, North Carolina, where buskers and drum circles form the soundtrack of the city's core.

Lake's career has since taken off—she's become a multi-year winner of Best Female Vocalist and Best Traditional Jazz Artist in *Offbeat* magazine's annual readers' poll and has worked in the studio with both Tom Waits and Alec Ounsworth of Clap Your Hands Say Yeah. Accordingly, she hasn't had much time to busk.

'No, not so much,' she says. 'I mean, I *would*, but I think it was 2009 when my career kind of started to take off and I got a lot of club gigs and started doing international tours. I love playing on the street and I would do it in a heartbeat again, but I just haven't really had the time for it. Also, I felt like it was time to give it away to the next generation. I've got other work now, so I feel, it's right to just hand it over to the slightly younger kids, you know.'

PRESENT-DAY NEW ORLEANS BUSKING

CHAPTER 16

TUBA SKINNY,
ROYAL STREET ROYALTY'

'I GOTTA TELL YOU,' says Robin Rapuzzi, who plays the washboard in New Orleans band Tuba Skinny, 'I travel all over the world with our band. Sometimes we're in big towns, sometimes we're in little towns. And I see a lot of towns that are struggling for culture, especially in America. And I always think, *If only their city council would consider street performing, they would have a much more peaceful downtown—a much more positive and communicative downtown area.* Street performing can really help the ecosystem of any city. I think that's something that people are missing out on across the world, but especially in America. Yeah, I think it would help the local economy too.'

Which is to say: the rest of America ought to look to what New Orleans—where street music is a way of life—has known for well over a century. 'Something that's important to be aware of is that a lot of the musicians in Tuba Skinny, including myself, we all performed on the street before that band existed—with other projects, or even sometimes by ourselves,' Rapuzzi notes.

It's true: Tuba Skinny's story is complex. But their history nearly all unfolded on the streets. The band—whose music is steeped in traditional jazz, ragtime, and pre-war blues—formed in the spring of 2009. Their origins trace back to three earlier Crescent City outfits, most notably Dead Man Street Orchestra and Loose Marbles. The former, a Cajun and old-timey music band, featured Shaye Cohn, Barnabus Jones, Todd Burdick, and Kiowa Wells. Future Hurray For The Riff-Raff singer Alynda Segarra also played in the band. When Dead Man Street Orchestra disbanded, Cohn, Jones, Burdick, and Wells went on to perform with Loose Marbles, eventually becoming the nucleus of Tuba Skinny by way of a few other intertwined line-ups, side projects, and band names. The bands received national press, including in *The New Yorker* and *Time*.

Rapuzzi, whose nickname is Itchy Ribs, plays an actual washboard—the kind originally used for washing clothes. It is not uncommon to see one being played on New Orleans's streets. 'Up in Cajun Country, they play, they play the *frottoir*,' he says, 'which means *the scratch* in French. It looks like armor, and it's stainless steel. They use spoons to play it.' The *frottoir* is made from corrugated metal, solely for use as a percussive instrument that hangs from the shoulders; many people play it with bottle openers rather than spoons.

In an article for *Offbeat* magazine, writer Geoffrey Himes posited that the earliest iteration of Tuba Skinny 'played for tips in [the city's] Jackson Square out of necessity more than choice.'[1] These days, the band's itinerary might extend to two or three weeks per year in legitimate music venues, but they 'keep returning to the sidewalks, because the group's personality is so grounded in those origins that they require regular doses to keep their character intact. Plus, it's so much fun.' It is not unusual to find Tuba Skinny busking in a city where they're due to play onstage to a ticketed audience just a few hours later.

Tuba Skinny's music is a modern iteration of the traditional jazz brass bands that preceded them. Their instrumentation is patently New Orleans: cornet, clarinet, banjo, *frottoir*, and, of course, tuba. Their music hearkens to the brass bands of the 1920s and 30s, incorporating elements of ragtime and blues.

How did the name Tuba Skinny come about? Perhaps the appellation shouldn't be surprising, coming from a city that gave the world Fats Domino and Trombone Shorty. Rapuzzi tells the story. 'There was a New Orleans musician named Tuba Fats [Anthony Lacen] who sadly passed away. He was a performer in Jackson Square and around the city. He also toured abroad. But he fought for performing rights and carried the soul of traditional New Orleans music—he was a big representation of that. The reason [our] band is called Tuba Skinny in part is because our tuba player, Todd Burdick, used to bike toward the French Quarter to go busking and with the band, and he *is* skinny, so locals would yell out, *What are you, Tuba Skinny?*'

The late Anthony 'Tuba Fats' Lacen, who lived from 1950 until 2004, had in fact become something of a spokesperson for the buskers of New Orleans. 'I don't need to be a millionaire,' he told *Offbeat* in December 2000. 'If I want to play on the street, that's my business. We're not beggars, we're not homeless. I play in Jackson Square, and I do it because peoples love music and I love to see peoples enjoy music. People come to New Orleans to hear the music and they don't get it up and down Bourbon Street. It's not there anymore.'[2]

In a profile of Tuba Fats for the *Gambit*, Katy Reckdahl wrote, 'About a decade ago, Quarter residents really began to demand limits on music in the streets. . . . Lacen's role was one of a peacemaker . . . when NOPD Captain Ernest Demma headed up the French Quarter's Eighth District, he often went to Lacen's bench in Jackson Square to get help resolving, say, a trombone bleating in the Quarter in the wee hours. "I cannot say enough good things about him," Demma says. "And besides that, he was a good musician."'[3]

Nick Spitzer, host of the public radio program *American Routes*, saw Tuba Fats frequently in Jackson Square, and shared the following remembrance:

> Tuba Fats' greatest legacy was not the sound of his horn playing for tips or on parade, but the way he shared his love of music, his ever-changing ensemble and his positive attitude with tourists, natives, and musicians alike. So it was that players from the great brass bands were there for the funeral parade: Tremé, Rebirth, and Dirty Dozen, and many others. A line of tubas, a man with a red tuba, all the celebrants filled with sorrow, but also exalting Tuba Fats with signs and pictures, in fine suits and fancy dresses, hot colors and cool hairdos. They were alternately somber or cheered as the mood of the music changed: slow dirge, medium hymn, fast march. Probably 2,500 made their way with the horse-drawn casket to the French Quarter, down Bourbon Street—a rare honor, due to Tuba's daily play on Jackson Square—where tourists gawked and clamored. A somber stop at St. Louis Cathedral, where a priest blessed the bier while those who knew Tuba Fats cried out his goodness. Starting up and out of the Quarter the several blocks long throng sang 'Down By The Riverside' with the line *'Ain't gonna study war no more'* resonating about life here and abroad. By the time we reached Tremé, the crowd was down to 1,000 of the most exuberant still singing in the receding daylight.[4]

Tuba Fats was not only a fixture in Jackson Square but also an advocate of street performance and a protector and mentor to those who followed in his footsteps. He continued to tour nearly until his death, and when he was no longer able to participate in parading with second lines, funerals, and such in his final years, a bench in Jackson Square became his headquarters.

According to *Legal Affairs* magazine, when he died, on January 11, 2004, 'Thousands of mourners and hundreds of brass band musicians gave him a traditional jazz funeral, walking and dancing behind his horse-drawn casket as it passed through the streets of his hometown of New Orleans.'

WHEN TUBA SKINNY BUSK as a full band in New Orleans these days—which is significantly less often than they used to, given their cross-country touring concert itinerary—they favor the French Quarter's Royal Street.

'As a group, we don't busk as often as we used to,' says Rapuzzi. 'But we've been fighting it in City Council, having discussions with, like, the district police who run the French Quarter—police captains and chiefs change every year. And now Royal Street is a pedestrian mall. And that's the best spot. That's where we've always played. We had to figure out the flow and what time to get the spot to beat the other groups. So we would often play at St. Peter & Royal, or at Toulouse & Royal.

'In the heyday of our busking on Royal Street, there was no marketing at all. We would just decide to go out there one or two days a week. And we would hold the spot early in the morning, and then we'd play for, like, two hours—sometimes longer. But at a certain point, you need to learn to share the spot. So we'd help hold down the spot together, and then we would trade off—one group would play for two hours, maybe eleven to two, and then the other group would play from two to four, when the street opened back up. But you had to claim your spot each time.

'We play inside clubs in New Orleans more than we busk these days,' he's quick to clarify. 'That's partly due to the city shutting down the Royal Street pedestrian mall for so long. Royal Street has not always been available to street performers, even though it's a part of the municipal code. So, myself and some bandmates, along with other members of our street performing community, have had to have meetings with the city council members and the police, as well as MaCCNO.

'MaCCNO has been creating a lot of these meetings between the street performers in the city. Now Royal Street is open again, the street performing. And they even have some signs out there; they do not say that it's open to street performing, but they do say that it's a pedestrian mall. So that's better than nothing.'

The MaCCNO to which Rapuzzi refers is the Music And Culture Coalition Of New Orleans, a registered 501(c)(3) nonprofit corporation, which, according to its website, is wholly devoted to 'organizing, empowering, and advocating with New Orleans's musicians, artists, traditional culture bearers, and other members and allies of the cultural community.' Though the word 'busking' is not in its mission statement, advocating for and empowering buskers constitutes a good portion of its work. Its 'Guide To New Orleans Street Performance,' for instance, informs street musicians of their rights:

> You have the right to play a musical instrument in any public right of way, public park, or recreational area as long as you don't exceed an average of eighty decibels measured at fifty feet from the source. (Sec 66-203) You are allowed to perform on Bourbon St. only between 6am and 8pm. (Sec 30-1456) You are allowed to ask for donations during a performance, as long as it is not aggressively solicited. (Sec 54-412 & Sec 54-419) You are responsible for keeping yourself and your crowd from obstructing the normal use of public rights of way.[5]

Good citizenship, of course, is a two-way street. The organization also publishes a 'New Orleans Street Performers Code Of Etiquette' for musicians, which includes these guidelines, among others:

- You have an obligation to preserve the heritage of New Orleans music and culture.

- Do not block doorways of any businesses or residence and audience should do the same.
- No one 'owns' a spot, it is however acceptable to ask another performer how long they plan on staying at a spot, without being demanding or rude.
- Pedestrian traffic should not be obstructed in any way.
- Welcome new performers and teach them the rules.

The current ordinance has evolved much from 1959 when, according to the MaCCNO website, 'the first unified city code bans musicians from playing on city streets from 8pm to 9pm,' or even from 1977, when a 'city ordinance prohibiting street performance on Royal Street was declared.'

MaCCNO executive director Ethan Ellestad, whose vocational background combines nonprofit work, urban planning, and community development, cites the ultimate dichotomy between enforcement and embracement. 'We were in a meeting, and there was a picture of Tuba Skinny in the official tourism marketing of the city. The headline banner was *Tuba Skinny Performing On Royal Street* or *Spring Fling In New Orleans* or whatever, right? That was the headline image of the tourism—while they were being shut down for performing on Royal Street by the police. So there's a police car, paid for by New Orleans & Company. The same people doing the advertising were paying for the law enforcement agency that was shutting them down from performing. This is a mismatch that can be pretty common. Everybody loves to talk about how much they support music, but then when it comes down to, like, changing the policy or actually doing anything about it, well, then it's a different story. We try to [point out] that hypocrisy.

'A lot of times, we find that performers get lumped into kind of the nuisance category, with street performers seen as vagrants,' he adds. 'And so we really are working hard to try to change that narrative that can come out of folks as well, because that dictates how they're treated by law enforcement from my policy.

'The city markets performers. They absolutely market that as part of the sale of New Orleans—visit New Orleans where music is on every street corner, like Doreen Ketchens playing in front of the houses on Royal Street. It's the images they use.'

Along with nearly everyone you're apt to talk to about New Orleans busking rights, Ellestad eventually mentions civil rights attorney Mary Howell. 'We base our work on *her* work,' he says. 'She's the star of the work that we do. We follow her lead. She's defended a lot of these folks.'

Take, for instance, Grammy-winner Trombone Shorty, né Troy Andrews, who in the 1990s was detained by law enforcement for playing music. He was ten years old and already playing alongside his musical family: elder brother James Andrews III and cousins Glenn David Andrews and Travis Hill, aka Trumpet Black. (To further illustrate the musicians' tender ages, Hill reportedly lost a baby tooth during the arrest.) Trumpet Black died in 2015, while the rest went on to carve their own legacies.

'In the 90s, they [were enforcing] the noise ordinance in the French Quarter,' Trombone Shorty told the *New Orleans Times-Picayune* in 2023. 'Some of the older musicians hipped us to it, like, If we see the police, bring the volume down. But this particular day, we were playing in front of the Cabildo. [Police approached] with a decibel meter, and they said that we were playing too loud. They put us in the back of the police car and drove us downtown. By the time we got there, [attorney] Mary [Howell] was there, so we didn't spend too much time there. We walked in and walked out; they had to call it a protection arrest because we were so young. Our parents were there to pick us up.'[6]

'It was a public-relations disaster, as it fully deserved to be,' opines musician and DJ Marc Stone, who's lived in town for more than thirty years. '[Troy's] always been a very poised, graceful person.'

Mary Howell has defended the rights of musicians like Andrews for more than forty-five years. A native of southeast Missouri, Howell began as a musician herself, playing guitar in a folk band. But she came to New Orleans for college.

'When I first became aware of the street performance culture in New Orleans was in the 1960s,' she says. 'I was at LSU, and we would come down to the French Quarter and Babe [Stovall] was playing.'

Germane to her future practice in civil rights and musicians' rights, Howell worked early on with a noted attorney in the city, Ben Smith. 'Smith, his law partner Bruce Waltzer, and long-time civil rights activist Jim Dombrowski were arrested for sedition by the State of Louisiana in 1963 for advocating integration. The arrest led to a famous US Supreme Court decision, Dombrowski v. Pfister, where the court threw out the state court prosecution for having a chilling effect on speech in violation of the First Amendment.

'In addition to his civil rights work, Ben was president of the Louisiana ACLU. Ben always saw the fundamental connection between civil rights and civil liberties. The First Amendment was an important part of Ben's practice, as it has been for mine,' she says. 'It was a whole different scene in the late 60s and early 70s. There was no Royal Street pedestrian mall. Chartres Street in front of the St. Louis Cathedral was still open to traffic. Babe Stovall, sometimes joined by other players, would sit on a bench inside Jackson Square, and it was just magic—the thought that you could walk into that public place and sit or stand in that beautiful park and hear this amazing music was just sort of astonishing. It was one of the few places where families with children could hear live music since children couldn't go inside bars where alcohol is served. Also, back then, bars with live music were really smoky. And on the street, of course, there is no cover charge. The whole situation, in these beautiful outdoor settings, was really a wonderful experience ... and still is.'

Howell is part of an ad hoc group of local attorneys who provide pro-bono legal assistance to street musicians, as well as for traditional New Orleans culture bearers in the second line and Black Masking Mardi Gras Indian community, all of which takes place on the public streets of the city.

'I'm not aware of any other city in the US that has such a vibrant live music street culture as we have in New Orleans, and street music in the Quarter is an important part of that. A unique feature of the New Orleans busker scene is that permits are not required for musicians and street performers in the French Quarter. While there are specific ordinances governing decibel levels and a questionable 8pm curfew on Bourbon Street, a street performer doesn't need a permit in the Quarter. They are also not confined to specific locations.

'We always say about New Orleans that we don't have garage bands, because we don't have garages. So the streets are really important,' she concludes. 'And in street performance, if you're not any good, you don't last.'

GEORGE 'BONGO JOE' COLEMAN

CHAPTER 17

AMERICAN PRIMITIVE

WHERE MOST OF THE street musicians profiled in this book play guitar, banjo, harmonica, or perhaps a wind instrument, George Coleman—known to his outdoor audience as Bongo Joe—sang, spoke, whistled, and bantered, all while accompanying himself banging on a fifty-five-gallon oil drum.

Bongo Joe was born in Haines City, Florida, on November 28, 1923. Orphaned at an early age, he grew up in Detroit, where he first performed music—including a stint with Sammy Davis Jr. By the 1940s, he'd moved to Houston, where he played percussion in a local ensemble. In time, he took to the streets—of Houston, Galveston, and eventually San Antonio, where he gained a following playing on the city's RiverWalk, outside the site of HemisFair '68, near the now-defunct Joske's department store. Along with his oil-drum percussion, Coleman would sing—though it was more a precursor to rapping, with witty and frequently bawdy turns of phrase—through a pickup microphone through a small amplifier powered by car batteries.

Jim Beal Jr., who before his retirement would serve nearly a quarter-century as a music reporter for the *San Antonio Express-News*, used to see Bongo Joe as a teenager. 'He was outrageous, loud, and sometimes reminded me of the classic rodeo clown with mismatched kind of clothing,' he recalls. 'He was a statement of *something*. He was a showman—and he was pretty darn good percussionist. One day, a guy who I was playing in a garage band with at the time, said to me, You know, Bongo Joe always whistles in a minor key. I hadn't thought of that!'

Equally unusual was the way Bongo Joe arrived from his home, off of San Antonio's Broadway, to his street shows—not by car or van but by bike. 'He had all that stuff on a small motorcycle, almost like a moped,' says Beal. 'It wasn't a Harley–Davidson and it wasn't a bicycle—it was somewhere between. And somehow he jerry-rigged his moped to carry his oil drums.

'He lived in a tourist court—you know, those stand-alone motels with a kitchenette—in one of these wooden buildings [that] of course is long gone, but not far from downtown. Maybe ten, twelve, fourteen blocks from where he lived to the middle of downtown, where he set up nightly. He was like a living tourist attraction, almost like the guy with the parrots on Fisherman's Wharf or the gutter punks on the street in New Orleans with the boa constrictors. But it wasn't the kind of thing where you would go and hang around and listen to Bongo Joe play all night. You would encounter him on the way to a river-block bar, or tourists walking around, back and forth from the Alamo to their hotels, and that part of town was a big tourist attraction. So you would see him. He was just there.'

In an interview with San Antonio musicologist Larry Skoog for the Arhoolie Foundation's website, Coleman—a man of few words, as the interview demonstrates—explained the origin of his unusual instrumentation in the early 1950s: '[I was] just trying to get a job as a drummer, and I couldn't get the job unless I had my own drums. I tried to make a loan from several sources to buy drums … my first job, and couldn't get the money so I got some cans and fixed them up like drums and started playing on street corners in Houston.'[1]

While he may have appeared the ultimate outsider artist, his jazz influences ran deep, revealing a lucid context for jazz. He listed his musical heroes to Skoog as 'Dave Brubeck, Stan Kenton, Erroll Garner, Fat Wallace, Chick Webb, Gene Krupa, Stan Kenton, Duke Ellington, Johnny Hodges, Flip Phillips, Dizzy Gillespie, and this Mexican guy … I can't think of his name right now.'

It was in 1968 that Chris Strachwitz, founder of the legendary blues, folk, and roots music label Arhoolie Records, traveled to San Antonio to record what would be Bongo Joe's only LP, subsequently described by *AllMusic* as 'hilarious' and 'edgy.' One track, 'Innocent Little Doggie,' became an underground radio classic in both Texas and the UK. 'Nobody took him seriously,' Strachwitz told the *San Antonio Current* in 2022. 'He was just a street entertainer. But he was absolutely brilliant.'[2]

Attesting to the album capturing what he'd heard on the streets of San Antonio, Beal says, 'The melody line was his vocals. And he was just banging on the drums, and whistling and then some singing. What you heard on that here on that record is exactly what he did. He was what you might have called an American primitive.'

In addition to—or more likely as a result of—the intrigue surrounding his Arhoolie album, Bongo Joe did occasionally perform outside of San Antonio, notably for nine years at the New Orleans Jazz & Heritage Festival. On one occasion he accompanied Dizzy Gillespie … as a pianist. Beal remembers attending JazzFest one year, surprised to see the local musician onstage. '*What the heck,*' he recalls thinking, '*I travel all the way from San Antonio to New Orleans, and there's Bongo Joe playing at New Orleans JazzFest!*'

In 1976, Bongo Joe performed at several stops along the Gerald Ford presidential campaign. Two years later, he helped local authorities capture an alleged shoplifter—an incident recalled in a 2017 story by Josh Baugh of the *San Antonio Express-News* that references a 1978 article from the same newspaper:

> 'Bongo Joe apprehends suspect in strange way' explains that Bongo Joe helped in the arrest of an alleged shoplifter. According to the story, the suspect stole some jewelry and sunglasses and then threatened a store worker with a knife. As the suspect fled, he ran past Bongo Joe, who pulled up on his moped next to a patrol car and asked the officer why that man had run past him. The cops told Bongo Joe the man was a suspect in a robbery. 'With that information, Joe moved up alongside the breathless suspect and asked if he could give him a ride. The breathless person nodded yes and he, too, climbed on the bike,' the story said. 'Joe said he told the man he looked like he needed a cup of coffee and would buy him one.' The story continues, saying that patrol officers pulled up next to the bike and inquired if everything was okay. Joe apparently gave the officers a wink. 'Finally, at Fourth Street & Broadway, Joe ploughed to a halt and got off the sagging moped,' the story said. 'The trailing officers immediately closed in and apprehended the suspect as he tried to get away.' Later that night, Bongo Joe was back at his spot near Alamo and Commerce streets, banging on his drums.

This incident wasn't Coleman's only display of street extemporization. In 1987, a heckler brandished a knife at the street percussionist. In self-defense, Coleman shot him in the shoulder. Beal likens the incident to the infamous moment when Texas Outlaw country singer Billy Joe Shaver shot a man in self-defense. According to Baugh:

In the mid-1980s, Bongo Joe found himself on the wrong side of the law after he shot a heckler at point-blank range with a .44-caliber handgun. In April 1983, Bongo Joe was playing to a crowd of about thirty people, including the heckler. According to a police sergeant quoted in a newspaper article about the incident, the heckler 'made a threatening motion which Joe interpreted as an attack,' the story said. The victim apparently walked to the nearby McDonald's after he was shot and was then transferred to Medical Center Hospital and was treated for a bullet wound to the chest, the story said. Bongo Joe was jailed overnight on a third-degree felony charge and then was released on his own recognizance, according to one newspaper article. Another report said someone posted a $5,000 bond for him. ... Ultimately, Bongo Joe received five years' probation for the incident.[3]

At one point, Coleman's home along the San Antonio River was threatened with demolition, and he very nearly left San Antonio for his former home of Corpus Christi. By then, however, he had become a significant enough phenomenon that a group of local supporters were able to find him new living quarters within the city.

As he notes in San Antonio filmmaker George Nelson's twenty-minute documentary, *Bongo Joe*, 'If a thing is not elevating or progressing, it ain't alive. 'You ain't living if you ain't doing ... and if you ain't progressing, you ain't living. And, of course, if you ain't doing, you're dead. You'd be surprised at the walking dead we stumble across daily.'[4]

Coleman's career came to an end in the early 1990s when he was diagnosed with diabetes and kidney disease. He passed away in 1999, at the age of seventy-six. He is fondly remembered by Texas country singer Gary P. Nunn, who gave him a shout-out in his 2008 song 'What I Like About Texas.'

Today, busking is allowed in many public places in Downtown San Antonio. The city's website notes that 'Downtown public pedestrian spaces on sidewalks in public right of way and City-owned parks will be available for busking.'

'After Bongo Joe, a couple of local singer/songwriters were trying to get busking legalized, and they did it,' says Beal. But while he relishes the development and the way it has enlivened the city's public spaces, he cautions, 'This ain't Royal Street in New Orleans, where you can make a living, you know.'

POI DOG PONDERING

CHAPTER 18

ALOHA TO AUSTIN

POI DOG PONDERING play a blend of folk, rock, soul, and world music—and a bit of inevitable island influence. The band's busking roots can be traced back to their early days in Hawaii, where they started out performing on the streets of Honolulu, playing their music to passersby and gathering a strong local following, before relocating to Austin, Texas, and then to Chicago, Illinois.

'I grew up in Hawaii,' says lead singer and songwriter Frank Orrall, who founded Poi Dog in 1984 and is the group's only constant member. 'I moved there when I was three years old [from Sac Peak, New Mexico], then I went to Europe when I was probably about twenty-two, and that's where I first saw buskers. So it went in my head; it was like, *Oh, wow!* In Paris and Amsterdam and stuff, I would see buskers, and it wasn't really something that people did in Hawaii.'

It also occurred to Orrall that, in busking, there was strength in numbers. 'I noticed that when I first started busking [and] I was just by myself, everyone looks at you like you're panhandling. But we were five people— one California woman, a Frenchman, one New Zealander, and two Hawaii local boys—so they gave us the time of day. People are curious about your story. So that was kind of a thing that helped us. Busking by myself [was] hard going, for sure . . . finding a quiet place [is important]—places that have a resonance behind you, like the open front of a movie house.'

When the original band came together, they test-marketed their act on the streets of Waikiki. 'There were not many places to play original music in Honolulu,' Orrall explains. 'Most bars wanted you to play cover songs, as there were so many tourists. Playing on the street allowed us to play whatever we wanted and served as a great way to work out new songs (without the pressure of the stage). Right out of the bag, we had a really big crowd going one evening—and a beat patrolman came and arrested us. There were three of us playing, and they arrested us for peddling. They had us down on our knees handcuffed, and the crowd was bewildered that we got arrested. And then the squad cars came to pick us up. [Drummer] Sean Coffey was younger. He was seventeen. So he went to juvie [juvenile detention center]. And me and Kalea went to County. Shawn had to spend the night, but me and Kalea got out—we were in there with a guy from Canada who tried to stab his girlfriend, but they let us out after about four hours. The next day, then they set a court date for us, the judge just read everything and said, Case dismissed.'

When Orrall asked if it would be okay to go back to the streets to play, however, the judge replied, 'I wouldn't if I were you. They're just trying to clean up Waikiki. They'll arrest you again.' Besides, Hawaii had become a dead end in the band's career development.

'In Hawaii, there's not many places to play,' Orrall continues. 'You're usually you're playing fifty percent covers, because you're playing for tourists a lot of the time. So, when I started writing my own songs, I started playing them on the street in Waikiki. That was like the place to go play—and it was kind of emulating that European experience. And then, around that same time, The Pogues came out, and The Pogues are an acoustic band, you know, using acoustic instruments with post-punk mentality. So it kind of went in my head: *Oh, you can do that.* So that's that and then we started enjoying playing on the street, and we thought that it would just be a nice way to go across the United States, across the continent, and have an adventure—and that's exactly what we did. We did it for a year. We flew to the mainland and bought, like, a GMC Suburban in January of 1986, and started playing on the street. And it was pretty hard going for a long time.'

The band's first stop was Los Angeles, as they had signed with Santa Monica's indie-credible Texas Hotel Records (also the home of albums by Henry Rollins and Vic Chesnutt), for whom they would record seven albums. The label also owned a retail record store that carried independent releases.

'[Texas Hotel] gave us an in-store,' Frank recalls. 'We did that, and then we'd play [other locations in] Los Angeles, where it was really rough to find a place to play. We would sleep outdoors; we'd drive outside the city and drive down like San Diego and sleep along the beach there and on eucalyptus groves, and then come back up and play in Santa Monica. Then we went up to San Francisco and had a great time there, but we're making very little money—just barely anything to get gas in the tank.

'It wasn't until our car broke down in Davis, California, and we played in front of a college coffeehouse—that's when we discovered a new mode. There were students there that were more our age. We were a little bit older, probably in our mid-twenties, but they were inviting us to play their college party. They let us sleep on their floor. You know, they were kind of we were making, you know, like, seventeen dollars. So that kind that became a model, and we started doing that.'

The band might have stayed in California, but wanderlust got the better of them. So, from San Diego, they set their sights on the city known as the 'Live Music Capital Of America,' Austin—by car, west by southwest.

'So we're going up the Western Seaboard, and we're playing college coffeehouses by now,' Orrall explains. 'Everything's going kind of smoothly. We're like, *all right, cool*—you know, we didn't have to sleep outdoors as much. We're having a nice adventure. We [went] up to Canada, and we came back down, and we're just staying along the Western Seaboard— Seattle, Oregon—and then we got down to San Diego. We knew we wanted to go to Austin because we had friends of ours who were from Hawaii, like the tattoo artist Rollo Banks, who was always telling us [it was an] amazing music scene. New Orleans was high on our list, too, and we wanted to see it. So we started crossing the States.

'We started in San Diego, then we went into Phoenix. We started pawning—one of us pawned a camera, another, a trombone—kind of like a boat throwing stuff off the ship. But we were not catching up [to our expenses], and it's a long way from El Paso to anywhere. So, in El Paso, we decided we were gonna start picking up hitchhikers and then ask them to contribute for gas. We picked up this guy who looked a little rough and tumble—he looked like a trucker, actually, but there was a little bit of an edge to him. We picked him up, and then we said, Hey, can you contribute to gas? He said, If you get me to San Antonio, I'll give you forty dollars.

'We were enamored of this guy because he knew so much about the road. He taught us how to flick the lights before you pass, and to let a truck come in after they pass you. We felt like we were having a Kerouac-ian moment—a moment when [you're with] someone who knew something, the little secrets of the road in America.'

The band's singer, Abra Moore, did not have a good feeling about the rider, however, and Orrall admits he should have heeded her intuition. 'We got to San Antonio about three in the morning or something like that, he went to make a phone call, and then, you know, we never saw [him again]. He left, and we realized he wasn't coming back. So we drove into Austin.

'It's now pre-dawn. We didn't know the town at all, and that's our usual mode of assault: you get to the outskirts of town, sleep, and then go to the college coffeehouse, take a shower, and then go play on the quad. So we're we pulled up, and it was cold. This was in December of '86, and I was cold, so I slept on the hood of the car where it was nice and warm, because the engine had been running all night. I woke up to a cop shaking me. I started making excuses right away—*Oh, sorry, I was tired, and we pulled over*—and he said, No, it's okay, just making sure you're still alive. I came up here and found a guy with four bullet holes in his head a month ago.

'So there we were in Austin. We went to the college coffeehouse, got some coffee, got cleaned up, and then we played on the [University Of Texas] quad. And, miraculously, we made that forty dollars we needed. We closed the [guitar] case and went to the store and bought groceries. We ended up staying in Austin for two months after that … we'd been on the road by then for five or six months, something like that … sleeping outdoors half the time and sleeping on people's floors the rest of the time. And that's how we grew to know the town and wound up back there after we finished the [cross-country] trip.

'There was really only one place that in Austin [that] we used to play, and that was Guadalupe Street, the Drag, on the university side, across the street from Captain Quackenbush's—a great coffee shop—or in front of Quackenbush or the Austin Film Society building. East 6th Street or South Congress were always too noisy. And the thing about the Drag is that you could play on the street, or you could play up inside the college, like toward the Cactus Café, and get a little further away from the road. And, yeah, the burritos were fifty cents each.'

In 2022, longtime Austin journalist and scene observer Michael Corcoran wrote about Poi Dog's years in Texas's capital city on his Substack blog:

In late '86, Frank and Abra and a couple other haole scruffs made it to Austin. 'Our truck was on its last legs, we were completely broke and hadn't eaten in two days,' Orrall remembered. When Poi

Dog set up next door to the Co-op, they were like no other buskers Austin had ever seen . . . they identified more as beatniks than hippies, but they also had a very melodic sound. People danced. Frank had a strong pop voice . . . and his lyrics came right from the heart. But after an hour that first day only one guy had tipped them, tossing a couple bills in the open guitar case. 'I went over to get the money, and it was two twenty-dollar bills,' Frank said. 'That's when we decided to stay in Austin a little while.'[1]

After that, Orrall notes, 'we continued on to New York and more solid busking. And then we just stopped busking, really.' By then, the band had albums on both Texas Hotel and the ultimate major label, Columbia. Orrall and the ever-evolving Poi Dog Pondering spent the next five years as residents of Austin, followed by twenty-seven in Chicago. By the time they hit the Windy City, they were for all intents and purposes out of the busking business.

'We'd immersed ourselves so completely in busking for a full year, living one hundred percent off the change in the guitar case,' he recalls. 'It was a beautiful and rugged adventure: sleeping outdoors and on floors, existing on coffee, bread and cheese, pasta, burritos, and tacos. Seeing lots of cities and small towns, from the nitty-gritty inside out. I satisfied my curiosity completely. The only way I think I would want to do it again is in Europe . . . that would be a fun way to explore Europe!

'The camaraderie that we forged with that group of people on the trip . . . it was really just a means to travel and see the continent, you know. Everyone gets to their moment [upon which] they don't think they can go on anymore. And then they make, like, twelve dollars. That'll buy a box of pasta, a bag of peas, a bottle of olive oil, and some salt and pepper—and you can make some pasta.

'And by then, you know, everyone's cool again.'

LUCINDA WILLIAMS

CHAPTER 19

HAPPY WOMAN BUSKING

THE YEAR 2023 was a pivotal one for the multiple Grammy Award–winning singer and songwriter Lucinda Williams, a performer whose music was once described by NPR music critic Ann Powers as being 'deeply informed by tradition [yet] determinedly individualistic and envelope-pushing.'[1] She reemerged after a two-year absence with both a new album (*Stories From A Rock N Roll Heart*) and a memoir (*Don't Tell Anybody The Secrets I Told You*). It was a career triumph. The banner year was also a personal triumph, following her recovery from a debilitating stroke in 2020. By 2021, she was back on tour. 'I'd like to think I'm coming through it all a stronger person,' she says.

While recent years have seen Williams headline venues like the Ford Theater in Los Angeles, Nashville's Ryman Auditorium, and Colorado's Red Rocks Amphitheater, she relishes a chance to look back to her formative years as a street singer.

The daughter of poet and literature professor Miller Williams, young Lucinda moved throughout the South as a child and teenager. 'My dad was teaching in different colleges and universities,' she says, 'and that propelled us to move around. He would teach for a year or two here or a year or two there until he achieved tenure at the University of Arkansas.' One of the cities in which Professor Williams took a job was Macon, Georgia. It was there that Lucinda saw the blind street singer Reverend Pearly Brown. Her father brought home his album, and she immersed herself in his music.

Later, when her father became tenured at University Of Arkansas, Williams she caught wind of the emerging music scene in Austin, Texas. 'I met this guy at the folk music festival in Arkansas—I believe it was the Eureka Springs Folk Festival—and he had gone down to Austin,' she recalls. Then he got in touch with me and was all excited and just beside himself about this town he discovered: Austin! He said, You've gotta come here and check it out, it's so beautiful and magical and wonderful! And so I went, and it was beautiful and magical and wonderful back then. You know, it was kind of like a little San Francisco almost. It sort of had that vibe about it, you know, and you just felt like your tribe was there—lots of hippies … they used to call them cosmic cowboys.'

So Williams packed her bags and went to the city that would in later decades become known as the Live Music Capital Of America. She made camp on the city's Guadalupe Street.

'I remember they called it the Drag,' she reflects. 'It was right by the campus there, and there were a couple of streets where vendors would set up their wares—jewelry and what have you. And the city allowed live music—I didn't have to get a permit. It was just accepted and understood that musicians could go there and set up next to the vendors and do their thing. And so that's where I would go.

'I would have my guitar case open for people to throw tips into. And somebody took a picture of me that has circulated around Austin all these years. It's in one of those books that goes back to those days—a picture of me in a long skirt and a big floppy hat that looks like it's from that era. I'd moved to Austin in 1974, so it would have been probably the next year or two.'

When she first arrived in Austin, she stayed with friends who were renting a house nearby to the Drag. 'The Armadillo was open at that point, and they had a lot of live music there,' she says. 'And then at some point there was a guy—Bruce Wallenzik—who put me up in his place for a little bit. He always credits me with coming up with the idea [of] the Armadillo Christmas Bazaar that they started back then. Musicians would come and set up and sing.'

John Kunz, who opened what became Austin's most famous record store, Waterloo Records, in 1982, remembers seeing Williams playing on the Drag. 'There were always people hanging out on the Drag and the 23rd Street market,' he recalls. 'The hippie vendors would set up and sell their wares and their art jewelry and canned vegetables and that sort of thing. So there were a number of people there. But there was something about her songs—and also how cute she was—that caught my eye. The couple of times I caught her there, I didn't have any money to put in a guitar case. I wanted to ask her out, but I didn't feel there's good *pro quo* about putting money in the guitar case and getting a date. And then when I *did* have money, I never ran into her again. So, other than maybe the tip of my hat and, *You sound great*, there wasn't any interaction between us. But in talking with her years later, I've always [wondered] what it would have been like if we'd gone out.'

Among the highlights of her stay in Austin, Williams cites seeing two legends of Texas blues—Mance Lipscomb and Lightnin' Hopkins, albeit not busking. She attended the latter's memorial service in 1982. She moved around a lot in those days. A few years later, she had made camp in another busker haven: New Orleans's Jackson Square. 'I was one of those people who, you know, if I heard about a place and it was cool, I'd wanna go there and check it out,' she says. She also spent time playing at San Francisco's Fisherman's Wharf, and in New York's Washington Square Park—a buskers' hub since the 1950s.

'When I was a kid—like, twelve years old—and just starting to play guitar, I wanted desperately to be in New York and be in that scene, because I would read about it and it just sounded so magical to me,' she adds. She finally got her chance as an adult. One day, while playing her own music in Washington Square, Williams followed a beautiful voice she heard from afar. It was that of a fellow busker, a North Dakota native who'd made her own way to the Big Apple.

'I remember hearing this woman's voice wafting through the air one day,' Williams remembers. 'It's just this gorgeous voice, and it was this woman named Susan Osborn. She and I became real good friends in New York City, and I lived in her apartment for a while, and that was great. We ended up doing shows together.'

Williams was evidently not the first to be taken in by Osborne's voice. According to the *Islands Sounder* newspaper, 'New York photographer Harold Feinstein was walking home in the rain when he heard a voice. It was sweet and heavenly, so he stopped to listen ... [he was] was so moved that he became a patron of Osborn's, giving her half of his earnings from every photograph he sold, with the promise that she would write more material.'[2]

In summation, Williams says, busking was 'a good way for me to learn how to project my voice, [to] just practice singing and attract attention. It was like being on the stage ... you had with immediate and instant audience.'

VIOLENT FEMMES

CHAPTER 20

WHAT MADE
MILWAUKEE
FAMOUS

FOR THE VIOLENT FEMMES, 'desire was the mother of invention,' according to founding drummer Victor DeLorenzo.

The acoustic 'punk-folk' trio—'one of Milwaukee's biggest claims to rock fame,' according to the city's *Journal-Sentinel* newspaper—are best known for their 1983 self-titled debut album (featuring the alt-rock hit 'Add It Up') and its 1984 follow-up, *Hallowed Ground*. Following six subsequent LPs and a five-year hiatus, they reunited with an altered lineup at the Coachella Valley Music & Arts Festival in 2013.

The Femmes' distinctive sound, which combines singer/songwriter Gordon Gano's raw, emotive vocals and frenetic guitar playing with Brian Ritchie's melodic bass lines and occasional use of exotic instruments like the xylophone and the didgeridoo, quickly gained a following among Milwaukee locals. As Ritchie notes, however, the members' musical origins predate the birth of the Femmes.

'Victor and I had been playing on the street with a bona-fide railway hobo named Doorway Dave,' he recalls. 'We loved it, and the lifestyle led to many unexpected and unpredictable outcomes. Shortly after meeting Gordon, we introduced him to this practice, which incidentally was not common in Milwaukee and was perceived as a form of begging. We had friends who saw us playing who would cross to the other side of the street or avert their gaze in order not to be associated with us. On the other hand, children, older people, and inquisitive people in general would stop, allow us to entertain, and sometimes throw a coin in Gordon's guitar case. Importantly, it taught us that we could entertain anyone and not have to pander to specialized rock subcultures.

DeLorenzo, who left the band in 1993, picks up the story. 'We were used to rehearsing in my cold, damp basement on Milwaukee's east side. Once it got to be spring and summer 1981, we took it upon ourselves to solve the problem in a way—we decided we would go out on the streets. Gordon had an acoustic guitar, [and] Brian had an acoustic guitar that he put bass strings on. But it didn't really cut the mustard. So finally he got an Ernie Ball Earthwood bass, which is a large, almost like a mariachi-style acoustic bass guitar, and we were ready then. I just had a snare drum with brushes, so we were very portable. And we figured, *Hey, it's nice outside, let's get out of the basement. And let's find some places to play*. We found two places in particular that were very advantageous to us because they had good acoustics.'

Those two places were beneath the marquee of two Milwaukee theaters—the Oriental and the Downer. 'The Oriental was an arthouse theater, plus they also had live music from time to time. It was a really nice theater. I remember seeing Hawkwind and John McLaughlin and the Mahavishnu Orchestra with Jeff Beck there. They had so many great, great shows at that theater. And then, eventually, the Violent Femmes played *in* that theater, too!'

When they started, the Femmes rarely if ever performed with

a set list, preferring to sequence their songs as the spirit struck. A lot of this spontaneity and fearlessness came from their street band roots. 'We decided to play out on the streets because the idea of busking was attractive to us,' DeLorenzo explained in 1983, when I interviewed him for *Trouser Press* magazine. 'It got us in touch with really playing instead of hiding behind a shroud of electricity. Besides, none of the clubs wanted to book us at the beginning.'

'It was a lot of fun because it honed our performance skills. When you're playing for people walking by on the street, if they like you, they'll stop and listen. And if not, they'll keep walking. So it's very easy to tell when you have the audience's attention. If you're lucky, maybe they'll even throw some coins or some dollar bills into your open guitar case, which was usually sitting in front of us.

'We were playing a lot of those songs because Gordon had this magic notebook. A lot of the songs [from] the first day ended up on *Hallowed Ground*, our second album. I think we had quite a repertoire of music that we could play on the street.'[1]

The Femmes built a following and pocketed occasional spare change. But one night, beneath the marquee of the Oriental Theater, their luck changed.

'We were just making our normal rounds,' DeLorenzo recalls. 'I'm not sure if it was a Friday or Saturday night. We make our way over to the Oriental Theater—underneath the marquee there was pretty good acoustics, so we are just out on the street. The door opens, and I'm playing, and he stops me and introduces himself—James Honeyman-Scott of The Pretenders. He goes, Hey, I really liked the way you guys sound. You remind me of this group that's kind of taken off in England now called The Stray Cats. (They're from New York, but James had seen them on the road.)

'He listens to us for a while, then he goes back into the theater. [Meanwhile], we're continuing our little concert underneath the marquee of the Oriental. And then the door opens again, and this time a whole group of people come out, and there was a curb right behind or right in front of where we're playing. So this group of people starts leaning back on the cars and listening to us. And finally we get to a point in our performance where we do a song called "Girl Trouble," and it has this refrain, *Girl trouble, I've got girl trouble up my ass.*

'The woman that is leaning against one of the cars just starts laughing— she just loves that song. When we finish the song, she comes over and introduces herself. She says, Hi, my name is Chrissie [Hynde], would you like a gig tonight? And we said, Yeah, sure, we're playing on the street, and we'd love to have a gig somewhere. She says, Well, how would you like to play here tonight? And we say, You mean at the Oriental Theater? And she goes, Yeah, we're playing here tonight, and if you want to come in and open up the show for us—maybe play, like, three songs—we'd love to have you.

'They had another opener—I think they were called The Bureau, an English soul band with horns. Then the lights go down and everybody's expecting to see The Pretenders, who we knew nothing about. We didn't know who The Pretenders were—I mean, we were listening to avant-garde music, classical, and jazz…hardcore country music…we were into blues. We weren't really into, like, modern popular music.

'The lights go down, the lights come up, and we walk out with snare drum, acoustic bass, and acoustic guitar, and start playing our three-song set. And people when we first started walking out there are booing, because some people probably thought, *Oh, these are these jerks that play on the street. What are they doing here?* It's funny because, nowadays, when you talk to people that say that they're at the show, they said that they loved us, but we definitely heard a lot of boos!

'By the end of our little three-song set, we received a decent amount of applause, and then we left the stage. Chrissie said we could have some food backstage and something to drink and watch the show, so that's what we did. And then, of course, the next day we were back on the streets. We found that you could have a magical and immediate connection with strangers walking by, or sometimes they'd stop and have a listen or even throw some change into the open guitar case. Busking fine-tuned our performance skills and shaped the way we seduced the audience. From the streets of old Milwaukee to the sellout shows at Carnegie Hall and the Royal Albert Hall in London!'

Back in 1983, bassist Brian Richie told *Trouser Press* magazine, 'We're always putting ourselves in danger. Most bands have their little song list taped to their monitor, and say, *This is a tune from our EP . . . one, two, three . . .*' Today, he says of busking, 'Musicians face myriad performance opportunities in the course of their careers. Concert halls. Nightclubs. Weddings. Parties. TV. Competitions. Dances. The most misunderstood and maligned performance format is busking. Many people and even entire municipalities look upon busking as begging, a nuisance, noise pollution. But in fact it can be a joy for both musicians and listeners if it's done properly. Unfortunately, it seldom is.

'Artists make extravagant noise about their pursuit of freedom. Busking is the epitome of unshackled freedom. Imagine: a musician unencumbered by technology, playing, or singing anywhere they can fit, moving on when boredom or the cops intervene, changing musical direction at will. Sounds fun, right?

'I am a purist about busking. It must be acoustic, or else it's fraudulent. Any musician can drastically improve their musicianship and technique by the simple act of acoustic busking. Drawing real sound out of your voice and instrument in the face of traffic and other ambient noise is a challenge. Musicians playing a variety of instruments of disparate volume levels and learning to use dynamics to accommodate each other is rare in this world of close-miking and digital mixers. Learning how to engage an audience without relying upon volume to inundate them is a key to developing the theatrical sense that separates introverts from performers. If you can grab a random audience on the street, you can do it anywhere.'

Ritchie is generally not enamored of what he sees on the streets today in the name of busking. 'Unfortunately, the buskers of today are bastardizing what could be a noble pursuit through the immobility of staking out and guarding key spots,' he says. 'Amplifying pillow-talk voices in an invasive manner, instead of learning how to project. Assaulting listeners for blocks around with shrill scraping on their piezo pickups ... among other unnatural means of gaining perceived advantage in the modern cityscape.

'Choosing to turn busking into a downscale replica of a pub stage or concert hall in public space deprives musicians and listeners alike of the opportunity to experience something unique. Doubtful The Pretenders would have been impressed with the Femmes if we were all plugged in and whispering into mics while feebly plucking Flying Vs through battery-powered Marshall stacks.

'If anything,' he concludes, 'conventional gigs should strive to resemble busking, not the reverse.'

PART
FOUR

CALIFORNIA

For me, it's an argument for keeping some kind of wild space available for artists. It's important for a graffiti artist to have a wall where they can do an amazing mural, and the city won't control it. Like, just go for it. [Busking is] our graffiti art. It's so crucial to just have at least one space like that. **EILEN JEWELL**

PETER CASE

CHAPTER 21

NERVES OF STEEL

SINGER/SONGWRITER PETER CASE has left an indelible mark on the music scene, consistently displaying his prowess as a skilled musician and storyteller. Initially known as a member of the new wave rock band The Nerves in the late 1970s, he went on to form The Plimsouls, a power-pop quartet that achieved critical acclaim and a mid-charting pop hit. However, it is Case's subsequent solo recording career that's showcased his musical versatility and songwriting depth. His albums blend rock, folk, and blues influences and underscore his ability to craft poignant and introspective songs.

Throughout his career, Case's music has continued to evolve, his life experiences and artistic growth reflected in every song. He's become a consummate American troubadour. Though he wrote his first song at the age of eleven ('Stay Away'), his music career began in earnest in 1973 when he dropped out of high school in Buffalo, New York, moved cross-country to San Francisco, and immediately began performing on the streets. It was a transitional time for the city once described by *San Francisco Chronicle* columnist Herb Caen as 'Baghdad By The Bay': the late-60s hippies had largely dispersed, the late-70s punk scene that begat the Mabuhay Gardens venue and the 415 Records label had not yet taken hold, and the dot-com bubble would not explode for another twenty-three years.

'I started playing on the street Union Square . . . just like that,' Case recalls of his baptism by fire. 'The pushback against it from the cosmos is great, you know, when you start singing in a place where the public is, that is not really for singing. It's a trip, but there was a whole culture of street music and street performers in San Francisco when I got out here, including Shields & Yarnell, a group of mimes, and they were drawing huge, huge crowds on the street. And there were some other guys called the Broadway Strutters, and they drew really big crowds on the street—they were like Dixieland. So I jumped into playing on the street and playing in Union Square. I met a guy who showed me some stuff, and then he took me on the cable car over the hill and showed me you can play over at Fisherman's Wharf during the day.'

At the time, Case was living in what he describes as 'a junkyard, in an abandoned truck . . . I didn't own a car. Oh, man. I went to a heliport in Sausalito. Nearby was a junkyard. There were abandoned trucks in the junkyard, and I picked up an old abandoned bus. I moved into the bus and had a sleeping bag and a couple changes of clothes in there. You could take showers at Maritime Park, down by the swimming pool.'

Undeterred by his living conditions, Case spent his days plying his craft as a street singer in this strange but culturally vibrant city. 'You can make enough money to live,' he reasoned, 'and it enabled me to be a full-time musician and not have to really be part of society, accepted as a marginal character who played on the street and lived in a junkyard. I was able every day to go out and just play music all day. I would go out at noon, and I'd play until two in the morning. I would play [during] the day sometimes at Union Square, Fisherman's Wharf . . . I tried the Financial District, and

that wasn't very good. But at night I would go to Broadway—Broadway &
Columbus was kind of my place. You get real strong playing on the street
in a lot of different ways.'

Though he was an outsider, Case met many entertainers of renown
who also chose outdoor San Francisco as their stage. 'I remember one
guy showed up, and he played like this kind of mambo blues that was
just incredible. He was an African American guy with a steel guitar, just
traveling through. And then there was a guy named Coco, who played
washed a bass with a harmonica. He sounded a lot like Sonny Boy
Williamson. He was an old, old man, and he was really great. There was a
guy you might have heard of, Norman Yancey, and he played calypso—he
was at the corner of Broadway and Ghirardelli Square. There was also a
guy they called the Automatic Human Jukebox. I forget his actual name. I
knew of him. He lived and he was in a box all day, like a pretend jukebox,
and you put money in it and a window would go up [and he would] play
trumpet songs, you know?'

One of the first people Case met in San Francisco was Michael Wilhelm,
guitarist in one of the city's first psychedelic bands, The Charlatans (whose
membership at one point included Dan Hicks). Case recalls their first
dialogue. 'He comes up to me—and, you know, he's all dressed like Bo
Diddley, wearing leather, and playing on the street—and he says, I need
a singer for my band. You could be the singer? He was playing folk clubs.
He was a surviving San Francisco artist [from] the psychedelic era. Mike
was on his own with a band called Loose Gravel, but he would go out on
the street. And he wanted me to possibly sing in this band. I was eighteen
or nineteen. I couldn't drink in clubs at that point. He took me up to this
place with Coffee Gallery in North Beach, right near Grant & Green—a
lot of people that played in the street would also go up and play at the
Coffee Gallery. It was a legendary place.'

Case also met beat poet, musician, and satirist Bob Kaufman at the storied caffeine emporium. 'I played alone on the street, and then there'd be team-ups with other people,' he says. 'I learned a lot from all those people, and I learned a lot singing on the street. You get real strong, rhythmically and performing-wise. And I learned how to deal with people going by, because crowds of people would be going by, and you get on their wavelength and pull them in.'

Although he would first become identified with new-wave power-pop via The Nerves, a more powerful pop sound with The Plimsouls, and later the full range of singer/songwriter sounds as a solo performer, Case came to San Francisco with a very different musical palette. 'I played two different strains,' he says. 'I played a lot of different music, just like I do these days. I've always loved blues music, you know, so I was playing some songs by Lazy Lester. I did Elmore James material. I knew a lot about Mississippi John Hurt, but you couldn't really play that on the street. But I did play Elmore James on the street. My repertoire would be those kinds of things.'

Case would also play 'things that were more classic' like Wilbert Harrison's 'Kansas City' or The Drifters' 'Save The Last Dance For Me,' as well as his own rewrite of The Kingston Trio's 'Scotch & Soda.' Around this time, he met an older street singer from Texas named Crazy Horse Danny, a fan and friend of Houston psychedelic band The 13th Floor Elevators, and the two developed an entire set of Elevators material. 'That was pretty weird,' he says, 'but *he* was really weird, and we really enjoyed it.' (Tommy Hall, an original 13th Floor Elevator, later migrated to San Francisco and lived in yet another street singer's basement in San Francisco's Haight-Ashbury district for a while.)

AMONG THE PEOPLE Case met while performing in outdoor San Francisco was his future bandmate in The Nerves, the late Jack Lee. By now it was 1974, a few years before punk and new wave indelibly reshaped the musical landscape.

'Jack would walk by every day when I was playing on the street,' Case says. 'I never really saw him play on the street [himself], but I guess he did once; I think it didn't go that well for him. But I was out there every day for a few years. This other guy that was his buddy was Pat Stengl, and he was one of the original Nerves. [Pat] was a busker. So, The Nerves were me and Pat and Jack for a while. Jack wasn't that much of a busker, but he was very friendly to it. At one point, we were even considering having The Nerves break out on the street, as buskers—like, having a thing where we played [at] lunchtime. One of our concepts was to have the group start, like, a busking mania thing.'

Case used to station himself not far from Lawrence Ferlinghetti's City Lights Bookstore. One day in 1974, beat poet Allen Ginsberg crossed Columbus Avenue and sat in with Peter and his accompanists. 'He comes across the street and he's like, Hey, you guys, my name's Allen. Could I sit in with you? I'm like, Sure, whatever. We introduce ourselves and he goes, You guys play some country blues? So we started playing it. You just start making up songs like people walking by this. Nobody really picked up on who he was at all. It was like tourists, girls going into work at the Condor Club [a legendary North Beach strip bar], street winos, and Marines. You know, just all kinds of people walking back, and, like, nobody picked up on it, and he's out there singing "Stay Away From The White House." He was really fun to play with. We even asked him for a name for our group, and he looked across the street and there was a sign that said *Roaring 20s*, so he said The Rockin' 20s. It was great to hang with him. It was very cool. It was like he just was doing it for the love of the game—he just liked to be out there.'

Case took full advantage of his frequent proximity to the West Coast's most famous bookstore. 'I used to go into City Lights every day and basically read my way through the store. You know, I dropped out of high school, so that was basically my education. I ran into Ferlinghetti on the sixtieth anniversary of the store—I used to actually go in and during the day sometimes to sleep in there, with my head down on a book, you know—they would just let me hang out, really, and I just read my way through a lot of different sections of the store. And I thanked him for that.

'Bob Kaufman was a literary figure, and he'd be out on the street, and Dan Hicks would come down and get my face, like, Let's hear something good, and then he'd go, I don't wanna hear that a minor-[key] crap. He was a really weird guy. He used to make fun of my Hush Puppies. I had Hush Puppies that I'd gotten from a thrift store because I was always broke.

'That was the adventure of playing on the street,' he adds, though it wasn't always a storybook adventure. 'Terrible things would also happen on the street. I've been coldcocked while I was singing, you know? I've had guys try to rob me, and we'd get in brawls out here—knives, all kinds of stuff.'

Then there was local law enforcement. In San Francisco at that time, the police generally left acoustic musicians alone, but plug in and you might be asking for trouble. 'One time we were out there with an electric—it was a column Mike Matthews Freedom amp—and it ran on, like, an insane number of batteries. The really big D batteries, loaded up with just tons of them, and then it would sound like a Marshall for about half an hour.

'So we're out there, rocking on this amp, but we have it set up so that there's like a coat over the front of it, and the cords are going down the coat and up the sleeve of the coat. A cop came down and said, You guys aren't playing electric, are you? We said, No, sir.

'It's odd that he couldn't tell that it was electric—it sounded so electric—but usually we just played acoustic back in those days. And that's when I learned to sing *really* loud. Like Michael Wilhelm used to say, I'd be on the corner of Broadway & Columbus, and you could hear me up all the way up on Grant Avenue, which is two city blocks away.'

Case reflects on the last time he had to play on the street in order to put food on his table. 'The last time I played on the street because I needed to was July 4, 1976,' he recalls of America's Bicentennial celebration. 'Me and [future Nerves drummer] Paul Collins busked in Fisherman's Wharf, and that was because we were broke and needed to buy food or something. And that was the last time I did it kind of *desperately*. I've done it a number of times since then, but more just for fun.'

AT SOME POINT, Case reconnected with Jack Lee, and The Nerves were born. 'Jack was just really hungry to, like, make a million dollars. And he instilled that in me: *We can do this*. It was really fun and exciting while it lasted. Also, I had to focus a lot more than I had before, and actually write songs. I'd started writing songs in '65—ragtime songs, talkin' blues, all kinds of stuff. Right up to The Nerves, where we focused on two-minute songs. Those are hard to write, in a way.'

The Nerves released a critically acclaimed four-song EP that helped shape the American new wave. Case contributed the song 'When You Find Out,' while Lee's 'Hangin' On The Telephone' would become a global hit for Blondie. By 1978, however, The Nerves had gone their separate ways. Case soon formed The Plimsouls.

'I learned a lot from [The Nerves],' he says, 'and to work with Jack was intense and crazy. But I wanted to have a band that could blow the roof off the place live—which maybe The Nerves didn't quite have the chops for. I wanted to expand the influences again. And ever since then, I've been expanding the influences that I had before I was before I was in The Nerves.'

The Plimsouls played together from 1978 to 1983, breaking ground that The Nerves were never able to, including a major label contract with Geffen Records and two albums (1981's *The Plimsouls* and 1983's *Everywhere At Once*) that dented the *Billboard* charts. By 1986, the band had split up and Case had signed a solo contract with Geffen, releasing an eponymous solo album that year. Three years later, he released a follow-up with the intentionally unwieldy title of *The Man With The Blue Post-Modern Fragmented Neo-Traditionalist Guitar* (usually referred to as simply *Blue Guitar*).

It was at the Los Angeles release celebration show for that album that Case found himself working the streets again. This time, however, the scene was the sidewalk along Sunset Boulevard, in front of a sold-out headline gig at Hollywood's trendsetting Club Lingerie, and the busking was borne of triumph rather than of necessity. 'The club was sold out, and they said they were they weren't letting more people in. So I went out and stood in front and played! I knew how to do that from being a street musician. In fact, a lot of things I did as a solo musician in my early days were things I knew how to do because I was capable of playing in weird areas. I was one of the first people to walk into radio stations with a guitar and sing on the radio. Now everybody does it. So that's what we did [in front of Club Lingerie]. Along with Marvin Etzioni [Lone Justice] and Willie Aron [The Balancing Act], we played on the street in front of the club, and it was super fun. We did the entire concert out there. It was a great experience.'

In 2023, Case's story was definitively told in Fred Parnes's documentary *Peter Case: A Million Miles Away*. Case also wrote a memoir detailing his life as a homeless busker. The book, titled *As Far As You Can Get Without A Passport*, was published in December 2006 by Everthemore Books' For Now imprint and featured a foreword by X's John Doe. It is now out of print, with used copies commanding upward of a hundred dollars—if you can find one at all.

FANTASTIC NEGRITO

CHAPTER 22

THE POWER IN
NOT CARING

EVERYTHING LOOKED PROMISING for Xavier Amin Dphrepaulezz in the mid-90s. In 1993, under the *nom de guerre* Xavier, he signed a reported million-dollar contract with Interscope Records' founding chairman, Jimmy Iovine, releasing his debut album, *The X Factor*, three years later. Interscope was the hottest label of the day, home of multi-platinum hits by Eminem, Dr. Dre, Nine Inch Nails, U2, No Doubt, and Enrique Iglesias. Its sales accounted for nearly one third of Universal Music Group's twenty-seven percent share of the US music market.

The album failed to launch Dphrepaulezz's career. But that was hardly the worst news. On Thanksgiving 1999, the artist found himself in a near-fatal car crash that left him comatose for three weeks and affected his ability to play guitar. 'I fishtailed and rolled over four lanes of traffic,' he later told the *Guardian* newspaper.[1] He was thirty-one years old. The accident left his arms and legs badly fractured.

'And then I stopped,' he recalls. 'I got out of doing all that I did with touring and trying to be famous back then. I went back home to Oakland and quit. I sold everything and became a marijuana farmer with no interest in playing. I think that when I stopped wanting it. I just said to myself, *You know what, I think I'd like to just play on the street because it feels very good.* It wasn't for money. It wasn't for anything. I thought it was over. I was like, *I'm never pursuing that again.* I just wanted to play on the street because it felt very honest and beautiful and therapeutic and fun.'

So, for the artist who'd soon be known as Fantastic Negrito, busking was not a first step. It was a way to restore a sense of purpose following a disastrous major label experience and a debilitating accident. It was also a chance for him to rethink his musical direction. Where the Xavier album had hearkened to Prince with hip-hop inflections, Dphrepaulezz now reconnected with his earliest influences, which he describes as 'Southern music and, you know, the Black roots. Country-blues artists as well. I forgot about [trying to make it],' he says. 'I got into this music because I really enjoyed it. And it was lots of fun and gave me satisfaction, but I didn't want to chase the whole fame and record deals anymore. I just wanted to really connect on the streets with people trying to make it home from work.'

Dphrepaulezz could be found playing music in front of Colonial Donuts in Oakland's Lakeshore district. Sometimes he'd cross the Bay and play at San Francisco's Powell Center, or at 25th & Mission in the Mission District. It almost didn't matter where he made camp. 'I was just playing because I just love being out there,' he recalls. 'There's a lot of power [in] not caring, not wanting things, and that's how busking was for me. I was just really feeling life.'

It was during this time that Dphrepaulezz adopted the name Fantastic Negrito. '[The name] made some people uncomfortable—and that made it even better,' he proclaims defiantly. His long recovery from the accident and his early days of busking had given him time to gather perspective on his major-label experience. 'I'd spent my twenties and thirties chasing this thing that I could never get. Now I was a guy in his mid-forties. I wasn't chasing anything. And I wasn't yet aware of how powerful that would become. And how it's powerful now to keep reminding yourself: *Don't chase this stuff—be very true to the spiritual side of it.*'

Dphrepaulezz had taken to busking as a midlife antidote to the star-maker machinery to which he'd been a party in his twenties. 'Being a grown-ass man [on the streets], there's a complete opposite side of the spectrum to how you're approaching an instrument or playing. You have to really connect with these people who don't care about you playing out there. And there's something very powerful about that, every day, to know that. These people [on the streets] don't even care about what you're doing, so if you can connect with them, that's very powerful.'

Not all of his friends and family saw it that way. 'I knew some people who were a little embarrassed for me,' he shares. But others were captivated. 'I remember there some women from Saudi Arabia that used to come to hear me secretly. They'd sit there. They didn't want anyone to know that they were there. That was something that I really never forgot—these women from Saudi Arabia were so transfixed with what I was doing. And they'd sit there, admiring what I was doing. But they were like, *No one can know that we saw this.*'

One day in 2015, a street observer suggested that Fantastic Negrito enter NPR's inaugural Tiny Desk Contest. He submitted a video and—against all odds—became the prestigious annual contest's first winner. At first, however, he'd been reluctant to enter. 'I wasn't looking for any of this,' he says. 'When someone asked me, do I want to participate in Tiny Desk? I was like, *No, actually.* I just had no interest. I didn't think what I was doing really matched with NPR was about. I had a lot of feelings about that, and finally I was talked into it, and I did a one-take performance that beat seven thousand people—which I'm still in shock about.'

Tiny Desk was the start of what became an organic second music career for Fantastic Negrito. He won his first Grammy Award in 2017, when *The Last Days Of Oakland* was named 'Best Contemporary Blues

Album.' He won again in the same category two years later with the follow-up, *Please Don't Be Dead*, and for a third time in 2021 with *Have You Lost Your Mind Yet?*

Needless to say, Fantastic Negrito has since then toured the world, playing ticketed shows in respected indoor venues, but he continues to busk every opportunity he can. 'I definitely still do it,' he says. 'Especially in places where I'm not known. I was in Japan for a month [in 2023], and I was always playing on the streets. I just sneak around to the little places where I can go … at, like, three in the morning. Whenever I can do it, I do it. It's one of the most honest moments you can have.'

WILD MAN FISCHER

CHAPTER 23

NOT SHY ANYMORE

LARRY 'WILD MAN' FISCHER was a Los Angeles singer known for his eccentric, unpredictable behavior who gained notoriety for his idiosyncratic style of street performance during the mid-to-late 1960s and into the 70s. Though his early street singing days may not have been as extensively documented as his later musical collaborations (including those with Frank Zappa and Barnes & Barnes), they played a key role in establishing his reputation as a wild and unpredictable persona. His unconventional approach to singing on the streets of LA—usually spontaneously, *a cappella*, without a guitar—ultimately contributed to his status as an outsider artist. In its 2011 obituary, the *New York Times* called him 'a strange, intermittent, and often ill-fitting celebrity.'[1]

Fischer was discovered by Frank Zappa, who spent three months in the studio with him and produced his first album, *An Evening With Wild Man Fischer*, in 1968. Though in the words of the *Independent* newspaper it was 'a period curio rather than a seminal work on a par with Beefheart's *Trout Mask Replica*,' Fischer's album is an example of the late-60s boundary-pushing in which Zappa played a key role as both an artist and a label owner.[2] Guest performers on the album include producer Kim Fowley, DJ and 'Mayor Of The Sunset Strip' Rodney Bingenheimer, and the GTOs (Girls Together Outrageously).

Pamela Des Barres, known as Miss Pamela during her years with the GTOs, remembers seeing Fischer in LA. 'The only place I often saw him play was on the Sunset Strip,' she says. 'Up Holloway, and from Doheny to, like, Crescent Heights. He would wander up and down with some form of instrument. I don't know what the heck he was playing. It must have been [a guitar], but he really couldn't play it—he was just making sounds with whatever instrument it was and singing those songs we're so familiar with. That's how Frank discovered him,' she adds. 'He was already doing his thing up and down the street.'

But there was a darker side. 'He got very angry about the fact that he wasn't making money from the album. He just thought that he should be rich. He carried the album with him and complained about not making any money from it. A lot of people would avoid him. He was never clean, and he was often very combative. So you'd try to avoid him, although the GTOs loved him in our way, and we championed him to people. We never bad-mouthed him or anything.'

Fischer later recorded Rhino Records' inaugural release. Rhino, now a division of Warner Music Group, was then the independent label of the Rhino Records store on Westwood Boulevard in West LA. The year was 1975, and Fischer's record was called 'Go To Rhino Records.' The concept is simple: '*Go to Rhino Records on Westwood Boulevard*,' Fischer sing-screams. '*They have nice people there / They'll show you where the records are.*'

Bill Mumy of the musical duo Barnes & Barnes, best remembered for their Dr. Demento hit 'Fish Heads,' produced the second and third of Fischer's three Rhino LPs and remained in close touch with him for seven years. 'I watched him spontaneously combust and just start singing multiple times and in multiple places—it could be inside a restaurant, or it could be out on the street because he was manic, depressed, paranoid schizophrenic,' recalls Mumy, who is also an actor best known for playing Will Robinson in the 1960s TV show *Lost In Space*. 'It really affected when he was either [feeling] too low to do anything, or when he was so high he couldn't contain himself. I typically remember being at Norm's restaurant on Pico, near Sepulveda. My friend Scott was actually in the restroom using the toilet, and Larry poked his head over the stall and said, *Do you know who I am?*

Wild Man sang loudly and passionately on the streets of West Hollywood, often in front of the world-famous Whisky A Go Go music venue, attracting both curiosity and bewilderment from passersby. His songs—notably 'My Name Is Larry,' 'Merry-Go-Round,' and 'Not Shy Anymore'—were bizarre and unconventional, reflecting his aberrant if fragile mindset.

Harold Bronson, one of two founders of both the Rhino Records retail store and later the Rhino Records label, later included a diary entry in his memoir, *Time Has Come Today*, about a phone call he received on February 22, 1999:

> I got a call from Bob Merlis, Warner Bros Records' head of corporate communications. Eric Clapton is in town for the Grammy Awards presentation. During his visit with Russ Thyret, head of the label, Eric recalled, fondly, his encounter with Wild Man Fischer on the Sunset Strip during Cream's first tour of the US, when they played the Whisky A Go Go in September 1967. Clapton paid Wild Man ten cents—his going rate—to have him sing a song. He asked Russ, 'Whatever became of Wild Man Fischer?' I told Merlis [that] Wild Man no longer sang, and rotated among flophouses in LA. He drops into our office once a year to collect his royalty check.

Bronson's partner in Rhino Records, Richard Foos, first encountered Wild Man as a high school student. 'I'd see him at T's Beach, the beach that Beverly Hills High School students would stake out—Uni High would have the next beach over,' he recalls. 'And [Wild Man] went up and down the beaches—that was his day work, [performing on] the beaches. Then, at night, he would be on the Sunset Strip, which was mobbed with tens of thousands of people at the time. He would go up and down the Strip, playing songs for between a dime and a quarter.

'One day I saw him when I was at Wallichs Music City [an iconic music store in Hollywood from 1940 to '78], going through the record section. By then, he had become legendary in my mind. Plus, I had never met a rock star before. He came up to me and said, Have you heard my album?'

Foos remembers helping the USC's concert booker organize a Wild Man Fischer concert. When he called Wild Man's number, Larry's mother answered the phone.

'Why would you want to talk with Larry?' she ranted. 'He's a bum ... he's no good.' She went on, Foos recalls, to give him 'his whole history of everything he had ever done wrong: Even in high school, he was a horrible student, you know?'

One of Foos's abiding memories of Fischer was his fluctuating self-esteem. 'One minute he'd say, Nobody cares about me. And a minute later, he'd say, I'm as good as Paul McCartney, aren't I?' Eventually Rhino Records recorded an album, which Foos and Bronson produced.

Musician Chris Bailey—drummer for Phast Phreddie & The Precisions, The Hollywood Rivieras, and The Groovy Rednecks—remembers Fischer well.

'When I moved to LA in 1978, one of my roommates at our house on Sunset & Mansfield, across from Hollywood High School, was a doorman at the Star Strip club on La Cienega,' he says. 'One night, he brought

Larry home after the strip club closed. Larry was a street wanderer, and the roommate knew who he was. Soon, Larry was sleeping on our front porch and hanging around, when he wasn't wandering the boulevard whipping his piece of rope that he carried around.

'On Halloween, we bought a cheap bag of hard candy, but no kids showed up in our hooker-filled neighborhood, so Larry ended up eating the entire bowl of candy and woke up with several aching teeth. I gave him my tube of Ora-Gel to stop his childlike complaining. He was mostly a harmless guy—unless someone said something wrong. Then he would explode. There was no talking him down. He wasn't a physical danger, he would just storm around, yell and wave his arms. We would just show him the door. He stopped coming by after a few months.'

Pamela Des Barres remembers an indoor show that turned into an outdoor busk. The scene was LA's prestigious Shrine Auditorium, one-time home of the Grammy and Oscars ceremonies. The Mothers Of Invention, The GTOs, Alice Cooper, and a band called Ethiopia were on the bill. And Wild Man Fischer was formally on the bill. Yet he seemed to gravitate to the outdoors more than to the venue's indoor stage.

'He got up onstage and started singing his songs—warbling, shouting, really . . . singing wasn't his specialty,' she recalls. 'During "Merry-Go-Round," he started going around and around like a merry-go-round horse on the stage singing it. At one point he jumped down off the stage and sang all around the perimeter. Then he went all around the inside of the building, and then outside the freaking venue, with [the audience] waiting for him to come back. I can only imagine what the people *outside* the Shrine thought of this guy running around there singing. And then he came running back into the venue, got back up onstage, and finished the song.'

Fischer was a frequent visitor to San Francisco, where he would busk amid the cable cars. Mike Nold, nowadays a marriage and family therapist, worked in a record store back in the early 1980s—'still a coveted job' back then, he says. The store was on Market Street, 'the same block as the cable car turnaround at Powell. I recognized Larry, and we quickly became friends . . . sort of. He began singing on the street at the entrance to the store. Sometimes annoying, sure, but always a mix of sweetness and lunacy, which to all of us workers at the store became endearing. Eventually, he moved inside the store, where we stocked plenty of his album. He would stand by the bin with his record and sing selected songs. Sold a lot of albums, mostly to bemused tourists. If they bought it, of course, an autograph and maybe an additional performance. One day he was gone, and we all missed him.'

Fischer spent his final years in an assisted living facility. He was only sixty-six when he died of heart failure at Ronald Reagan UCLA Hospital. In 2005, a documentary about his life was released, entitled *Derailroaded: Inside The Mind Of Wild Man Fischer*. It premiered at the South By Southwest Film Festival in 2005 and has since been released on DVD and streaming platforms.

TED HAWKINS

CHAPTER 24

SOUL AMID
THE SUN, THE SKY, AND THE SURF

TED HAWKINS'S SINGING CAREER was fraught with false starts. Born on October 28, 1936, in Biloxi, Mississippi, Hawkins faced many challenges throughout his life, including imprisonment and institutionalization—charges that varied from drug possession to theft. Thankfully for all of us, his musical talents helped him gain the upper hand on his demons. Heading to Los Angeles during the mid-60s folk boom, he eventually found his way to his longtime roost of Los Angeles's Venice Boardwalk.

Hawkins had begun his musical journey as a teenager, learning to play guitar and honing his singing skills. He'd been particularly moved by the music of Sam Cooke, which he'd heard just after completing reform school. After serving time in prison, he pursued his passion for music and started performing on the streets as a means of survival. Busking enabled him to share his talent and connect with people on a more personal level. His outdoor recitals showcased his powerful and soulful voice—audible from blocks away—which captivated audiences and drew attention to his hybrid of folk, soul, blues, and gospel influences. In time, he gained recognition for his exceptional talent, and his performances began attracting larger crowds with the passing years.

Nearly every Angeleno has walked Venice Boardwalk at one time or another, whether on a Saturday morning in the summer or while showing the promenade to out-of-town visitors. It's a world-renowned carnival of sun worshippers, bodybuilders, and merchants hawking bikinis, sunglasses, vaping paraphernalia, pizza slices, and ice cream. Hawkins's sonorous voice was hard to miss, even above the walkway's obstreperous din. Who was this soulful folk singer, or this folky soul singer, his voice marked by equal parts ache and hope? Harry Perry—the roller-skating Sikh-garbed singer and guitarist who, like Hawkins, serenaded visitors to Venice—says he'd see Hawkins 'every day. It was just his voice and his charisma. He had such a charisma.'

Hawkins's son, Ted Hawkins III, remembers the frenzy at the Hawkins household each Saturday morning. 'Me and my father would wake up in the morning on a Saturday morning, and I remember eating a bowl of cereal really quickly before me before we left for the beach. He was really big on the *hurry up and go!* type of thing. So we had to get out of there. It was sometimes me and sometimes me and my little sister. We would have to go quickly to get on the bus and make it to that spot at Venice Beach on Thornton. He had a certain spot on Ocean Front Walk and Thornton Avenue that he'd monopolize for about eight hours. We just happened to get lucky and get there all the time.'

Part of Ted III's job was wrapping his father's hands before he played guitar. 'Me and my sister would get there and help him set up, maybe get him some water. If he was hungry, we'd get him some food. But the main thing was making sure his hand was wrapped with a glove and tape. That's because he would play his guitar so hard that he would cut his hand up. He would cut his fingers and get blisters, and everything is bleeding, and it was just horrible. So he would wrap it up [in advance], and, to avoid all the explaining, he would put that glove over it.'

Ted III is clear that the blistering and bleeding did not come from pyrotechnic lead guitar soloing so much as the sheer number of hours per day he'd play. 'He never picked all; he was a strummer. He didn't know how to walk the strings, as he would call it. But he would definitely strum the hell out of that guitar to an open C.'

A fringe benefit of being his father's assistant is that Ted III and his sister would pilfer the money bucket where passersby left dollar bills and change. 'We got to reach our little hands in his bucket of money to get whatever we wanted out, you know, and we would go buy pizza and ice cream,' he recalls. 'The beach was our playground, man. We were just having a ball. It was really a lot of fun.'

The worst part of a beach day, Ted III recalls, was returning home to Inglewood. 'We're coming back home from Venice Beach, walking the streets of [South] LA with everybody looking at us, you know. But as kids we kind of felt protected because, you know, [we had] this big old six-foot guy, 230lbs. But it was still bad out there! Once we got home, [we'd] throw the money on the bed and throw it up in the air. We were too young to realize that it really wasn't that much money. But it was enough money for food and a couple other things that we needed.'

In the early 70s, Hawkins was 'discovered' by producer and musicologist Bruce Bromberg, who then lost track of him for a time during the singer's subsequent prison term and a bout with heroin addiction. Finally, in 1982, an album entitled *Watch Your Step*, produced by Bromberg before Hawkins's imprisonment, was released by Rounder Records. In his 'Consumer Guide' column, *Village Voice* critic Robert Christgau called its fifteen tracks 'little dramas of passion, tenderness and betrayal are stamped with the sin-and-redemption of a lived life.'[1]

Hawkins's life continued to be marked by ups and downs, but Ted III says that his father kept his demons out of family life. 'Everything that he went through, as a child and as a grown man, he never, we didn't get those as residuals. He didn't show them to his family. The man walked around with a smile 24/7 after everything he went through as a child and as an adult. Somehow he never lost that smile, nor hope. As he would say, hope is the mother of all men. That was my daddy!'

Following some time at California Medical Facility, Hawkins came to England at the urging of radio personality Andy Kershaw. He then returned to the US and his turf on the Boardwalk. It was during the early 90s that he received his biggest break in what was truly an 'only in Hollywood' moment. Geffen Records A&R scout and in-house producer Tony Berg was told by his production client and close friend Michael Penn about a singer he had recently heard outside his beachfront house.

'There's a guy singing outside my house and he's incredible,' Penn told Berg.

'That was my first inkling of Ted,' says Berg. 'We didn't do anything immediately. He just told me the guy was out there and was great. Michael even said, I think he's the greatest singer I've ever heard.

'Cut to about three months later,' Berg continues. 'Michael was asked to play a benefit at a club in Santa Monica called At My Place. He and I walked into the soundcheck, there was a guy onstage singing and playing, and I turned to Michael and said, I think this guy's the greatest singer I've ever heard. And Michael said, That's the guy . . . that's the guy who I've been telling you about!'

Berg had brought the four-time platinum-selling artist Beck to the label, as well as Wild Colonials, Black Rebel Motorcycle Club, and At The Drive-In. Prior to that, he'd produced Penn's album *March*, from which the hit 'No Myth' emanated. 'I was in the process of talking to David Geffen and the people there about joining Geffen Records,' he says. 'And coincidentally to that, there was a young A&R guy at this is completely unbeknown to me at the time named Todd Sullivan who had heard Ted busking in Santa Monica, and he approached him independently [of me]. So there was just this perfect confluence of people and times and places. And we worked it out that Todd then became the A&R person [and] I produced it, because I was joining at that very moment.'

How did the venerable David Geffen feel about signing a street singer? 'David and Ed Rosenblatt, who was the president of the label, were so good at what they did and so responsive to artists, and that was really what they fostered as a philosophy in the building,' Bergs explains. 'They embraced Ted right from the beginning.'

In 1994, Berg brought Hawkins into his backyard studio to record what would be his highest-profile album, *The Next Hundred Years*. Joining him on the record were such session legends as Jim Keltner, Greg Leisz, Little Feat's Bill Payne, and Berg himself. Jim Washburn, in his hometown review for the *Los Angeles Times*, noted, 'Like [Sam] Cooke, there is a smooth huskiness to his voice, but with more sadness coloring it, and a disquieting nakedness of emotion. Unlike the far-ranging subjects of Hawkins's earlier songs, most here deal with love or the lack of it ... [he pours] a stunning amount of emotion into his own songs.'[2]

Fifty-eight at the time he recorded for Geffen, Hawkins was aware of his mortality. His guarded excitement over what was ostensibly his big break was palpable, as witnessed in the song titled 'Big Things,' in which he sings, '*Too soon my life will be through / Got no time to stop and pick up your flowers.*'

He did still have time for busking, however. According to manager Nancy Meyer, who continues to look after the Ted Hawkins estate, 'Once, after the release of *The Next Hundred Years*—even though we had a busy schedule for him—he found his way down to the Third Street Promenade for an afternoon of busking. The Geffen crew found out about it and called me in sheer panic, telling me he should not be out on the street, now that he is a major label artist—the optics weren't good. I had to break that news to Ted, and I think we had a laugh about it. Ted had many friends and fellow buskers/performers on those streets, and the humble man that he was, he felt a connection to those working so hard for their livelihood. He could not walk by a busker without dropping a few coins— or dollars—into the hat. We were in Cambridge, Massachusetts, together when he played the House Of Blues there, and walking around Harvard Square, I saw him pull out what he had in his pocket and drop it in the guitar case of a street singer.'

Ted III feels his father was a force of nature. 'I thought my daddy was a genius, the way he carried himself. The way he interacted with people was amazing. There was something about him that was beautiful if you knew him. I feel people saw that beauty in him, and the exchange of energy that he gave to people and they gave back. I didn't have a crystal ball; I couldn't have known how great my father would become as a child, but I knew he had the potential, and he was good enough to become great.'

STREET RELIEF, WILD SPACES, ROLLERBLADES

CHAPTER 25

THE BUSKERS OF VENICE BEACH

HARRY PERRY, THE SKATING SIKH

It was one of my first perceptions of Los Angeles. The year was 1984. I'd just moved to the Miracle Mile district from Chicago's Wrigleyville enclave, and I took my obligatory first stroll down Venice Boardwalk on a Saturday morning. My biggest takeaway, as I emerged from the sensory-overloading beachfront carnival, was a singing, roller-skating guitarist in a Sikh's white clothing, white turban, and knee pads. I didn't yet know the man's name. But I *did* know, then and there, that I'd arrived in La-La Land!

Little did I suspect that the musician, whose lyrical name was Harry Perry, was a Midwesterner also—from Detroit, the Motor City, to be precise. He'd been friends with that city's revolutionary rock ambassadors, the MC5. According to Wayne Kramer's memoir, Perry headed to the West Coast after becoming romantically entangled with one band member's girlfriend and wanting to avoid some of the band's drug trafficking convictions. He'd received some cajoling to move west from Tony Netwon, a musician, producer, and former Motown executive known among other affectations for his opulent taste in automobiles. But how, he wondered, would he make a living? LA seemed to work a little differently from Detroit ... or anywhere else for that matter.

Perry did manage to score a part in a stage production of *Hair*, and later in Shakespeare's *Two Gentlemen Of Verona*. Plays, however, have opening and closing dates. How would he pay his rent once the curtains closed? 'It was like, *That's over, and there's not another stage*,' he recalls. 'I'd had some experience of experience with Shakespeare. But in order to play a whole part, it's such a hard thing to go and audition for it and pass—there's gonna be people who are *really* good at it, and that's their thing.'

A revelation came to him one day while he was carousing the city's Westwood neighborhood. There he laid eyes on another fellow Detroit expat, a mime named Eg Mayhem. 'I couldn't believe that he was doing this weird mime stuff and people were giving him money!' he recalls. 'And then I saw him a little bit later and I couldn't believe he was driving an expensive sports car! I said, Hey, how did you get that car? He said he does his mime thing on the streets of Westwood every day and had a new car and a nice apartment. I mean, things were different then—for two hundred dollars a month, you were, like, living at the top of this town. For eighty or a hundred dollars a month, you could live at the beach in a nice apartment.' (Today, a similar apartment might set you back $3,000–4,000 per month.)

Perry knew that showbiz was for him. But he hadn't yet found his niche in entertainment's capital. So he signed on to work construction while he continued to observe the LA dynamic. He was the only non-Spanish-speaking worker. 'I couldn't speak any Spanish, but the guy who was running the whole show spoke just enough English. And he offered me six dollars an hour. I used to work in Detroit for six dollars. And yeah, I work all day with those people, all day in the sun, and then they stop for lunch, and they gave us apples and peanut butter sandwiches and Kool-Aid ... for thirty minutes, right? And then we went back to work until 6 or

7pm. At the end of the day, the dude was paying us in cash, and he goes, We have to take out three dollars for lunch!'

That didn't wash with Perry, who continued to search for his LA niche. It came to him one day in a rather unlikely place: a garbage can. 'I took this a little bit of money from construction,' he says, 'and I walked up toward Hollywood Boulevard, because it was active, even though the buses made it so you couldn't breathe because they didn't have all the [smog] restrictions back in the early 70s. I stood on the corner of Hollywood Boulevard and Highland Avenue and started walking back down the street toward Sunset. *And there was a guitar in a garbage can!*

'It was busted—I guess some homeless guy just got sick of it. It had three strings and a crack inside. So I took a little bit of that money I had and got some glue at the store and glued a patch over the hole. I sang a song that I still sing now. It's called "I Wonder What A Man Might Do On Mars?" I made it up right on the spot. That was the first song I sang in Hollywood on the street.

'By the end of the day, dude, I was, like, *hippie rich*. I had maybe, like, thirty-five or forty dollars or so. That was so much money back then. The rent was only a hundred and something dollars for my apartment on Seward Street.' Perry and his girlfriend celebrated with a shopping spree at the Hollywood supermarket known among locals as Rock'n'roll Ralph's.

Just prior to his busking epiphany, Perry had begun to work with a manager and agent who demanded he sign a lifetime contract. Perry wisely refused. 'It came down to, *You're signing with me, you're gonna sign a lifetime contract*. And that freaked me out. I said, How about fifteen years? Ten years? He said, No, you're gonna sign a lifetime contract. And that just freaked me out. So now I have no gigs, because he wasn't gonna book me anymore, because I wouldn't sign. Anyway, Alice [his girlfriend] was down here at the beach, and by this time I was making vinyl 45s, because it was my idea to be my own record label.'

So where along the way did he develop his longtime persona as the turban-wearing Sikh on roller skates on Venice Boardwalk by the oceanfront? It was Alice who first suggested he wear skates, to which Perry retorted, 'I'm *not* gonna wear skates at the beach!' Eventually, he relented. 'You know, the beach is crowded on the weekend,' he says, 'with everybody trying to roller skate. And good-looking girls can sometimes get you to do things that normally you wouldn't do! So I did it...I wore the skates, and I got out there.

'Before long, there was this dude, Chris Morris, the CEO of Rollerblade. He saw me out there, skating with the guitar and being crazy and he said, Look, dude, give me those skates. I'll give you rollerblades. Just wear my skates.

'That sounded like a deal to me, because keeping skates functional is so expensive and so difficult. So that's why I started wearing skates. I had no intention for it to become an image—it was just sort of a metamorphosis.'

The white Sikh outfit had a more spiritual origin. Perry was taken by a friend to a luncheon that segued into a meditation session in Downtown Los Angeles. 'There was this guy all dressed in white, and that just seemed so weird,' he recalls. 'We started doing yoga, and that really worked for me. I felt exhilarated—without the drinking and the smoking and all that. We did the session, and I felt exhilarated. So I kept going back there. That's how the turban and all that stuff came about because I went to the Sunday luncheons, and they gave me a turban and started giving me the white clothing.'

As a result of that meeting, Perry remains devoted to health and fitness, regularly running and practicing Kundalini yoga. Then there are his kneepads—probably prudent for someone who skates for hours at a stretch. 'There were some guys from the Detroit Red Wings that came to eat, and they saw me on the skates, and that's where I got the big pads— the guy went to his car and brought me out a set of Goldilocks kneepads, and that's why I started wearing the big pads. That's where that part of my look came from.'

Perry is also known for his white electric guitar with a graphic of a target on it. 'Eddie Van Halen used to have a cover band that played at the Whisky, and they'd have these parties out in Pasadena. I asked him where he got that guitar, [and] he told me about the guy who was making them. And that's when I got the essence of that guitar, which looks like it does because it had a rosewood neck. And they made Brazilian rosewood a protected species—you have to get a permit in order to travel out of the country with your guitar. So instead of you going through that, I just had Carruthers put a different neck on the guitar. So that's how that guitar came into being. It was all part of the metamorphosis, based on things that were going on in LA. It wasn't deliberate, it just became a part of the way that I looked and dressed and everything, because of circumstances.'

With the Harry Perry persona nearly in place, he gave some hard thought to how he'd make a living from that point forward. His preceding experience with auditions and booking agents made him realize that independence was the best route forward. 'My question was: *How do you pay your bills? How do you exist in a town where people treat entertainers just like they're doing you a big favor?*'

He reflects on his family's friendship with Redd Foxx, and how young Harry always thought he'd move to Hollywood to work for the ribald comedian. Upon arrival, many years later, he realized the town didn't work quite that way. 'So what's the solution?' he pondered. 'If somebody at one of these [venues] gives you a gig, it's forty-five minutes a month and a half from then. And you have to bring all these people that are gonna drink— all for the couple hundred dollars they're gonna pay you, right? You make the club money. And then what do you do the *next* day?'

According to Perry, the Venice Beach of 1970 bore little resemblance to the way it looks today. 'They had like a lot of parking lots where there are buildings now. Like, where there's a Starbucks down at the beach? That was the Hell's Angel parking lot. It wasn't even a building. It wasn't even a parking lot. It was just like a little grass, grassy park.'

Perry has had good days and bad days in Venice. 'A bad day is when you're on your skates and some racist creep with a big dog and a bullhorn chases you around. He won't let you do your work, shouting from the bullhorn into your ear. You're on your skates and he's trying to trip you. I won't even mention his name.'

A good day? 'The best break I got—I still receive money from it—is when I sang in this 1993 movie called *Point Of No Return*. I sang one of my songs to Bridget Fonda, skating down the street. They cast me in that movie. They paid me a SAG day-player rate and actually gave me all the ASCAP money. They, they didn't, like, make me sign a release. So, for years, I received money from ASCAP. No other movie has really done that. The rest of them rip me off. [They] were just really righteous people who made that movie. To this day I feel blessed that that happened. That's like to me, that's more valuable than it would have been nice to be signed to a label.'

By then, Harry Perry had become a bona-fide tourist attraction on the Venice Boardwalk. But the economics of the music business had begun to change. 'There aren't quite as many street performers as there used to be,' he says. 'There are fewer of them now because there are no CDs. People don't have CD players. So there's nothing to sell. You can sell a T-shirt, but without the music it just doesn't click the same way. If you stand there and play your guitar, people might give you, like, two dollars. That's why I started selling 45s, but now there's no market for physical product. It used to be, you could sell CDs and make a living. Now they stream everything—Spotify [and] all those people have, like, ripped off all the performers. So you can't even make money standing on the street corner.'

That was only the start of Perry's trouble in paradise. In 1995, the *Los Angeles Times* reported, 'A federal judge on Monday preserved a Venice

Beach boardwalk tradition, issuing an order protecting street performers and vendors who said they had been unfairly ticketed by police for selling everything from CDs to politically inspired T-shirts.' Perry, who reportedly ticketed for selling CDs and cassettes of his music, was quoted in the *Times*, as saying, 'This is important to all of us, from the performers and the people who sell cause-minded T-shirts to the guys who accept tips for the sandcastles they make.'[1] The CDs, he adds today, 'were as first amendment as you could get because they *were* my speech.'

In the US Court Of Appeals Ninth Circuit, petition #4215, case #96-55545, it was noted:

> The court of appeals reversed a judgment of the district court. The court held that a municipal ordinance violates the First Amendment by limiting a ban on sales and solicitations in connection with protected expressive activity to persons lacking nonprofit status.
>
> In an effort to conform to a Supreme Court decision, appellee City Of Los Angeles passed an ordinance banning the sale of goods or soliciting donations in an area adjoining the Pacific Ocean, including the Venice Beach Boardwalk. There were two exceptions to the prohibition: the sale of printed matter usually sold by news vendors, and solicitation of donations and the sale of merchandise by a nonprofit organization if it bore a religious, philosophical, or ideological message or statement relevant to the purpose of the organization.
>
> Appellant Harry Perry is a musician and performance artist who solicits donations and sells recordings of his music.

Nonetheless, new economics beckoned new strategies. Perry decided to go to where the music is. Nowadays, he trails bands with loyal followings on the road, playing parking lots—the Grateful Dead, for instance, or Phish or Dave Matthews. 'People are there for music,' he explains. 'A lot of these bands' shows are places where you can set up, but this summer, it turned into some madness. [In the past] you could park for $20–40. Now it's, like, $125 … it's cheaper to Uber from a motel or something. And when I got to the Gorge Amphitheater [150 miles southeast of Seattle], you had to pay for camping, which was like $170 . . . and if you want [a] vending space, in order to do professional vending, it was anywhere from $1,500 to $3,000. And you have to pay them that money before they let you do it. So now I have to make enough money to travel from town to town and pay that amount. It's very competitive, *very* competitive to get a space in those lots.'

At least the Dead were busker-friendly. Other superstar attractions? Not so much. 'Usually, the parking lots are pretty well guarded,' Perry says. 'You can't just walk up and sell stuff. Why wouldn't I go to a Metallica show? Because there's security that will confiscate everything and throw you out of the parking lot. Only certain bands will let you. The Dead are one of them, and I guess somehow Live Nation has some arrangements where certain bands let people vend their stuff in the parking lot, but not all of them. Taylor Swift … believe me, there are people that tried to sell merch on her lot. Forget it. People have tried it. They were in for a rude surprise.'

In this new economy, with Perry finding an eager audience at concert sites, some of the original allure of playing music on the Boardwalk has lost its appeal. 'If I'm playing for somebody, and they hand me two dollars, I tell him, Just put it in your pocket, man—that doesn't help me.'

VICTORIA WILLIAMS

A singer/songwriter whose voice was once described by AllMusic.com as 'off-kilter,' Victoria Williams has released eight albums of her own and appeared on releases by Peter Case, Giant Sand, Joe Henry, Vic Chesnutt, The Jayhawks, and Jim White, to name a few. She is also the subject of a documentary, *Happy Come Home*, by the noted filmmaker D. A.

Pennebaker, while her 1990 diagnosis of multiple sclerosis helped inspire the establishment of the Sweet Relief Foundation. Founded in 1994, initially to aid Williams's own early medical expenses, the organization has since helped many other recording artists in need.

Williams lives in the desert these days, specifically the town of Joshua Tree, which sits in California's Mojave Desert, up the mountain and due northeast of Palm Springs. The area has long been an outpost for musicians: Gram Parsons of The Byrds and The Flying Burrito Brothers, Donovan, Keith Richards, Dick Cale, Eric Burdon, Mark Olsen of The Jayhawks, jazz singer Nancy Wilson—even Allie Wrubel, writer of the Walt Disney song 'Zip-A-Dee Doo Dah,' who spent his final years in adjacent Twentynine Palms.

Long prior to her life amid the yuccas and agaves—and before there were contracts with Rough Trade and Geffen, and later Atlantic and Mammoth—Williams busked on Venice Boardwalk. She arrived from Shreveport, Louisiana, in the late 70s and remained there into the early 80s. She went back to Louisiana for a time, hoping to start a band, but soon found herself back in LA—and specifically on the Venice Boardwalk.

'I was a lazy busker,' she confesses. 'I would busk [until] I made enough money to go down to the [nearby] Taurus Tavern to get something to eat. Sometimes I'd sit in at Taurus with [singer and guitarist] Sam The Man. I loved that guy. He also taught some guitar lessons from his house. There was also a band there called Andy & The Rattlesnakes.'

The Venice scene was very different back then, but Victoria was aware of Ted Hawkins and Harry Perry, as well as 'a very, very nice old Black man' named Uncle Bill. 'I had one of those little Pignose amps,' she says, 'a small little thing, and I believe I put my vocals through that. People seem to like it. They gave me a lot of money. This one fellow wanted me to do a record deal—I don't remember who it was with. But there was a fellow I'd met when I was in New York and who was in the music business. He read what the [proposed recording] contract said, and he goes, Oh, no, that's terrible—that's what they used to rip the Black people off in the 50s! He said, Let me hear what you sound like. So I just made a tape—made up some songs, which is what I always did back then. I hadn't written down any of my songs. He sent the tape to his friend Geoff Travis, and he offered me a record deal on Rough Trade Records. And that's how I got my first record deal. It was because I was busking, and somebody heard me playing and offered me a deal.'

As a result of that contract, she says, 'I went and toured Europe, opening for [other artists]. That wasn't a busking thing. This was like a real club tour. They had me open for Randy Newman in Europe.'

Eventually, Williams returned to Venice Boardwalk, but her revived busking career didn't last long as her Martin guitar got stolen. 'That was the only thing that was horrible that happened,' she recalls. 'Probably somebody took it to the pawn shop. I did check the pawn shops a lot before I went back to Louisiana.'

Then came Williams's brief return to the Bayou State. But whereas New Orleans is a bona-fide busking hub, Shreveport was not. 'I didn't busk much in Shreveport,' she says. 'I was in a band called The G.W. Korners. We didn't play out much. We played, like, deer camps out in the country. I didn't have a microphone. When the band went on break, I sang a song and a man at the deer camp gave me a hundred dollars if I sang [one more] song. I did, and the band let me keep the hundred dollars. So I bought a microphone.

'That probably has nothing to do with busking,' she acknowledges, 'but busking really helped me along there in the beginning. I was singing in front of people and got money for months, and I would have enough for bus fare and to eat and such.'

By 1986, Williams was back in LA, working as a chauffeur for clients including Stevie Wonder. She performed music with her then-husband,

Peter Case (himself a former busker), and was signed by Geffen Records—the same label that snapped up both Case and Venice contemporary Ted Hawkins. ('Ted Hawkins got really famous. I was so happy for him.') It was through Geffen that she released her first album, *Happy Come Home* (1987), its title track a paean to Williams's beloved dog, Happy. The LP was produced by Anton Fier of The Golden Palominos.

Promise turned to despair when Williams received her life-transforming medical diagnosis in 1992, but on learning that she lacked health insurance, an impressive collective of musicians who had become early fans of her music (including Pearl Jam, Lou Reed, Maria McKee, Lucinda Williams, and Soul Asylum's Dave Pirner) contributed tracks to a 1993 benefit album titled *Sweet Relief: A Benefit For Victoria Williams*. Several more Victoria Williams albums ensued. Although attending to her health has become an ongoing part of her life, Williams seems to have found a home in Joshua Tree, where the high elevations and clean air have helped her recover. It's not uncommon to find her sitting in with musician friends when they play desert shows.

Does anyone busk in Joshua Tree, which lacks a true town center and depends largely on auto traffic, I wondered? 'Yeah, over at the farmer's market,' she responds. 'Sometimes I'll sing with people who are busking, but I'm not taking any money or anything.'

EILEN JEWELL

Singer/songwriter Eilen Jewell has shared stages with Emmylou Harris, Wanda Jackson, and Mavis Staples. Based in Boise, Idaho, she has released nine critically acclaimed albums, her longstanding 'Queen Of The Minor Key' moniker inspired, as NPR has noted, by 'her penchant for both themes of hardship and her musical scale preferences.'[2]

While Jewell is a natural singer and songwriter, she's the first to admit she was not a born performer. Though she accompanies herself on guitar—

joined by her band featuring world-class guitarist Jerry Miller—piano was her first instrument. 'My first love was the piano, but I thought the guitar was more practical. You can bring it around to friends' houses and you can work on your songs together. But for me, music was really just something to do with friends. I was terrified of performing onstage because I'd been a piano student, and every year we had to have piano recitals. I loathed those things! I dreaded them all year long. I get so nervous. I'd mess up the song that I knew forward and backward.'

When Jewell started college in Santa Fe, New Mexico, music was an activity limited to her dorm room—until, that is, a friend suggested she join him as a busker in the city's farmers market. 'He was very outgoing and liked the spotlight,' she recalls. 'I was like, No, I don't wanna play in front of anybody. I hate that stuff. No audience, please. He said, No, it's fine, no one really listens, you'll just come and play…

'So I went there, and we played our songs. He'd kind of tricked me a little bit because some people *did* listen. They really liked our songs and gave us flowers or maybe a jar of jelly to show how much they liked it. I could see on their faces like that are things that we did make them happy. And it wasn't a big crowd—just a handful of passersby. So I got a taste of the positive side of performing where I'd only ever had the terrifying aspect and the doing-it-out-of-obligation side of performing. I got a taste of how much joy it could bring me to bring joy to other people.

'The following summer, [my friend] was out of town, so I decided to do it by myself, which was a pretty huge leap. And I really got the bug for busking.'

Jewell soon set her sights west. 'I was in Santa Fe, and my friend was now in Venice—not far from where he lives now today,' she recalls. 'And he said, Why don't you come out here to Venice Beach and busk this summer? So I moved out to Venice Beach for a summer, and every single day that was my job—my full-time job was busking in Venice.'

Playing in Venice definitively helped Jewell up her performing game. 'Busking taught me to have a tough skin—not to be offended when people don't stop and listen, or if people *do* stop for a long time and then don't throw anything in the guitar case. I met so many wild characters there, including other performers. There was a guy juggling a chainsaw—it was such an amazing variety show. It opened my mind to this world of possibilities.

'There are so many ways you can show your love of performers. Like, I remember there was this one guy whom I'm pretty sure lived on the beach and had covered his bike in flowers. His name was Roland. And he was covered head-to-toe with flowers. He would ride by me while I was playing, and when he'd hear a song that he liked, he would throw this huge container of flower petals on my head, and they'd all just rain down.

'On a good day, I would have flower petals plus a couple hundred bucks in my guitar case—and dozens of smiles and nods from people walking by. And, of course, the weather was always beautiful because it was LA in the summer, and I was right on the beach. At the end of the day, I might be able to buy an avocado to go with my beans and rice. So it wasn't highly lucrative. But it was enough.'

Clouds formed occasionally over the Venice sunshine, however. 'I did have a couple instances where people attempted to steal my money,' she says. 'I don't know whether they were drunk or what, but they'd move in slow motion, grabbing for the money out of my guitar case. And then there were sketchy male characters hanging around, and I didn't know what their intentions were. Sometimes they'd come up behind me. That put me on edge—it's one drawback to not having a stage. But I think the good days outnumbered the bad.'

It was in Venice that Jewell decided her next step would be to put together a band. She felt Boston—clear across the country—might be a good place to find musicians and develop a following in the clubs. So, in 2003, she made the move there and began to play open-mic sessions at clubs. 'That was kind of the next step up, after busking. I moved to Boston for the purpose of putting together a band, but in the meantime I was trying to be a busker again. But it was just too cold … [playing on] the subway was too miserable for me.'

Jewell did eventually become a club headliner. At one point, she caught the ear of Jim Olsen, owner of Signature Sounds Records in Northampton, Massachusetts, which has released seven of her nine albums to date. 'I first heard Eilen Jewell after I was tipped off by Peter Mulvey, who raved about her when they did a song circle together in Boston in the early 2000s,' he recalls. 'I made a point to go see Eilen at the old Club Helsinki on a spring night in 2005. I was expecting to see her solo, but she'd already put together the great band that she still fronts today. Her performance showcased not only her own excellent material but also an incredible range of covers, from Dylan to Bessie Smith, Charlie Rich, Billie Holiday, and more. It felt as though Eilen had absorbed the entire history of American roots music and seamlessly incorporated it into her art. It was an unforgettable night.'

While her live shows are mainly indoors these days, Jewell did get pressed back into busking service in 2008. 'There was a festival that had kind of a busking corner,' she says, 'and they scheduled us to play that little spot. It was totally unplugged but it was with my band. So we just played it real stripped-down—the bass player tried to play quietly, I tried to sing loudly, and the guitar player played an acoustic. It was *like* busking, but a more formal arrangement. It was a trip.'

Jewell often finds herself looking back on her Venice Boardwalk days. She believes it was a more hospitable location for buskers than Boston. 'I think part of what made Venice so special was that it was it was totally unregulated,' she reflects. 'You didn't need a permit. There was no red tape—it was just kind of free. I don't know if it's still this way, but it was like a free public art space. I kind of took that for granted, I guess. The

Santa Fe farmers market was the same way—they, they were like, *Oh, sure if you wanna set up in this corner, go ahead*. When I moved to Boston, you had to get a permit from the city. It cost money, and you had to display it, and you had to keep your decibels below a certain level.'

Jewell makes a larger point about the value of busking. 'For me, it's an argument for keeping some kind of wild space available for artists. It's important for a graffiti artist to have a wall where they can do an amazing mural, and [the city] won't control it. Like, just go for it. [Busking is] *our* graffiti art. It's so crucial to just have at least one space like that.'

And a bit of personal follow-up: years later, Jewell is now engaged to the friend who suggested she busk at the Santa Fe farmers market and in Venice. He still lives in Venice.

PART
FIVE

EUROPE

If you walked up there in the evening, the buskers of the entire city of Paris showed up, and I just thought, If I hang around, I'll learn how to play guitar. And I'll learn how to play songs. I tried to play my first terrace by myself, and I did a lunchtime crowd. And I made, like, thirty francs, which seemed like a really good day. **MADELEINE PEYROUX**

ELVIS COSTELLO

CHAPTER 26

WATCHING FOR DETECTIVES

SOME ARTISTS CAN'T get arrested playing on the streets. Elvis Costello disproved that axiom one history-changing day in the summer of 1977.

The British singer/songwriter, who had recently issued his debut single, 'Less Than Zero,' on the indie label Stiff Records, performed on the street outside the Park Lane Hilton hotel—also notable in pop history as the place where The Beatles first met Maharishi Mahesh Yogi in 1967—which was the site of CBS Records' London convention. Costello was furious that no American label had signed him. He'd attracted a streetside audience of roughly fifty, including Walter Yetnikoff (CBS Records International president), Matthew King Kaufman (Jonathan Richman's manager, who was reportedly yelling, 'Get down, Elvis!'), and Herb Cohen (Frank Zappa's personal manager, music publisher, and partner in his Bizarre and Straight labels). The scene was visited by a British police constable, who attempted to terminate the performance and disperse the assembled crowd.

According to a contemporary report in *Melody Maker*, Costello's manager, Jake Riviera, reportedly shouted at the officer, 'He's *not* busking, man! He's just singing in the street! You can't stop people singing in the street! These people are *enjoying* themselves, man! Look at them! They're clapping and singing!' Elvis was reportedly singing his heart out. Alas, he was arrested for 'unlawful obstruction,' despite having a soundcheck at Dingwall's scheduled for 4pm. Riviera, on the phone with his attorney, sought to free him. Thankfully, Elvis made the show (and remembered to include his song 'Watching The Detectives' in the set).

Forty-five years after the incident, the writer of that *Melody Maker* story, Allan Jones—later the editor of both the *Maker* and British music magazine *Uncut*—reflects on that fateful day in July. 'I'd been spending a lot of time at Stiff from the time they started in 1976,' he recalls, 'and in the summer of '77, 32 Alexander Street [Stiff's street address] was just one of the hippest places to be in London. I was around there a lot. And I suggested to Jake that I write a piece in *Melody Maker*, basically a day in the life of staff—that I go around, just sit around the office, and record whatever happened. And he kept putting me off and putting me off, and then late one afternoon, he called me up and said, You still want to do the story? If you do, be around here at nine tomorrow. Something's going to be happening.

'So I duly turned up. It was a usual morning of mayhem at Stiff. And then, about lunchtime, early afternoon, Elvis Costello turned up, he was carrying his Fender Jazzmaster guitar, and slung over his shoulder like a rocket launcher was a Vox practice amp. I wasn't sure what was happening. Very shortly afterward, The Attractions, who had only recently formed and were due to make their London debut that evening at Dingwalls, turned up. Nick Lowe was around somewhere.

'Suddenly, the whole [Stiff office] exploded with activity and Jake started shouting and ordering cabs. He pushed Elvis into the back of one cab, with his guitar and the practice amp, and then they drove off. Some more cabs arrived, and we all drove off after Elvis. At that point, I still didn't know where we were going or what was supposed to be happening, but we pitched up outside the Hilton Hotel, where CBS was having its annual London convention—and then I realized what was happening.

'*My Aim Is True* was due out, but there was already something happening around Elvis. You could just feel it. And Jake, I think, had already reached a decision that, as cool as it was to have Elvis on Stiff, if you wanted to make him the kind of international superstar that he thought Elvis his talent deserved, he was gonna have to place him on a major label. There was no way Stiff's operation was big enough to break in worldwide.

'So, we all gathered around outside the main entrance to the Hilton, and Elvis plugged in his guitar. He started playing, and Elvis is incapable of playing anything modestly. He was emoting like mad. You know, he can't be quiet, so he was just making a lot of noise, even though it was just his voice and his guitar. First of all he played "Welcome To The Working Week," then "Waiting For The End Of The World." And, you know, everybody thought this was just a gas. It was really great. And Elvis was putting everything into it. Of course, a small crowd had gathered, and there were some Japanese tourists, I think, who didn't know what the hell was going on. Eventually, somebody from the hotel came out. The security guard had a big argument with Jake and wanted us to move on. We all refused to move. Elvis was oblivious to what was going on. He was so into what he was doing.

'And, of course, Elvis had famously been turned down by every major record company. He'd gone along, sung them his songs, got no interest. But Jake was going to dare CBS to ignore him at this point.

'The security guard went off, and ... the convention started to filter out, and I remember they were all carrying these little picnic bags—I think they had a big fat *thank you* to Ted Nugent printed on them—so they all stood around and wondered what was going on. I'm not sure if any of them knew who Elvis was.

'Walter Yetnikoff, who was the king of CBS, came out. He seemed kind of baffled but very amused by what was going on. And it was all just building up rather nicely. And then a young policeman turned up. He looked very, very nervous. He wasn't sure what to do. And, of course, this was the summer of punk—the *second* summer of punk—so there was a lot of stuff going on . . . so there was always great alarm and panic around it. Anybody who looked remotely like a punk, which none of us really did, because we're all old pub-rockers, basically.

'Anyway, that policeman asked Elvis if he would move on. Elvis refused, and Jake was conspicuously the ringleader of this particular event. The policeman approached him and said he wanted him to stop playing and move on. And Jake said, Why, man, why? And the policeman said, you know, He's busking. Jake said, He's just singing in the street. Let him be. Everybody's enjoying themselves.

'The policeman didn't know what to do. He was on his radio for backup. Within minutes, a police car—three police cars, I think—and a police van came. I don't know what sort of situation they thought they might be getting involved in. The inspector duly turned up to take command of the crisis. He tried to get Jake to stop Elvis playing. Jake refused: *We're singing, we're dancing. There's nothing wrong with that. We're just having fun. Leave us alone.* The policeman just said, Right, I'm gonna take him in.

'But first of all, the policeman said, Please move along. So Elvis took a step to his right, which was moving along as far as he was concerned, but it wasn't nearly as far as the police officers were concerned. And in a very dramatic gesture, the officer grabbed Elvis by the collar and frog-marched him into the police van and basically just pushed him in the van, slammed the doors, and then drove off, at which point Jake realized there might be some trouble because there was a soundcheck at 4pm, and it was now about 2:30 or so.

'They took Elvis to Vine Street police station. We all rushed back to Stiff Records, where Jake was immediately on the phone. On one line, he had a guy named Glen Colson, who'd taken off in pursuit of the police van. On the other line, [Jake] had a guy called David Gentle, who was Elvis's lawyer. And he was like a hostage negotiator. *How are they gonna get him out?*

'As it turned out, the police let him go with a five-pound fine for, I think, lowball obstruction, and that was that was the end of his legal obligation. I think he had to go to court the next morning to make a brief appearance and plead guilty to the willful obstruction.'

By the end of the year, Jones notes, Elvis had left Stiff and signed to CBS. Jello Biafra—lead singer for the Dead Kennedys, co-founder of the Alternative Tentacles label, and political aspirant—who was in England during Elvis's street performance, calls it 'Jake Riviera's cleverest stunt of all.'

An American A&R rep for CBS, Gregg Geller (later an executive at RCA and Warner Bros), had seen Costello's street performance and would sign him to an American deal a few months later. He remembers Elvis's now-famous street serenade well.

'On July 26, 1977, my thirtieth birthday, my future wife, Hope Antman, and I, in the company of Walter Yetnikoff and [journalist] Lisa Robinson, exited the morning session of that year's CBS Records convention at the London Hilton on Park Row and encountered Elvis, his guitar plugged into a tiny amp, playing "Welcome To The Working Week." Another guy paraded back and forth in a sandwich board that said Elvis Costello and Stiff Records welcome CBS Records to London. A paddy wagon pulled up, and a couple of bobbies popped out and arrested Elvis and hauled him away.

'Needless to say, the event made quite an impression on me, and I made sure to acquire a copy of *My Aim Is True*, which had just been released that very week. I returned home with a stack of UK LPs, as was my custom in those days, but the Elvis album was the first to make it to my turntable, and it rarely left it for weeks thereafter. At some point I realized that not only could I enjoy Elvis, but I could sign him as well. And so I did.

'Or, as Elvis writes in his memoir, *Unfaithful Music & Disappearing Ink*, "I'd had to get myself arrested to get their attention." I'd likely have gotten around to listening to *My Aim Is True*, but probably not as quickly, had it not been for busking.'

GLEN HANSARD

CHAPTER 27

SWELL SEASONS ON THE STREETS OF DUBLIN

GLEN HANSARD'S STORIED CAREER as a busker dates back to his early years on Grafton Street in Dublin, Ireland. He was thirteen when he left school to busk. Back then, it might have seemed like an impossibly long road to Hollywood or to Broadway, but such an improbable bridge was built—half crown by half crown, pound by pound.

The urge to perform came early for Hansard, and came partly at the suggestion of his school principal. 'My headmaster was a radio DJ and he loved music,' he later told *Entertainment Weekly*. 'Whenever I'd get sent to the office for not paying attention or whatever, he'd say, You're a funny one. You can name the bass player on Neil Young's *Harvest*, you can tell me the track listing on Bob Dylan's *Street Legal*, but you can't tell me the square root of nine. You're obviously using your intelligence in an area that's not academic.

'He was quite smart. He said, You love music and you can obviously play, so why don't you start your career now? He encouraged me to leave school. He said, Take your guitar into town and start busking. His thing was that busking was where you learned your skills. He said, I can't guarantee you'll be famous, but if you start now, then you'll always be able to live from your guitar. And he was right. I have.'[1]

Hansard's busking days were influential in shaping his musical style and stage presence. He often performed with his guitar and drew inspiration from folk, rock, and traditional Irish music. Through busking, he honed his songwriting abilities and learned to captivate audiences with heartfelt performances. In the early 1990s, he formed The Frames, with whom he would go on to release seven studio LPs and two live albums. Around that same time, casting directors John and Ros Hubbard traveled to Dublin on behalf of the director Alan Parker, who was set to make a film about an Irish soul band titled *The Commitments*, based on author Roddy Doyle's 1987 novel. Hansard was cast as Outspan Foster, the band's guitarist.

Seventeen years later, he was cast by another filmmaker, John Carney, to appear in the 2007 movie *Once*. The film tells the story of Guy, a busker, and Girl, a young woman (played by Markéta Irglová), who meet after his hard-earned proceeds are stolen by a street thief. Girl is intrigued by both his music and his ability to repair vacuum cleaners. A romance ensues, complicated by the fact that Girl is married to another man in the Czech Republic; the film traces their musical and interpersonal union and their eventual parting.

Hansard's own experiences as a street musician heavily influenced the film, and he even contributed his own songs to its soundtrack. *Once* went on to achieve critical acclaim and helped propel Hansard's career to greater heights. In his *New York Times* review of the movie, A.O. Scott noted that it 'does not look, sound, or feel like a typical musical. It is realistic rather than fanciful, and the characters work patiently on the songs rather than bursting spontaneously into them.'[2] *Variety* observed that 'no money went up front for the songs written by Hansard and Irglová that have been integral to the film's success. Filming took place on the street and at friends' houses using natural light. Most importantly, low-budget didn't mean low-experience.'[3]

Hansard and Czech-born Irglová had first connected when The Frames played at a festival in the Czech Republic promoted by her parents. Their own romantic involvement did not blossom until the making of *Once*, but it lasted through 2009, bookended by two albums by their duo, The Swell Season. The union produced a #16 *Billboard* pop hit, 'Falling Slowly,' which went on to win Best Original Song at the eightieth Academy Awards. The soundtrack album from *Once* also won two Grammy Awards, Best Compilation Soundtrack Album For A Motion Picture and Best Song Written For A Motion Picture, Television Or Other Visual Media, a Critics' Choice Award, and an Independent Spirit Award, and appeared on many critics' Top 10 lists of the best films of 2007.

The ensuing theatrical production of *Once*, which premiered in 2011, received eleven Tony Award nominations in 2012, winning in eight categories, including Best Musical, Best Actor, and Best Book. The musical also won the 2012 Drama Desk Award for Outstanding Musical and the 2013 Grammy for Best Musical Theater Album.

Since the film's success, and with The Frames ongoing as a recording and touring unit, Hansard has used his celebrity to return to his street origins, this time on behalf of worthy causes, with his annual Christmas Eve Busk. Featured guests have included the late Sinéad O'Connor in 2012 and fellow Dubliner Bono of U2 in 2020.

The event returned following the COVID pandemic in December 2022 with co-stars Dermot Kennedy and Imelda May. Proceeds have helped provide food and shelter for Dublin's homeless population, which a 2016 tally estimated at over five thousand. The event, which also called attention to oppression in Ukraine, took place on the street in front of the Gaiety Theater on the city's South King Street.

'It's not our place to judge why people are homeless,' Hansard has said of his busking benefit events. 'It's our place to help shelter the cold and hungry. The rest is up to them.'[4]

BILLY BRAGG

CHAPTER 28

RIFF-RAFFIN'
THE TUBE

BRITISH SINGER/SONGWRITER, author, and political activist Billy Bragg boasts a significant background as a street singer. In the late 1970s and early 80s, he began his musical journey as a busker in London. He performed on the streets, in Tube stations, and in various other public spaces, singing his own songs and accompanying himself on acoustic guitar. Playing in public provided him with an opportunity to develop his performance skills, connect with audiences, and test his material in a live setting.

Bragg's busking repertoire often consisted of politically charged songs with themes of social justice, inequality, and working-class struggles. His heartfelt and passionate performances quickly garnered attention, and he became known for his blend of folk, punk, and protest music. Bragg's music carried a strong message, and his busking experiences helped him refine his songwriting and live delivery.

As his popularity grew, Bragg transitioned from busking to performing in venues and recording albums, but he has remained connected to his busking roots throughout his career, occasionally returning to the streets, primarily to support various causes. Those causes have varied from advocating for reform of the House Of Lords to forming the original British chapter of Jail Guitar Doors, its goal being to help rehabilitate prisoners through musical education. (An American chapter was launched by MC5 guitarist Wayne Kramer.)

Bragg has authored several books and recorded more than a dozen albums, including the 1998 LP *Mermaid Avenue*, a collaboration with the band Wilco commissioned by Nora Guthrie, daughter of American folk artist Woody Guthrie. Bragg and Wilco set some of the elder Guthrie's unrecorded lyrics to music. The album received a Grammy nomination that year for Best Contemporary Folk Album.

Bragg's prime busking years were 1981–82, when he was in his early twenties. 'It was around the time after my band [Riff Raff] broke up,' he recalls. 'I was living with some friends in West London, and when we ran out of money, I used to go out and do a bit of busking and not come back 'till I made ten or fifteen quid, which would get me through the next few days. A money spinner for me was Elvis Presley's "Can't Help Falling In Love." You could really let it hang in the air.'

There were several reasons Bragg preferred Underground stations to surface streets, among them shelter from the elements and the acoustics. 'In my day, one had to rely on the environment,' he says. 'My favorite place was at South Kensington. There's a long tunnel, probably about a mile long, that connects the subway station with the Natural History Museum, and also [runs] toward the Royal Albert Hall. It's a long tunnel and it has tiled walls—and that's really good for a little bit of reverb. I'd been in a band, so I knew I had to you know reach out to people as they went by. But that was that was kind of my sort of busking education there.'

Respect for other buskers was key. 'The tunnel also connected to the

Royal College Of Music,' he says. 'Sometimes you'd get cello players down there... viola players. Sadly, no one ever sat in with me. But I did get I did have a few encounters with people who [told me] was I was on I was on their pitch. So out of respect I had to move on.

'The thing about the tunnel at South Kensington was, you didn't have to worry about traffic noise,' he adds. 'You didn't really have to worry about the rain. It was quite a good spot. Just get there and stay there, really—an all-weather busking spot with good acoustics because people would hear you right up the tunnel. So if you're hitting a song they like, they get close, close, close, close, close, close.'

Addressing the sustainability of street performance, Bragg is candid. 'I wouldn't say I ever made a living [by busking], but I made enough money to get through the next few days.'

Bragg may have subsequently graduated to concert stages, festivals, and touring, but he considers himself a busker for life. 'The significance of busking in my career is that I am still basically a busker, you know—that's what I do,' he says. 'I was at a festival called Bearded Theory. It was a festival held in a field up in Staffordshire, in between Birmingham and Derby. It probably was about twenty thousand people, and I probably played to maybe twelve thousand people. I was on in the afternoon, and the whole time that I was onstage, I was more or less busking. What I mean by that is, I was dealing with the situation as it was presented to me.

'Now, when I'm in a gig where I have a soundcheck and it's my gig, I tune everything exactly as I like. If I'm having a bit of a problem, I'll have a word with a guy, and we'll sort it out. But when you're just thrown in with a fifteen-minute changeover, you've got twelve thousand people who want to hear you sing, you [just] start playing. And if the levels aren't right, and you can't quite hear the keyboard player as you'd like to, you just have to busk it.

'I hate being at festivals and watching artists spend ten minutes getting the ball back just right. I'm like, *Get on with it—we can hear you.* Or not. You can see if people hear it or not. [If] they can understand you, they're smiling. And that, to me, is busking. You're there to deal with the environment, wherever it presents. When you're busking, the environment changes all the time, people coming and going all the time. It's not a constant thing, right? You adapt to the weather and to everything. You have to suss out what's going on and adapt to that and do what you came to do in terms of what the environment presents to you, and that's how I am at most festivals. I'm doing it by the seat of my pants.

'[Busking is] a fundamental aspect of me, I guess. I'm of that same sensibility that I had in the tunnel, looking at people's faces, bending the set to fit into the moods, [all of which] I'm doing onstage, still. When I get to a festival—once we've gotten our stuff in—I'll go out and find a coffee or a burger or something, and I'll walk around the crowd and see if I can suss out what kind of mood the crowd is in. It can be in a different mood [because of] the weather . . . it could be all wet and miserable. Or it could be sunburned and a bit dozy. But you go out and you feel about, and then you come back, and you write the set you think fits the mood.

'The artists that I admire are the ones who are tuned into what's happening around them and are able to adapt to that, respond to it, and make it part of the show. *That's* busking to me. That's what I think of as busking. The skills that I learned on the street still inform how I perform. In certain circumstances, I fall back on that experience. I'm not fazed by it. Because I have something to fall back on and say, *Oh, yeah, I've been in this situation before, right?* Then there was only, you know, maybe a dozen people every five minutes. Now there's twelve thousand people, but it's still the same mindset I need—not to be intimidated, suss them out, see how they react, and if they're reacting positively, they can probably hear me, they're probably enjoying it. Trust your sound person, and just do a gig—and come onstage and everyone's happy. When everyone's smiling,

I'm good. That's money in the hat for me … I like a bit of that spontaneity. I like a bit of devilment, really.'

Bragg's time on the street, in fact, prepared him for his storied history of political activism. 'Somewhere I would find my busking skills coming out is on picket lines, because that's a lot like busking. It's the same sort of thing,' he explains. 'You're out in the open. You're also performing songs. We're walking by they're walking by in the picketers are out there trying to get some support with you.

'I was in Australia in March [2023] and I took part in Adelaide with a flash mob of women: fruit and vegetable pickers who didn't feel they were getting properly looked after and properly paid. So they did a kind of flash mob in a big supermarket in Port Adelaide. And they needed something to manifest themselves on the way in there, so they got me down to teach them the chorus of "Solidarity Forever." We marched in, singing that … then they all sang the chorus, and the song manifested them, so people could see that there was a load of us, and we were all there and we were all doing something. I was just walking in off the street [into] the supermarket, singing a song, and everyone's joining in singing with me—that was a very *busker* thing to do!

'You know,' he concludes, 'it's kinda like *engaged* busking, rather than passive busking.'

TYMON DOGG

CHAPTER 29

FIDDLING, STRUMMING, AND CLASHING

BRITISH MUSICIAN TYMON DOGG, whose given name is Stephen Murray, is known for his versatility. He is proficient with various instruments, including violin, guitar, and piano, and has been associated with musical genres ranging from folk to punk-rock. His influences are mainly American singer/songwriters: Woody Guthrie, Paul Simon, Leonard Cohen, Bob Dylan, and Randy Newman.

Tymon (which rhymes with Simon) gained recognition for his collaboration with The Clash during the late 1970s and early 1980s. He contributed violin and songwriting to several songs on the band's 1980 album *Sandinista!*, for which he wrote the track 'Lose My Skin,' a showcase for his high-pitched lead vocals and violin.

He has also released eight solo albums and worked on various music projects, from a single under the name of Timon on Pye Records to unreleased tracks for The Beatles' Apple Records with Peter Asher producing, Paul McCartney on piano, and James Taylor on guitar. He also toured with The Moody Blues, whose frontman, Justin Hayward, produced a second Timon single.

Not many artists take to street singing after they've played world-class venues, nor after they've gone into the studio with a Beatle. But for Tymon Dogg, it came down to a simple matter of economics. 'The first time I actually I was ever played in London was actually at the Albert Hall, supporting The Moody Blues,' he says with a sigh. 'After I'd done a nationwide tour in all these massive places. I didn't really have much money because we were the support act. You get your money and it's immediately spent on hotels and gone after a few months. So I thought, *I'll just go out [on the streets] and play some songs.*

'I was always quite romantic about busking,' he adds. 'I got down to the south of France when I was fifteen. And I played around Avignon and San Tropez. I ended up in Nice, working there for a long time on the Promenade, and I made quite good money—in today's money, it was, like, one hundred or two hundred pounds. At night, I'd play for an hour and a half, two hours—they'd be tourists coming by. And so I always had [busking] as my ammunition, as it were. It's a great way [to perform] if you if you need independence, and you want to work on something.'

Around 1971, Dogg was renting part of a house in London's Westbourne Grove when he met John Graham Mellor, who would soon come to be known as Joe Strummer. Mellor was a student at London's Center School Of Art. 'He was getting a bit fed up, you know, because this may have been *art* school, but it was *school*. And he needed money. So he was thinking, *I'll come out with some hang out with Tymon to get some money.*'

That was around the time Dogg decided to take up violin. 'I learned an instrument I've never played before,' he says. 'Because I thought if I was going to be standing there—totally ignored by people mostly—by the end of that two hours or whatever, three hours, at least I'm going to be a little bit better at this. If you play any instrument for two hours a day, something's going to start happening. He decided to take up the guitar, and I had a guitar. He was left-handed, but I only had my right-handed guitar. So he was playing that, and he would learn the chords to back up my playing the violin. We're basically standing in London learning our instruments—and we got to be pretty good pretty quickly. I got okay on the violin. And he, of course, became Joe Strummer!'

This was a full five years before the formation of The Clash.

The busking life threw Strummer and Dogg their share of setbacks. 'We got we got locked up a few times,' says Dogg. 'We had some very interesting times. But the great thing about Joe is, he was always a real optimist. He was just hanging out; his spirit was very much in songwriting. We'd play games: we'd be busking, and we'd say, Hey, let's see who can lean back the furthest without falling over while we're playing our instruments!'

'We had some fantastic times. Joe was very funny because he had a baritone voice, which is much lower than mine—mine is more the tenor/ alto area—and it was bloody loud. So I'd be singing the song, and there'd be this fog-horning in my ear. At one point, I said to him, Listen, why don't you stay here and I'll go and play somewhere else—that way, we have two places going at once.'

Public performance laws caught up with Dogg and Strummer in Holland. 'We got to Amsterdam to play some good paying gigs,' Dogg explains. 'I suggested we busk down the street and get a bit of money so we could go to a restaurant, because we had no money. The police came and were in plain clothes and said, You're under arrest, and they took the instruments. So we had no instruments for the gig. Joe went off and came back with a violin. It was some person's family heirloom—it was it was some old precious violin that some kid sneaked out of his mother's house.'

At some point, the Strummer/Dogg duo went their separate ways. 'I was ready to do my own show,' Dogg says. 'And he walked away. That's when he started his career. But it was great to work with a partner like him. He was optimistic. He made the best of everything.'

Strummer, of course, went on to form The Clash with Mick Jones, Paul Simenon, and Topper Heddon. And Tymon Dogg pursued his own career. In addition to releasing eight solo albums between 1976 and 2015, he has played on and/or produced albums by Ian Hunter, Ellen Foley, Poison Girls, El Doghouse, and Susannah Austin, as well as Strummer's post-Clash band, The Mescaleros.

The parting with Strummer augured the end of Dogg's tenure as a street singer. 'I didn't busk after that, really,' he says. But he credits his outdoor performances for helping him learn to project his singing. 'We just had to be loud, as we were drowned out. If we were inside the Tube, we had a nice echo. So that would help, particularly with an instrument like violin, which had a lot of sound to it.'

Dogg hasn't ruled out a return to the streets in the future, regarding it as something he can always turn to when he wants to refine new songs and new sounds. 'I was thinking to do some busking again, actually. Maybe I'll even work with somebody who plays classical,' he says. 'It's a great thing when maybe you haven't got any work or you're not getting any shows in clubs—a really great way to just keep on going. You can be making money while you're actually rehearsing. But mainly you're just playing and having a good time. If you're not doing that, it's hard work.'

MOJO NIXON

CHAPTER 30

LONDON CALLING

SINGER, SONGWRITER, and (latterly) satellite-radio DJ, Mojo Nixon carved a niche for himself thanks to his energy and his catalogue of jocosely irreverent songs.

Nixon was born Neill Kirby McMillan Jr. in 1957 in Danville, Virginia. Debuting on record as the frontman in a duo with washboard player Skid Roper (né Richard Banke), his sound was a bodacious hybrid of rockabilly, punk, country, and blues. His frenetic stage presence captivated audiences, while his humorous songwriting showcased his social commentary wrapped in a caustic wit, as songs like 'Elvis Is Everywhere' and 'Debbie Gibson Is Pregnant With My Two-Headed Love Child' became cult classics. His discography contains about fifteen albums, the first six with Roper. A documentary film titled *The Mojo Manifesto* premiered at South By Southwest in 2022.

Nixon's busking years preceded what McMillan called 'my Mojo Nixon revelation,' which occurred when he moved to London after graduating from Miami University, Ohio, in 1979. 'I was the only punk-rocker there.

An army of one. I graduated from college and moved to England. I lived in a squat in Brixton. My goal was to join The Clash. I was only twenty years old and had been playing guitar for a couple of years.'

Nixon had a ninety-day work visa and would take the Tube every day, where it occurred to him, 'I should go play, you know. A lot of times it was string quartets playing "Eleanor Rigby." I thought I could and should do that. And so I did. And I would make fifty to a hundred bucks an hour.'

For Nixon, how much money he produced depended on what songs he played. One of them was Hank Williams' 'Hey Good Lookin'.' 'I had kind of a rockabilly arrangement,' he recalled, 'and I was an American, and I was on a little bit of a Bruce [Springsteen] kick at the time. I'd seen Bruce three times in the 70s, in the summer of '78, so I was a Bruce-aholic. Another good song I would sing was "Runaround Sue"—you could hear me echoing through the halls singing, *Hey, hey . . . whoa!* Every now and then, people would join in with the *hey, hey!*

'To be honest, I wasn't *that* talented,' he conceded, 'but I was extremely rambunctious. I was just Kirby MacMillan, and I had my Guild T-50 electric guitar. I had the case open to people so I could get money. I was probably doing a couple of Clash songs and a couple of Bruce songs, and maybe a Woody Guthrie song. I think I might have been doing "Union Maid." But the song that *really* made the money was "American Pie." I could play it for an hour, straight through, without ever doing the slow parts. I could be singing the same verse over and over. They wouldn't know. I would make a hundred bucks if I played it on the Northern Line. Where I worked was Tottenham Court Road. That's where you'd really make the money. There's, like, seven verses, but nobody knew when it started or ended. It was just like me singing "American Pie," trying to make money so I could get some food.

'By the time I'd played it enough, I had also kind of figured out what all he was talking about in "American Pie." I had broken the code, you know. *Oh, oh, oh—the jester in the coat from James D, that's Bob Dylan. Oh, that's The Beatles!* So I was very, very happy with myself. Here I was, a *semi-talented* American, kind of doing an "American Pie," Bruce Springsteen–like on the Tube of London, and it went great. And then you move on to the next stop.

'You're supposed to go in and buy a ticket to get out,' he noted of London Underground protocol. 'I would go in with no money and hope I'd made [enough] to get out of the Tube; otherwise, I had to jump over the turnstile or something.'

THE ARTIST AND DJ later to be known as Mojo Nixon was living in San Diego when he and Skid Roper secured their first recording contract with Enigma Records. But he doesn't recall busking in Downtown San Diego, or along the beach. Rather, his next opportunity was a promotional stunt in Los Angeles, promoting his 1990 album *Otis*. By then, he and Roper had parted company.

Enigma arranged for Nixon to play the lead track, 'Don Henley Must Die'—Mojo's decidedly unflattering song about the Eagles' founding drummer and vocalist, featuring lyrics like '*Used to be in the Eagles / Now he whines like a wounded beagle*'—on the back of a flatbed truck right in front of Geffen Records. 'We played the song,' he told me, 'and then somebody from the label said, You realize [Don Henley's] not here, right? He [wasn't] there, but half the people who worked there—the young people—came out. There was a guy on the side writing down names of who was liking it, so he could tell David Geffen or Don Henley, you know: *Get rid of those people … they like Mojo!'*

More likely, Henley himself never became aware of the incident. In 1994, the Eagles released their reunion album, *Hell Freezes Over*. It was certified nine times platinum (for sales of more than nine million units) by the Recording Industry Association Of America. So you could say he got the last laugh. Not that Nixon didn't also do well for himself, going on to work as a DJ on SiriusXM's Outlaw Country station (famously elongating the *law* in the name of his station IDs), as well as performing on the channel's cruises and annually at South By Southwest.

My interview with Mojo Nixon was conducted on May 26, 2023. On February 7, 2024, he died suddenly and unexpectedly of cardiac arrest while on the Outlaw Country Cruise in the Caribbean Sea. His family issued the following statement:

> August 2, 1957—February 7, 2024, Mojo Nixon. How you live is how you should die. Mojo Nixon was full-tilt, wide-open rock hard, root hog, corner on two wheels + on fire . . . passing after a blazing show, a raging night, closing the bar, taking no prisoners + a good breakfast with bandmates and friends. A cardiac event on the Outlaw Country Cruise is about right . . . and that's just how he did it, Mojo has left the building. Since Elvis is everywhere, we know he was waiting for him in the alley out back. Heaven help us all.

MADELEINE PEYROUX

CHAPTER 31

BUSKING BY BENZ AND BARGE

AMERICAN JAZZ SINGER AND SONGWRITER Madeleine Peyroux is known for her soulful voice and interpretations of standards. A native of Athens, Georgia, born in 1974—six years before R.E.M. became that town's biggest export—she began her professional music career in her teenage years, gaining early experience by performing in the streets and cafés of Paris, France.

Peyroux spent her early years in Europe, living first in Paris and then in Athens, Greece. During this time, her busking experiences provided her with opportunities to connect with audiences, experiment with different musical styles, and develop the intimate, emotive approach that she is known for today. Her rise to prominence came with the release of her debut album, *Dreamland*, in 1996. Since then, she has enjoyed a successful career and has released several critically acclaimed albums, earning recognition as one of the leading voices in contemporary jazz.

Prior to that, young Madeleine had moved to Paris with her mother in 1987 after her parents divorced. She soon met a trio of older buskers from England. 'These guys had created this whole other world for themselves,' she recalls, 'but they were not a band. They were just like solo buskers that would mostly sit around and drink all day. They talked to me, and I was talking to them, and then next thing I know, they're like, *Come with us to Cannes.*

'And why did we go?' she asks rhetorically, 'Because it was film festival time, which means it's packed, and you can go and stand in front of a literally captive audience of people sitting at their tables and play your songs for them. That's the first time I passed the hat. I was just like, *Oh my God, there's a million people. And I'm gonna go up to these strangers?!* But I was learning that maybe you can get a few of them to be entertained. You *do* have a captive audience.

'I think they were making more money with me there than they usually would. But they drank too much. I had a big fight . . . beat one of the guys up. Then I took him to the hospital. And the next morning, I said, This is *bullshit*—I'm out of here, guys. I hopped on the train and went back to Paris. So that was my first tour of busking. But I was addicted by that time. I was like, *Wow, I've got to follow these buskers around.*'

Back in Paris, Peyroux discovered the Café Mazet, located on the city's Rue St. Andre des arts. 'If you walked up there in the evening, the buskers of the entire city of Paris showed up,' she says. 'And I just thought, *If I hang around, I'll learn how to play guitar. And I'll learn how to play songs.*' She decided to try it herself. 'I tried to play my first terrace by myself, and I did a lunchtime crowd. And I made, like, thirty francs, which seemed like a really good day. It would have been five or six dollars in 1989–90. That was me by myself. And I could only play two songs, you know?'

In time, she found collaborators. 'I joined a band that was out there, passing the hat for them. It was kind of a swing band. And I just asked them, Can I sing a song? And I ended up working with them. And, again, there was alcohol involved; not with them, but this time it was *me*. A band member told me, They're gonna have us back, but you can't come because you got drunk and you were only fifteen years old!'

Madeleine was technically homeless by then. 'I left school and left home. And then . . . I didn't really have a plan—I was just acting as if I could figure it out on the fly. And that wasn't working out for me, so I would end up sleeping in the subway overnight and just be, like, *Well, this wasn't very safe.* Or a park bench . . . that wasn't very comfortable.'

As she continued to observe the Paris streetscape, she discovered that some buskers led a very structured life. 'What I saw in Paris soon after starting on this was that there were professionals. There were people that got up in the morning, strapped on their guitar, and went out to the subway station and worked until 4 or 5pm. Then they took all that coin over to the Mazet, drank a little something, and went home and charged up their amp.'

Life changed the day that Madeleine Peyroux met Danny Fitzgerald, a native of Kingston, New York. He was stationed 3,552 miles east of his hometown in Paris, where he led the Lost Wandering Blues & Jazz Band, named after a Ma Rainey song. As she queried further, she found that Fitzgerald had a past in New York's beat culture, where his prose had been included in activist Abbie Hoffman's *Steal This Book*. Bob Dylan had slept on his floor. And there he was at the Mazet. 'He really should be known as the king of the buskers,' she says of her new friend, who was then in his fifties—decades her senior.

'He heard me singing around the busking neighborhood,' she remembers. 'And he told me, Someday you could sing with us. I was literally down to my last five francs. I bought a beer with it. And then I didn't know what to do. Winter was coming—it was the end of summer, and it was getting cold. Being an outdoor tourist-season busker was a losing game, and you had to know what you were doing. He obviously knew. He had a car. He had hats piled up all over the backseat inside. The car had a washtub bass. He always had a bunch of guys playing with him.'

Not only did this very successful busker have a car, he also had a boat.

'It was a *péniche*—a flatbed without an engine. We had it parked in the suburbs outside of Paris. It was beautiful out there. Quiet. Swans would come floating by. I mean, it was beautiful. And it was free. He never paid rent. He was supposed to, but they couldn't [enforce it.] Because of the combination of the French bureaucracy and the sort of obscurity of this specific type of lifestyle he created. It was like, *Who's the landlord? He's not there. He's gone. Sorry.* Every few years, somebody would come to the boat and say, You owe us money. I mean, it's not like we get mail,' she laughs.

'Anyway, he had a Mercedes—a big old brown Mercedes—and he would leave town all the time, and then I would see that Mercedes pull up in front of the Cafe Mazet. I was like, *Who drives up in a car these days that's a busker? This is awesome!*

'One day, I said I was completely out of money and, *hey, you told me I could sing with your band.* Like, in his face, you know? And he kind of looked; he was like, Okay, go ahead. I said, Go ahead what? He said, Audition. I was like, But there's no guitar. There's nobody playing. Aren't you gonna? Is there anybody to play?'

'No,' came Fitzgerald's response. 'Just do it.'

Madeleine describes what it was like to audition a cappella: 'To this day, I still try to wonder what it was like for him. Because I know what it was like for *me*. I'm standing there, kind of singing for my life. At that point, I had literally just nothing. There was no option. I couldn't go home to my mother. Why not? I don't know. But I had to do this. So I go, *Jeepers, creepers*, and I sing the whole thing snapping my fingers. And I got the bridge and the melody and all that, but the whole time I'm thinking, *How am I supposed to entertain this audience of one while the whole time he just looks at me?* Standing right looking me right in the face and we're like two feet apart. Oh my God, I was shaking!'

Fitzgerald informed her that she'd passed *his* audition, but now needed to audition for the other members of the band. 'And how do I do that?' she wondered. Fitzgerald told her: 'Well, you can come with us. We're going to leave town. *We're going to Holland.*'

'I'm like, Perfect. I have nowhere to live. Where do you sleep tonight or tomorrow or the next day? I've got no money. And for some reason I have no *guitar* at this point. What happened there? I think I got so drunk that I left my guitar outside of a bar. Oh my gosh. I then I had no money left… I was staying at this hotel. And he says, Yeah, we're leaving tomorrow.'

Madeline immediately told her Irish friend, Patter, about her tour with Fitzgerald's band. Patter knew of Fitzgerald and told her, 'Oh, that's great. Maddy. That's great. You're gonna join Danny's band! It's good for you. They're gonna love you and you're gonna do great.'

'So I go the next day and stand in front of the Mazet,' she continues. 'I wait for that car to show up. It's not there. *What's going on? What am I going to do? What time are we leaving today? I'm ready!*'

Fitzgerald, savoring a coffee at the Mazet, had decided to leave Paris the following day, so Madeline stayed on Patter's floor another night. The following morning, they left. 'We finally do get in the car,' she says, 'and we go to Holland—to a place called Eindhoven. It's where the jazz conservatory is. And there was a student in the jazz conservatory who absolutely loves being in Danny's band, but he's finishing his degree in jazz guitar. He's about twenty-something. All of us are young. I'm the youngest, but everybody's, like, eighteen through twenty-one. And then there's this bandleader who's fifty-five. So a little bit like, *What's Danny's deal?* But eventually I started singing and working with them.'

She also discovered that this band of buskers knew the tricks of the trade. 'They knew where to go and when,' she recalls. 'The thing that boggles my mind is that being a good busker [gives you] all the skills that you need for being an entertainer. You need to read the room, but they read a whole city and knew where [receptive listeners] were.'

Madeleine soon had her own take on the busking life. 'It's a thankless job in the sense that, when a culture doesn't appreciate it, they think you're begging,' she explains. 'It's the worst mistake, because good buskers are like maître d's—they're people who understand that you're in this place to enjoy your time on this planet. And Danny really believed that. He said that the purpose of life is to feel good.

'So we got in that Mercedes, and the five of us drove all over Europe, mostly Northern Europe: Holland, Belgium, Switzerland was a big one. You got four times as many francs there. Denmark was a big one, and it was always cold. And I was always like, Why can't we go to Italy and Spain? And they said, There's no money. It's great, people are really nice, but there's no cash.

'So we would go to these cold places. We went to Germany a lot— played in Stuttgart, Düsseldorf, Köln. And we would get gigs from audience members [who'd] fly us up to play a private party and pay for everything... ski resorts in the Alps. Danny was the one who made it he made it a show!

'They even made a movie about us,' she says. '*They* being a young film student who came to Paris and was looking for buskers to make a movie about, and they chose us and then they followed us around. We went to places we wouldn't normally go because of this moviemaker. We went to New York, and we went to play in Harlem, and they threw bottles at us and said, Get the fuck out of my stoop—you know you can't be playing here. And then we were in New York City. We didn't make any money in New York. Busking in New York was just... depressing.'

Shortly thereafter, Madeleine left Fitzgerald's merry band of buskers, but New York remains her home today.

Madeleine always tried to busk outside in the Big Apple. 'It's a lot to carry, to go down into a subway,' she explains, 'and you're competing with the trains. In New York, the trains are louder than they are in Paris. If you know where you're going in a tunnel, in the subway system, you can find a tunnel where you can get a decent sound. It's good to be away from the elements, but it's much more of a challenge. In Paris, you have walking streets. In New York City, we apparently couldn't find anywhere.

'You can usually find neighborhoods like SoHo, where there are a lot of rich people out walking and shopping and buying ice cream, so they're in a good mood, or there's a farmers market nearby.' She eventually found her New York niche as a 'subway morning busker,' but there was a downside: 'It's depressing because, in New York City, there is no respect for [those who] were, quote, *starving artists*. The idea of the starving artists is European. In Paris, if you're walking around with a guitar, people don't look you look at you with disdain.'

Paris itself was about to change in that respect. 'It was a golden age when I started busking with [Danny], because a few years later, the mayor of Paris outlawed it. All these little clubs used to have live music and then, all of a sudden, they had to have licenses. And all the gigs were kind of gone, and people were kind of leaving. I came back to New York to make a record or to just get . . . a GED.'

Little did she know she hadn't seen the last of Danny. 'He would come back to the United States once a year, [being] from upstate New York,' she says. 'And then they would drive all the way across the country and busk all the way out on the Venice Pier, and anywhere in between, and we were always trying to find out where the best place was to go. And he would do tours as a busker. Because he made so many friends, he would stay at people's houses . . . but there wasn't much money. And the older he got, the harder work [it became]. And they weren't making enough money really.

'And Mayor [Rudolph] Giuliani had a policy that you could arrest somebody within fifteen feet of an ATM for panhandling. We didn't know we were within fifteen feet of an ATM. They handcuffed us and roughed us up; it was ridiculous.'

Things were about to change significantly for Madeleine, who scored a recording contract with Atlantic Records in 1996. Now it was Danny who stayed on Madeleine's floor. In the ensuing years she has released nine albums, as well as appearing on an independently released 1997 collaboration with The Lost & Wandering Blues & Jazz band, *Spreading Rhythm Around*, under the pseudonym Moanin' Mary.

Did she ever look back at her busking life after becoming a respected recording and touring artist? Actually, yes. 'I *do* busk,' she explains, 'and I did busk during COVID. I was out there for money, just playing. It was the answer to COVID ... being outside and being comfortable with just gathering with other people, in a way, and so many people came up to me and said, We needed this so bad.'

She imagines that customs have changed for present-day buskers. 'You have to have Venmo or PayPal,' she surmises. 'And our bread-and-butter for a while was being able to sell a CD. We thought it was just a breakthrough. But carrying all that stuff around is no longer a thing. I guess the downside to busking was always that you have to spend so much energy on creating your life and your business—you spend so much time figuring out where you've got to go, where you've got to be, what you've got to bring, what kind of gear you can have, that you might forget to focus on the music itself. And you certainly don't have a lot of time to compose, let alone just perform and prep and perfect the art itself.

'If we could all just treat street performers with the respect that you would treat a professional and realize that there's really working, that would give everybody a leg-up. Like, we're not selling candy, right?

'And there are some amazing artists in New York. Most of the time they're in the subways. There are amazing singers, drummers in the hallways, dancers that get onto the train, young kids who probably have no resources whatsoever and can do the most incredible acrobatics on a subway car ... I just wish we could encourage that for our society.

'I don't know whether I'm being super-romantic about this, but this to me is what Utopia would have—a lot of buskers!'

PLAYING FOR CHANGE

'BUSKERS ARE IN THE JOY BUSINESS'

IN 2007, AWARD-WINNING music producer/engineer and award-winning film director and recording engineer Mark Johnson and film producer/philanthropist Whitney Kroenke Silverstein launched the multimedia project Playing For Change. Their production company spawned a separate nonprofit foundation devoted to promoting music and art education throughout the world. Since then, Playing For Change has recorded more than 150 artists in roughly fifty nations, primarily street singers.

According to the website for Concord Music, which distributed the first four Playing For Change albums:

> For ten years, Johnson and his team traveled the globe, with a single-minded passion to record little-known musicians for what would become Playing for Change—its name evoking the coins thrown to street musicians as well as the transformation their music inspires. They went to New Orleans shortly after the devastation of Hurricane Katrina. 'The city felt sad and desolate, yet the music never stopped,' says Johnson. 'The street musicians and music in the clubs kept the city alive and gave it a sense of hope ...'

Initially focusing on Los Angeles, New Orleans, and New York, in 2004 Playing For Change made its first documentary, *Playing For Change: A Cinematic Discovery Of Street Musicians*. More recently came the April 2008 premiere of its latest film, *Playing For Change: Peace Through Music*, at the Tribeca Film Festival in New York. In September 2008, the film won the Audience Award at the Woodstock Film Festival. Directed by Johnson and Jonathan Walls (*Automatic*), the documentary features over 100 musicians around the world, combining their distant voices into a powerful group of global songs.

Concord co-owner Norman Lear—also the creator of such groundbreaking sitcoms as *All In The Family*—was sold on the idea of releasing a Playing For Change album after watching Johnson's video footage. '[Lear] felt it was an important project, not just in terms of commercial viability but in terms of bringing people together through music and striving toward a more peaceful world,' the late Concord general manager Gene Rumsey told *Billboard* in 2009.[1]

'Playing For Change was born out of busking and born out of music on the street,' Johnson emphasizes today. 'I was a recording engineer in New York City, and I was on my way to work one day in a subway when I saw two monks performing in the subway. They were both wearing robes that were all painted white. One was playing a nylon guitar, the other singing in a language I didn't understand. I think *most* people probably didn't understand. But on this day, I watched everybody in the platform stop—everybody's watching this music.

'I looked around and I just had this epiphany, because there was a homeless man next to a businessman, a little girl next to an elderly woman. And everybody's so connected to this music. And then when the music ended, everybody gets on the train, they go their separate ways. But two things occurred to me. One, when the music played, all the things that made these people different disappeared. And the second thing was that the best music I heard in my life was on the way *to* the studio, and not *in* the studio. And that was the beginning of Playing For Change—the idea of, *Let's bring the studio to the people.*'

Johnson never found the monks again. 'I certainly looked,' he says, 'but I never found them. But that was the day Playing For Change was born, to bring the studio—the same equipment I used to use with Paul Simon—out into the streets [with] some cameras so we could document and record them in the moment. To me, you know, street music is one of the greatest art forms. It goes directly from people's hearts—you can walk by and listen to this music, and it can change your day. And changing your day can change your life. For me, one of the greatest gifts in a society is the street performer—and it's also one of the oldest professions.'

Johnson and Silverstein, his partner in the organization, moved from New York City to California. Johnson continues the story: 'I was a recording engineer here [in LA] for Jackson Browne, and I was on my way to work with him one day and I heard the voice of a street musician named Roger Ridley, one of the great street musicians of all time in the Santa Monica 3rd Street Promenade. And he was an old black man, similar to Ted Hawkins, but to me he had an even better voice. He sounded like Otis Redding on the street. So I had been thinking about how to take Playing For Change around the world, and I heard him singing the song "Stand By Me."

'I approached him and said, Hey, I wanna record you and film you playing the song, travel around the world, put headphones on other musicians and add them to the track. And he looked at me like I was crazy. But he said, If you come back, I'll play the song. And when I came back, he had a set break. And I said to him, Roger, what are you doing, singing on the street [when] you sound like Otis Redding? And he said, Man, I'm in the joy business—I come out to bring joy to the people.

'And to me,' Johnson adds, 'that summarizes the power of the busker because they really are in the joy business. You know, they bring joy to everybody who walks by them. They don't care if you're rich, poor, black, white, old, young—the music's for you. And to me, you know, so that really sparked the Playing For Change movement.'

Among the artists whose career received a boost via Playing For Change's efforts was New Orleans street singer Grandpa Elliott, profiled elsewhere in this book. 'Our first trip to New Orleans was in fact a mission to find Grandpa,' the organization's website notes. 'We knew of his reputation in the New Orleans street music scene and knew his voice would be a great addition. We made our way over to Royal and Toulouse, and found him entertaining a crowd on the corner. While he was on a set break, we approached him and struck up a conversation and introduced ourselves and the project.'

'You had Roger on the 3rd Street Promenade with Grandpa in New Orleans,' Johnson continues. 'And then the craziest thing happened on the show *America's Got Talent*. A woman named Alice Ridley comes out and sounds like Tina Turner and turns out to be Roger's sister. She's a busker in New York City. Amazing. By now, Roger had passed away, but I still had the track, so I went to New York and added her to the song with her brother and Grandpa.'

According to Johnson, the resulting video clip of 'Stand By Me' has been seen 'close to a billion' times in two hundred countries around the world. 'It's really a great thing,' he says, 'a legendary band, because it's James Gadson, drummer for all Bill Withers albums, and then Reggie McBride from Stevie Wonder's band. So I had this legendary band playing with Roger, Grandpa, and Alice.'

CHUCK GULLO IS a music industry veteran who began his career at A&M Records as a marketing executive, furthering the careers of Janet

Jackson, The Police, and Bryan Adams, among others. For eight years, he served as president of Scotti Bros Records, where he guided the careers of several gold and platinum artists, including James Brown and 'Weird' Al Yankovic. He then went on to launch Top Sail Productions with legendary radio personality Casey Kasem to release a series of compilation CDs titled *Casey Kasem Presents America's Top Ten Hits*. The packages generated over $23 million in sales.

A label dedicated to buskers might have seemed an incongruous next move for a music executive of Gullo's pedigree. But that was precisely his aim when he launched Music From The Streets.

'In my fifty years in the music industry, I was blessed to work with a lot of unbelievable artists,' he explains, 'So I decided I wanted to start a company with philanthropic intent—a company that gave back. I really believe we all need to do more in the fight against homelessness. I tied it to my passion for music and the love of street musicians and their incredible stories, and of course street musicians were pleased to be a part of it because they came into contact with the unhoused almost every day while performing on the streets. I believe that music unites us like nothing else and taps into all of our emotions, so why not let music be the driving force in the fight against homelessness?' As such, Music From The Streets partnered with four of the top nonprofits in the fight against homelessness: The National Alliance To End Homelessness, National Coalition For The Homeless, National Coalition For Homeless Veterans, and StandUp For Kids.

Gullo's concept involved not only a label but also a weekly TV show that would travel from city to city to find where some of the best street musicians perform. The goal was to showcase their talent, tell their stories, and provide them with well-deserved exposure. As he tells it, 'I have talked with many street musicians over the years, and I have always been moved by their extraordinary stories.' He created a sizzle reel to garner interest in the TV part of his venture. The video includes a subway busker named Lorenzo Laroc, who offers the following consummate quote about busking: 'If I made you late for work, then I've done my job.'

The COVID pandemic gave Gullo some 20/20 vision on the venture. 'When COVID hit, I could no longer garner interest for the TV show, and it was time for me to make a very difficult decision on the future of Music From The Streets. After six years in development, and after having personally financed the company all those years, I realized it was time to wind it down. The whole purpose was to create a TV show to give all of these great musicians the spotlight they deserved, and at the same time generate revenue for these incredible organizations fighting homelessness. Without the TV show, there was limited exposure for the artists, the organizations, and for the fight against homelessness.

'So, my obvious regret is not bringing the TV show to reality. However, I wouldn't trade the experience for anything. I met some incredible street musicians who shared some very emotional stories with me. I also became even more aware of the work that is needed by all of us in the fight against homelessness. It's not a sexy topic and is difficult for many to discuss, but if we all do just a little more, I believe we can make a difference.'

MARK JOHNSON MAY have first heard it when two monks played the New York subway, but busking is now a way of life for him, and Playing For Change remains an ongoing organization. 'Busking is one of the most important things in a society,' he says, 'and I don't think anything that profound is ever going to be easy. I don't think you get to be a street musician and get an easy life, because if you choose that profession, you're going to have extreme ups and extreme downs. But the crazy thing about it is, you're never gonna be able to measure your impact.

'The symbolism I used to use in my mind is somebody walking home from work, they had a bad day, and they see a street musician. They've got two choices, right? They can walk by him, go home, get in a fight with their wife, their little daughter looks out her door, she sees parents fighting. Or they stop to listen to the music, and they take in this incredible energy. They go home, they hug their wife, and their daughter peeks out and sees that. The world changes based on our actions.

'Street musicians give us a place to put our emotion and then reset ourselves, and in a busy world, you know, those things are precious, and I just think that all street musicians deserve this incredible amount of love and respect. But it is definitely a tough job.'

I thank him for taking the time to talk to me about busking for this book.

'Oh, man,' he responds. 'Nothing I'd rather do with my time. So, thank *you*.'

ACKNOWLEDGMENTS
'IF I MADE YOU LATE FOR WORK,
THEN I'VE DONE MY JOB'

I HOPE YOU ENJOYED this tour of music on the streets, past and present.

A few random closing thoughts, if I may.

I've walked by several buskers during the writing of this book. (While there are not a lot of buskers in my current home of California's Coachella Valley, I spent a summer month in San Luis Obispo, whose deceivingly urban downtown has many of them.) I made it a point to throw at least a dollar into every guitar case, even if the musician was on break or frankly couldn't carry a tune. I probably always will.

Nearly everywhere I traveled as I wrote this book, I'd tell the locals what I was working on, and they'd excitedly ask me, 'Oh, are you aware of …?' Some of those suggestions became chapters (Tymon Dogg is one example). I'm keeping a running list for volume two. And if you're wondering 'but where is …?' I've probably already thought of that musician. (There were also a few who, via their managers or publicists, declined to be interviewed.)

THANK YOU to a few individuals who understood what I was attempting and helped in ways large and small: Michael Ackerman, Mary Katherine Aldin, Eric Ambel, Joel Amsterdam, Liz Antaramian, Billy Boy Arnold, Brian T. Atkinson, Duve Alexander, Stephen Baird, Kendal Beahm, Jim Beal Jr., Greg Beets, Tony Berg, Peter Blackstock, Scott B. Bomar, Harold Bronson, Georgane Calyanis, Mark Caro, Jim Catalano, Lori Cheatle, Danny Clinch, Aaron Cohen, Andrew Cohen, Bill Dahl, Jim Dawson, Jeff DeLia, Victor DeLorenzo, Tim Easton, Ethan Ellestad, Donica Elliott, William Lee Ellis, Holly Elson, Jeff Fasano, Bruce Fessier, Danny Field, Jenni Finlay, Jim Flammia, Richard Foos, Hillel Frankel, Aaron Fuchs, Gregg Geller, Brendan Gilmartin, Jeff Gold, Robert Gordon, Michael Gray, Jason Gross, Mark Guarino, Chuck Gullo, Adam Gussow, Craig Havighurst, Josh Hecht, Cynthia Herbst, Raoul Hernandez, Larry Hoffman, Bill Hutchinson, Mary Howell, Patria Jacobs, Mark Johnson, Allan Jones, Regina Joskow, Elliott Kendall, Adam Klein, Sonya Kolowrat, Bill Kopp, John Kruth, Amy Kurland, Lisa Labo, Allen 'Charmin'' Larman, Peter Leak, Thom Lemmons, Arlee Leonard, Trevor Laurence, Thom Lemmons, Robyn Loda, Nick Loss-Eaton, David Menconi, Dana Miller, Chris Morris, Griff Morris, Jim Neill, Mojo Nixon, Todd Novak, Robert K. Oermann, Lynn Orman, Tom Osborn, Jim O'Neal, Cheryl Pawelski, Reverend and Breezy Peyton, Chris Phillips, Bridget Piekarz, Playing For Change, James Porter, Domenic Priore, Robert D. Pruter, Bruce Boyd Raeburn, Jan Ramsey and *Offbeat* magazine, Scott Ambrose 'Bullethead' Reilley, Brad Rosenberger, Mark Rubin, Tamara Saviano, Ben Sandmel, Dick Shurman, Val Shively, John Sinclair, R.J. Smith, Tim Sommer, Chris Stacey, Marc Stone, Danna Strong, Gene Tomko, Billy Vera, Ross Warner, Murray Weiss, Jim White, Reid Wick, Chris Willman, John Wirt, Jonathan Wolfson, Melanie Young, and Andrew Zax.

Special thanks to Nancy Meyer for a conversation that—very inadvertently and serendipitously—spawned the concept for this book.

Heavenly thank you to Blind Arvella Gray, the first (and most authentic) street singer I ever saw.

And to the two women in my life: my wife, Sharon, and my mother, Sorelle, a nonfiction author herself.

SELECT BIBLIOGRAPHY

BOOKS

Laurence Bergreen, *Louis Armstrong: An Extravagant Life* (Broadway Books, 1997)

Ira Berkow, *Maxwell Street: Survival In A Bazaar* (Doubleday, 1977)

Peter Case, *As Far As You Can Get Without A Passport* (Everthemore Books, 2006)

Ben Cohen and Davis Greenwood, *The Buskers: A History Of Street Entertainment* (Davis & Charles, 1981)

Philip Groia, *They All Sang On The Corner: A Second Look At New York City's Rhythm & Blues Vocal Groups* (Phillie Dee Enterprises, 1983)

Adam Gussow, *Busker's Holiday* (Modern Blues Harmonica, 2015)

Johnny Keyes, *Du-Wop* (Vesti Press, 1987)

Robert Palmer, *Deep Blues* (Penguin, 1982)

Robert Pruter, *DooWop: The Chicago Scene* (University Of Illinois Press, 1996)

Robert Scotto, *Moondog: The Viking Of 6th Avenue* (Process, revised 2013)

Richard F. Shepard and Vicki Gold Levi, *Live & Be Well: A Celebration Of Yiddish Culture In America, From The First Immigrants To The Second World War* (Ballantine Books, 1982)

Billy Vera, *Harlem To Hollywood* (Backbeat, March 1, 2017)

Brian Ward, *Just My Soul Responding: Rhythm & Blues, Black Consciousness And Race* (University Of California Press, 1998)

ARTICLES

Cary Baker, 'Blind Arvella Gray: Blues Over A Tin Cup,' *Chicago Reader*, January 7, 1972

Cary Baker, 'Chicago Street Singers,' *Living Blues*, issue 11, winter 1972–73

Stacey Leigh Bridewell, 'Five Questions With Meschiya Lake On Her Move To Cork, Ireland,' *Offbeat*, May 30, 2018

Frederick Dennis Greene, 'Doo-Wop,' *Encyclopedia Britannica*

Elizabeth Lyttleton Harold and Peter Stone, 'Reverend Gary Davis,' *ACE Is Cultural Equity*, April 30, 2005

Geoffrey Himes, 'Tuba Skinny Stays On The Street,' *Offbeat*, September 2014

John Kruth, 'I Am The Light Of The World,' *Please Kill Me*, March 31, 2023

Bunny Matthews, 'Tuba Fats: Livin' La Vida Loca,' *Offbeat*, December 2000

Kris Needs, 'The Tale Of David Peel, The Dope-Smoking Hippy Who Became The King Of Punk,' *Classic Rock*, March 22, 2016

Amanda Petrusich, 'How Moondog Captured The Sounds Of New York,' *The New Yorker*, December 9, 2019

Joel Rosen, 'How The Beatnik Riot Helped Kick Off The 60s,' *Weekend Edition Saturday*, April 9, 2011

Nils Skudra, 'Meet The Faces Of Durham: Reverend Gary Davis,' Museum Of Durham History website, February 9, 2021

David Whiteis, 'Maxwell Street Blues,' *Chicago Reader*, October 13, 1988

Dirk Wissbaum, 'The History Of The Street Buskers,' *Big City Rhythm & Blues*, October–November 2022

WEBSITES

Chicago.gov, 'History of Maxwell Street Market,' www.chicago.gov

Cynthia Haring & World Nation, worldnationgroup.com

Maxwell St. Foundation, maxwellstreetfoundation.org

MACCNO: The Music & Culture of New Orleans, maccno.com

Street Arts & Buskers Advocates, buskersadvocates.org

ENDNOTES

INTRODUCTION

1. Ben Cohen and Davis Greenwood, *The Buskers: A History Of Street Entertainment* (Davis & Charles, 1981)
2. José A. Pascualm, *Diccionario Crítico Etimológico Castellano E Hispánico* (Gredos, 1954)
3. Dirk Wissbaum, 'The History Of The Street Buskers,' *Big City Rhythm & Blues*, October–November 2022
4. Kenneth Silverman (ed.), *Benjamin Franklin 1706–1790: The Autobiography And Other Writings* (Penguin, 1986)
5. Richard F. Shepard and Vicki Gold Levi, *Live & Be Well: A Celebration Of Yiddish Culture In America, From The First Immigrants To The Second World War* (Ballantine Books, 1982)
6. Drew Kent, liner notes to *Blind Lemon Jefferson: The Complete 94 Classic Sides Remastered* (JSP Records, 2003)
7. Robert Palmer, 'Big Apple Grapevine: Professor Longhair's Legacy,' *Real Paper*, February 23, 1980
8. Joel Rosen, 'How The Beatnik Riot Helped Kick Off The 60s,' *Weekend Edition Saturday*, April 9, 2011
9. Kris Needs, 'The Tale Of David Peel, The Dope-Smoking Hippy Who Became The King Of Punk,' *Classic Rock*, March 22, 2016
10. 'Welcome To Buskers Bunkhouse,' buskersbunkhouse.angelfire.com
11. John Stanton, 'Stop The Royal Street Standoff,' *Gambit*, March 9, 2023
12. Scott Snowden, 'Promenade Struggles With Talent-Optional Performers On The Public Street, *Santa Monica Daily Press*, September 15, 2023
13. Stephen Calt, liner notes to *Reverend Gary Davis, New Blues & Gospel Vol. 1* (Biograph Records, 1971)
14. Fran Spielman, 'Reilly Softens Street Musician Ban To Avoid Almost Certain Defeat,' *Chicago Sun-Times*, March 29, 2017
15. 'Street Performing In Austin,' austintexas.gov
16. Bret Anne Serbin, 'City Discusses Street Performances As A Way To Keep Missoula Weird,' *The Missoulian*, December 1, 2023
17. Jason Lamb, 'Street Performers Want Clarity On Law Banning Some Performances,' News Channel 5, Nashville, December 5, 2017
18. 'Top 40 Glen Hansard Quotes,' quotefancy.com

CHAPTER 2

1. Cary Baker, 'Chicago Street Singers,' *Living Blues* issue 11, winter 1972
2. Cary Baker, 'Chicago Street Singers,' *Living Blues* issue 11, winter 1972
3. David Whiteis, 'Maxwell Street Blues,' *Chicago Reader*, October 13, 1988

CHAPTER 3

1. Brian Ward, *Just My Soul Responding: Rhythm & Blues, Black Consciousness And Race* (University Of California Press, 1998)
2. Frederick Dennis Greene, 'Doo-Wop,' *Encyclopedia Britannica*
3. Michael Hann, 'Dion: When I Heard My Album Sober, I Thought, Wow—Heroin Didn't Touch It,' *Guardian*, June 16, 2020

CHAPTER 4

1. Clayton Maxwell, 'Deep Ellum Clues: Searching For The Spirit Of Blind Lemon Jefferson And The 1920s In Dallas,' *Texas Highways*, December 2021
2. Robert Palmer, *Deep Blues* (Penguin, 1982)
3. Elizabeth Lyttleton Harold, interview with Reverend Gary Davis, April/May 1951
4. Nils Skudra, 'Meet The Faces Of Durham: Reverend Gary Davis,' Museum Of Durham History website, February 9, 2021
5. David Menconi, 'Buskers And Music At The Crossroads,' ourstate.com, August 31, 2020
6. Simeon Hutner and Trevor Laurence (directors), *Harlem Street Singer* (2013)

7   John Kruth, 'I Am The Light Of The World,' *Please Kill Me*, March 31, 2023
8   Jim Pettigrew, liner notes to *It's A Mean Old World To Try To Live In* (Rounder, 1975)
9   John W. English, William Vanderkloot, Robert L. Williams, *It's A Mean Old World*, via Folkstreams

CHAPTER 5

1   Patricia J. Campbell and Alice Belkin, *Passing The Hat: Street Performers In America* (Delacorte Press, 1981)
2   Joel Feinberg, *The History Of NYC Busking: General Admission* (Eportfolios & Macaulay, 2018)
3   Robert Hawkins, 'Industry Cannot Go On Without The Production Of Some Noise: New York City's Street Music Ban And The Sound Of Work In The New Deal Era,' *Journal Of Social History*, volume 46, issue 1, fall 2012
4   Joel Rose, 'How The Beatnik Riot Helped Kick Off The 60s,' *NPR Weekend Edition Sunday*, April 9, 2011
5   William Grimes, 'David Peel, Downtown Singer And Marijuana Evangelist, Dies At 74,' *New York Times*, April 19, 2017

CHAPTER 7

1   Paul Nelson, liner notes to *Oliver Smith* (Elektra Records, 1966)

CHAPTER 8

1   Jim Farber, 'His Work Sems Endless: Music Stars Pay Tribute To The Incredible Life Of Moondog,' the *Guardian*, September 26, 2023
2   Amanda Petrusich, 'How Moondog Captured The Sounds Of New York,' *The New Yorker*, December 9, 2019
3   Ljubinko Zivkovicso, 'Moondog: Takin' To The Streets,' *Living Life Fearless*, January 2015
4   Jason Gross, 'Moondog,' *Perfect Sound Forever*, May 1998
5   Mark Swed, 'Living By Rules—It's Madness,' *Los Angeles Times*, January 27, 2008
6   Phillip Glass, 'Remembering Moondog,' foreword to Robert Scotto, *Moondog: The Viking Of 6th Avenue* (Process, 2013)

7   Robert Scotto, *Moondog: The Viking Of 6th Avenue* (Process, 2013)

CHAPTER 10

1   Peter Blackstock, 'The Lord Of Sixth & Brazos,' *SXSW Scrapbook: People And Things That Went Before* (Essex Press, 2011)

CHAPTER 11

1   Historic Woolworth website, woolworththeatre.com

CHAPTER 12

1   Barry Mazor, 'Old Crow Medicine Show: Making The Ghosts Walk Faster,' *No Depression* no. 49, January–February 2004

CHAPTER 14

1   Sarah Ravits and John Stanton, 'Songs In The Streets Of life: Celebrating The Long History Of Buskers In New Orleans,' *Gambit*, February 25, 2002
2   Henry A. Kmen, 'Old Corn Meal: A Forgotten Urban Negro Folksinger,' *The Journal Of American Folklore* vol. 75, no. 295, January–March 1962
3   Laurence Bergreen, *Louis Armstrong: An Extravagant Life* (Broadway Books, 1997)
4   The Busking Project, buskers.guide, April 14, 2021
5   Elijah Wald, liner notes to *Snooks Eaglin: New Orleans Street Singer* (Smithsonian Folkways Records, 2005)

CHAPTER 15

1   Charles Kerault, *Charles Kerault's America* (Putnam, 1995)
2   Sheila Stroup, 'Grandpa Elliott Small Debuts At New Orleans Jazz Fest Today,' *New Orleans Times-Picayune*, June 25, 2019
3   Stacey Leigh Bridewell, 'Five Questions With Meschiya Lake On Her Move To Cork, Ireland,' *Offbeat*, May 30, 2018
4   Gwen Thompkins, 'Meschiya Lake, An Honest-To-God Modern-Day Chanteuse,' *Music Inside Out*, undated

CHAPTER 16

1   Geoffrey Himes, 'Tuba Skinny Stays On The Street,' *Offbeat*, September 2014
2   Bunny Matthews, 'Tuba Fats: Livin' La Vida Loca,' *Offbeat*, December 2000
3   Katy Reckdahl, 'Big Man Gone,' *Gambit*, January 19, 2004
4   Nick Spitzer, 'Love & Death At Second Line,' *Southern Spaces*, February 20, 2004
5   'Know Your Rights While Performing,' from the MaCCNO *Guide To New Orleans Street Performance In French Quarter And Marigny*
6   Keith Spera, 'Let's Talk With Trombone Shorty: Casket Dancing, Alcohol Abstinence, Arrested For Music,' *New Orleans Times Picayune*, June 16, 2023

CHAPTER 17

1   Larry Skoog, 'Bongo Joe Interview,' The Chris Strachwitz Collection, arhoolie.org, 1968
2   Bill Board, 'Will Musician Bongo Joe, Who Entertained Downtown San Antonio For Two Decades, Be Lost To Obscurity?,' *San Antonio Current*, March 8, 2022
3   Josh Baugh, 'Bongo Joe Was A Colorful Street Musician,' *San Antonio Express-News*, December 13, 2017
4   George Nelson (dir.), *Bongo Joe* (Maverick Video, 1972)

CHAPTER 18

1   Michael Corcoran, 'Poi Dog In Austin: Frank's Abra Years,' *Michael Corcoran's Overserved*, May 20, 2022, michaelcorcoran.substack.com

CHAPTER 19

1   Ann Powers, 'Lucinda Williams, Live In Concert,' NPR, December 7, 2016
2   Colleen Smith, 'The Latest And The First: Susan Osborn Working on Two Special Recording Projects,' *The Islands Sounder*, April 4, 2016

CHAPTER 20

1   Cary Baker, 'What Made Milwaukee Famous Made Winners Of The Violent Femmes,' *Trouser Press*, August 1983

CHAPTER 22

1   Pete Paphides, 'Fantastic Negrito: The Drug-Dealing Hustler Who Became Bernie Sanders's Favourite Bluesman,' *Guardian*, August 2, 2016

CHAPTER 23

1   Margalit Fix, 'Wild Man Fischer, Outsider Musician, Dies At 66,' *New York Times*, June 17, 2011
2   Pierre Perrone, 'Wild Man Fischer: Outsider Musician Who Was Discovered By Frank Zappa But Could Never Transcend His Psychiatric Disorders,' *Independent*, July 22, 2011

CHAPTER 24

1   Robert Christgau, 'Ted Hawkins: Consumer Guide Reviews,' robertchristgau.com
2   Jim Washburn, 'Album Review: Ted Hawkins, *The Next Hundred Years*,' *Los Angeles Times*, June 23, 1994

CHAPTER 25

1   Martha Groves, 'LA City Council Again Passes Restrictions On Venice Beach Performers,' *Los Angeles Times*, April 10, 2008
2   Joe Kendrick, 'Eilen Jewell, Crooked River: The Songwriter Strikes A Balance Between Heartache And Triumph,' NPR #NowPlaying, February 28, 2003

CHAPTER 27

1   Barry Dviola, 'Once Star Glen Hansard Gets Personal,' *Entertainment Weekly*, August 29, 2007
2   A.O. Scott, 'Some Love Stories Have A Better Ending Than The Altar,' *New York Times*, May 16, 2007
3   Jon Weisman, 'Once Upon A Time: How To Make A Movie On A Shoestring Budget,' *Variety*, July 18, 2007
4   L.V. Anderson, 'Watch Bono And Glen Hansard Busk For Charity In Dublin,' *Slate*, December 27, 2011

EPILOGUE

1   Mitchell Peters, 'Peaceful Dreams: Playing For Change Promotes Music As A Unifying Force,' *Billboard*, May 16, 2009

INDEX